Relative Grief

of related interest

Love and Grief
The Dilemma of Facing Love After Death
Catherine O'Neill and Lisa Keane
ISBN 1 84310 346 X

Finding a Way Through When Someone Close Has Died
What it Feels Like and What You Can Do to Help Yourself
A Workbook by Young People for Young People
Pat Mood and Lesley Whittaker
ISBN 1 85302 920 3

Without You – Children and Young People Growing Up
with Loss and its Effects
Tamar Granot
ISBN 1 84310 297 8

The Inspiration of Hope in Bereavement Counselling
John R. Cutcliffe
Foreword by Ronna Jevne
ISBN 1 84310 082 7

Attending to the Fact – Staying with Dying
Hilary Elfick and David Head
Edited by Cynthia Fuller
Foreword by Andrew Hoy
ISBN 1 84310 247 1

Someone Very Important Has Just Died
Immediate Help for People Caring for Children of All Ages
at the Time of a Close Bereavement
Mary Turner
Illustrated by Elaine Bailey
ISBN 1 84310 295 1

Relative Grief

Parents and children, sisters and brothers, husbands,
wives and partners, grandparents and grandchildren talk
about their experience of death and grieving

Clare Jenkins and Judy Merry

Foreword by Dorothy Rowe

Jessica Kingsley Publishers
London and Philadelphia

First published in 2005
by Jessica Kingsley Publishers
116 Pentonville Road
London N1 9JB, UK
and
400 Market Street, Suite 400
Philadelphia, PA 19106, USA

www.jkp.com

Library of Congress Cataloging in Publication Data
A CIP catalog record for this book is available from the Library of Congress

British Library Cataloguing in Publication Data
A CIP catalogue record for this book is available from the British Library

ISBN-13: 978 1 84310 257 1
ISBN-10: 1 84310 257 9

Printed and Bound in Great Britain by
Athenaeum Press, Gateshead, Tyne and Wear

Contents

Acknowledgements

This book would simply not exist without the co-operation of the contributors.

Given the sensitivity of the subject, we have been overwhelmed by people's willingness to speak about their experiences of death and grief. A casual mention of the book in general conversation often resulted in people – women in particular – spontaneously talking about their own experience of bereavement.

When we started approaching people, we fully expected rejections. In fact, we had hardly any – and those who did turn down our request usually had solid reasons for doing so, and did so regretfully.

We are immensely grateful to all those who did agree to be interviewed: for their openness and honesty, and for giving their time so willingly. In most cases, the interviews took place in the person's home, occasionally in an office and once over the telephone. Subsequently, we would send the interviewee a written account to check for accuracy, stressing that we wished to retain the individual 'voice' and their way of telling their story and expressing their feelings.

We have been much impressed by people's integrity and dignity in talking about something so powerful and often so distressing. It is difficult in a book of this nature to communicate the strong emotions that characterised many of these interviews.

Some people were moved to tears – often years after the death. There were other obvious signs of struggle as people tried to put into words the inexpressible. A book like this cannot hope to capture the breaks in the voice, the silences, the photographs shown, the diaries and poems read aloud. But those very signs of emotion – and the silences that sometimes occurred – speak eloquently of people's honest attempts to come to terms with their loss, to express deep emotions and to share their sorrow and the lessons they have learnt. We are so very grateful to them for that.

Foreword

Dorothy Rowe

Death is the elephant in the living room – the huge thing that everyone knows is there but no one mentions. Fear keeps us silent. We fear the physical aspect of death, the body becoming still, silent, cold, and then decaying, but even more we fear the annihilation of the person, what we call 'I', 'me', 'myself', which is what makes us unique. We fear not just the annihilation of the person we love but our own annihilation. Talking of his brother's death, Rony Robinson said, 'You lose a bit of yourself in the process of somebody dying'.

There's no way of knowing beforehand which bit of yourself will disappear when someone close to you dies. My friend Jean Flanagan had emphysema and I knew she was dying, but when the news of her death reached me I found myself utterly distraught with grief because I suddenly realised that Jean had known about my erstwhile marriage in a way that no one else did. Both of us had married fascinating, entertaining, exciting men who often behaved like wilful, selfish, naughty schoolboys. Jean and I could discuss our husbands in a way very different from the way we spoke about our husbands to other people. There was so much which we didn't have to explain to each other or try to excuse. When Jean died a significant part of my story was lost. I was left like the only speaker of a newly extinct language.

Each person is unique, and the part of our person which we lose in each bereavement is unique. Consequently, the grief one person feels is quite different from all the different kinds of grief which others can feel. No textbook on 'Death Education' or 'The Stages of Grief' can encompass what each individual endures. By letting each of the people in this book tell their story in their own way Clare Jenkins and Judy Merry have shown the individuality of grief. These stories remind us how wrong it is to say to someone who is grieving, 'I know exactly how you feel', or to say to oneself, 'My grief is greater than everyone else's'. The stories show too that the dead belong to no one. All we possess are those parts of our own stories which we shared with those we grieve for.

Yet, out of all the unique stories in this intensely compassionate and humane book, comes the understanding that, alone as we are in our grief, such suffering shows us that what matters most in life is the love we have for one another.

Introduction

Queen: Thou know'st 'tis common; all that live must die,
            Passing through nature to eternity.
Hamlet: Ay, madam, it is common.

(Hamlet, Act 1, Scene 2)

Death is not, of course, just common. It is inevitable. Everybody has to face their own death and most people will have to face the death of someone close. Yet most of us would prefer not to think about death until it comes too near to ignore. As a result, it may leave us feeling shocked and numb. We may cast about wildly for something to make sense of what has happened, asking, 'Why me? Why him or her? Why now?' And what we sometimes forget, in the pain of grief, is the grief other people are feeling.

Although bereavement can be a very isolating experience, any death usually touches many people. An adult who dies might be a wife, mother, sister, grandmother – or a husband, father, brother, grandfather. A child is not only someone's son or daughter, they are also a grandchild and often a sister or a brother. This book sets out to show how grief can feel from these different perspectives.

We have spoken to people with a wide range of experiences of death and bereavement, from children as young as six to a woman in her eighties. Some deaths are very recent; others happened decades ago. There are mothers and fathers who have lost children; husbands and wives who have lost spouses; brothers and sisters who have lost siblings; grandparents and grandchildren; partners and friends.

Among them are a widow and her two children expressing their feelings about the sudden death of their husband and father; the mother and sister of a murdered young man reflecting on his loss; a grandmother and grandfather talking about the death of their young grandson.

The book also includes individuals reflecting on more than one loss. Where an earlier bereavement has significantly affected a later death, we have included both experiences in the relevant chapters. Rose Dixon, for instance, has lost both a grandchild and an adult daughter:

> I felt that the death of my parents was very much the death of my past and my childhood. I think that the death of my husband – if it happens when I'm still alive – I see that as the death of the present… But I see the death of my child and my grandchild as the death of my future.

Different perspectives

When grief is at its most painful, it can be difficult to appreciate someone else's perspective. After every interview, we sent the written account to the person concerned. In the case of Rachel Osorio and her husband, Tim Whewell, they had talked separately about how they felt when their three-and-a-half-year-old son, Jethro, died. After reading both versions, Rachel wrote:

> It seems to me that the two accounts make more sense than either one would on its own – and the huge differences between them might convey something of the vast gulf of loneliness and non-communication that can happen within families in these kinds of situations.

Sometimes we forget that we do not have the monopoly on grief. Without anyone realising it, grieving can sometimes become competitive. Cheryl Craggs's husband, Glenn, died when she was pregnant and she found the relationship with her in-laws difficult to cope with:

> They thought their grief was the worst. I thought mine was. This is a common thing amongst people who are young widows. The in-laws think they're the chief mourners at the funeral, but in fact you all are. We're all grieving.

More than one person told us how death, instead of bringing family members together, could drive a wedge between them. Some of the mothers we spoke to talked about the need to talk endlessly about their child's death, whereas some fathers found talking too painful. More than one bereaved sibling felt they had no right to talk about their grief when they saw how badly affected their parents were.

Karen Rea remembers as a six-year-old desperately missing her elder sister, Elaine, but feeling unable to show her emotions in front of her parents:

> I got it into my head – being six – that I couldn't do anything now to upset them…I was really missing Elaine, but I thought, 'I don't want to burden them with that…, so if I keep telling them I'm fine, then that's something less for them for them to worry about.' Little did I know that they were upset because I wasn't talking about it.

Such misunderstandings can last years. Tim Bentinck, the actor who plays David Archer in *The Archers* on BBC Radio 4, was 13 when his father told him his mother had killed herself:

> His shoulders were going up and down and I thought he was laughing, because I'd never seen him cry. I said, 'You beast!' and pushed him away, because I thought it was just a silly joke.

For years his father lived with the thought that Tim blamed him for his mother's death – not that he had mistaken tears for laughter:

> We never spoke about that conversation until a few years before he died – this was about 35 or 40 years later – and I said, 'You…didn't think that I blamed you for Mum's death, did you?' He said, 'Yes.' I'd always thought he'd realised that I thought he was laughing… He felt it was his fault and he'd held that inside him all those years.

One particular group whose grief can often be overlooked is grandparents. Yet they are not only mourning their grandchild. They are also sharing their child's suffering. They may feel they have to be strong, hide their own hurt, while their child may be trying to shield them from the worst of *their* grief.

A grandmother said how deeply hurt she was that her daughter didn't turn to her when her child died:

> I just couldn't get near and I resented the fact that it was friends she spoke to and not family. She had a friend who only lived up the road from her and she did her crying there. But I wanted to be the one to console my daughter… I felt as if I'd lost her for a while and that I was grieving on my own.

Range of experiences

We have deliberately included accounts from people who are not strictly 'family' – there is a chapter on Partners, another on Friends – because these days a partner can have the same commitment to a relationship as a spouse and, in a society which is so mobile and where families are geographically fragmented, the ties of friendship can often be stronger than those of family. But families can sometimes exclude people who believe they were very close – sometimes the closest person – to the person who has died. Richard Scarborough's partner, Paul, died of an AIDS-related illness. He said:

> If either my mother or my father dies – and they're both now in their late seventies or early eighties – I can't imagine that it could possibly be worse for either of them losing the other than it was for me to lose Paul. They would never, ever understand that.

Vera Percy's partner, James, died when they were on holiday together. Both were in their early eighties.

> I wasn't invited to the funeral, but I went. …And nobody looked at me. At the crematorium the minister turned to James's daughter and said, 'You were with your father when he died, weren't you?' And I wanted to shout, 'No, she wasn't. I was with him.' But I didn't.

Every death is unique and so is every response to death. It is impossible in a book this size to convey the whole breadth of human experience. All this book can hope to offer is snapshots of grief. But those snapshots include accounts of different types of death: natural causes, genetic conditions, accident, suicide and murder. They also reveal a range of emotions, from anger and guilt to relief.

How people cope

We asked all the people we interviewed, 'What does it feel like to lose a child – or a grandchild? A sibling or a spouse?' 'What effect did that have on your grief and the relationships of those closest to you? How did you cope with it?'

How *does* a woman cope with the sudden deaths of her mother, father and only sister, and the elimination of all that family memory? How does a man deal with his father's suicide? How do parents come to terms with the sudden collapse and death of their daughter on the day of her graduation ceremony, or with the knowledge that their son jumped from an eighth floor window after taking LSD? How, we wondered, does the manner of the death influence the length and intensity of bereavement?

Unsurprisingly, a sudden death can have far greater immediate impact than an expected one. There is no time to prepare, to say goodbye. There can be greater shock and pain, more opportunity for bewilderment, anger and regret – the 'if onlys', the 'what ifs'. As Cheryl Craggs said:

> I'm choosing a coffin when I should be looking at prams. I'm staring at the Yellow Pages trying to find a funeral director, when I should have been buying a cot.

In two instances of sudden death – one a car crash brought on by an undiagnosed heart problem, another a suicide – the people we talked to had spent years suppressing their anger. In both cases, that anger was finally unleashed by writing a letter – one, a letter to the dead brother, the other, replicating the suicide letter left by a father. The act of writing helped both people face what had happened and start the process of recovery.

When the death was some time ago, people talked about how their grief had changed over the years. Jeremy Howe's wife Elizabeth was murdered at an Open University summer school. He likened the initial impact to an atomic explosion with his family at the centre. Twelve years on, he says:

> As you get further from the epicentre, time-wise, the ripples get less, but it doesn't mean that they've gone. They're always there. Grief is no longer the dominant feature of my life.

Catherine Thompson's only sister died when she was hit by a car 18 years ago and her parents also both died suddenly. Grief is no longer the dominant feature of *her* life, yet she still mourns their loss, their continuing absence:

> It's no comfort, but grief doesn't go away. Not if you truly love somebody and they are part of the fabric of your life. It doesn't ever go away, it can't go away. It's how you learn to cope with it that's important.

For Catherine, prayer and the community of her local church have proved a great comfort and help, as they are to many people. There are examples here of people coming to terms with their bereavement through their commitment to a mainstream religion. Others develop their own belief system or are confirmed in their atheism. There are accounts of the birth of faith and of the death of faith.

Matthew Douglas's grandmother died after a long and painful illness:

> I used to believe in something after death, but now I don't. Her death changed my view. I thought, 'If there's a God, why would they let somebody die in such a horrible way?'

Legacies

Despite the pain and indignity that can accompany a death, the dying can teach us valuable lessons. And each life, no matter how short or uneventful, has meaning.

As Tim Whewell says of the death of his young son, Jethro:

> The formulation we came up with afterwards – because you do need to have something like that – was that it was a small life but that it was a life nonetheless. And it was a life that contained all kinds of things. Everybody's life contains some things and not others, some sensations and experiences, some good and some bad. And his life was also a mixture of those things.

We wanted to reflect this fact – that each of us, no matter how insignificant our life, has an effect on others. That effect may be big, it may be small, but every life leaves its legacy, and not just on those who are closest.

Rony Robinson recalls the surprise he felt by the turn-out at his brother's funeral:

> He was clearly immensely popular. So the fact that he was liked, and as much as he was, that was a great consolation.

This view is echoed by Jamie Bosworth, who has also lost a brother:

> The funeral itself was overwhelming, really. I expected it to be busy but not as busy as it was…there were probably about 1500 people there. It knocked me back a bit really, but it was good, it gave us a lot of strength, that so many people were supporting us.

Other people's reactions

One thing that causes people pain when they are bereaved is the lack of acknowledgement of what has happened. Time and again, people said that a simple 'So sorry to hear about your father/wife/son' was more helpful than avoiding mentioning the person who has died.

People talked about the hurt, distress or anger they felt when a friend, neighbour or colleague crossed the street to avoid talking to them, or never mentioned what had happened. When Glenis Stott's daughter died, some friends and acquaintances were too embarassed to speak to her:

> People used to bring cards and they'd run down the path and push them through the letterbox and run away again so they wouldn't have to meet us.

Katie Boyle, a well-known face on British television, is irritated when her grief is equated to illness:

> People sometimes said to me, 'Are you feeling better?' And that drove me mad. 'You must be feeling better now.' And I'd say, 'But I haven't been ill. I've lost Peter.'

Others pointed out the comfort of cards, letters or phone calls, of people being intuitively sensitive and practically helpful. John Suffield's son, who shared his name, was murdered in a particularly violent way. Two days after the murder, a young priest came round:

> He had the greatest compassion of all, because he never said a word...and he admitted, 'I don't know what to say. ...I just feel so much sorrow for you, but I'm here.' ...That was marvellous, because I didn't know how to handle it either and I didn't want somebody to come in and say, 'I know what to do on these occasions.' He became one of the family. If visitors came in, he made them welcome and offered them cups of tea. He went round to the chip shop for us. The man who admitted he didn't know what to do for us, did everything.

Again, the message is of human contact, help in small, practical ways, the importance of a touch, a hug.

Strange behaviour

The shock of bereavement can lead to people behaving differently, badly, madly, at least in the initial stages. Some people talk of becoming obsessive about their other close relationships. Others, often men, talked about wanting to get into a fight, to find a physical release for some of their pain. Ed Farelly, whose wife died just after the birth of their second child, remembers:

> …driving around…and thinking, 'I just hope somebody gets into an argument with me. Just give me the opportunity!' I'm five foot five and not remotely violent. I'd probably have been beaten to a pulp!

Other people find themselves doing strange things, acting totally out of character. One woman recalls putting the milk bottle in the hall and her shoes in the fridge. Jeremy Howe, a BBC producer, looks back now in some amazement at when, four years after his wife Elizabeth died, he made a television film about his grief, which involved returning to the room at York University where she was killed.

> You totally lose perspective. People must have thought, 'This guy's a nutcase.' …I kind of needed to go and see where she'd got killed, and the only way I could think of doing that was by taking a television crew with me! …God knows what my crew must have thought – what kind of madness was I in the grip of? I was unstoppable. *It* was unstoppable.

To talk or not to talk?

Cheryl Craggs felt an urgent need to talk to complete strangers about the sudden death of her husband, Glenn, when she was pregnant with their first child. After she'd had her baby she remembers being in the park one Sunday morning:

> There was a couple there and I just found an excuse to bring it into the conversation and talk about it. I felt the need to tell people about what had happened to me, because I didn't want them to think that I was a normal single parent. I might be alone, but it was not out of choice.

Others – again, often men – retreat into themselves, preferring to keep their grief to themselves. When we approached Tim Whewell, for example, to request an interview, he told us:

> I'm not actually sure what, if anything, I've got to say. I've never sorted out what I think, and I think you need something moderately articulate – not totally raw stuff such as you might give a psychotherapist.

Many of the men we spoke to recognised their reluctance to talk about their feelings but felt their silence was often misunderstood. It was simply their way of dealing with their grief.

The passing of time

When we interviewed the psychologist and writer, Dorothy Rowe, about the death of her father, she pointed out that when the psychiatrist Elisabeth Kübler-Ross identified particular stages of death, dying and bereavement, she was simply observing those stages, and recognising that people pass through them at different times and at different speeds:

> But what Elisabeth Kübler-Ross had simply noted as observations has now hardened into dogma, and you're supposed to go through these stages like you're doing it properly. It's analogous to teaching women how to give birth, and all these women trying to do everything perfectly feeling upset afterwards because they haven't done it properly. They've got a live, healthy baby, but they didn't do it the way they were taught to do it.

As Jeremy Howe said, when also asked for advice:

> Trust your instincts... Take each moment as it comes... And just put one foot forward at a time... You do get through it. And the advice I'd give to people – and it's terribly pat, is – it will get better. It doesn't mean you love that person any the less. It's just that time passes and you adjust to it.

There is a general recognition among those who work with bereavement that life is never the same again after a death. But while that might sound – and feel – insupportable, time after time in our contact with bereaved people we found messages of hope, of triumph over despair, of a recognition that, no matter how traumatic the death and its effect on those left behind, the passing of time can ease the pain.

Joe Lawley, one of the founders of The Compassionate Friends, talked about how easy it is to feel that you are not recovering from the impact of grief. He described meeting parents whose grief was more recent than his own:

> They'd look at you after a bit and think, 'They're not as bad as me' and we'd look at them and think, 'We're not as bad as them.' Because the grief is difficult for you to gauge. You wonder, 'Am I getting better?'

The death of someone you love can be a life-changing experience. In the initial stages of grief, it can seem wholly negative. But these accounts show how people can turn that negativity around, force it to become positive. Some people, as a result of bereavement, have changed their lives completely. Others have simply changed their perspective on life. In nearly every instance, death has emphasised just how precious life is.

Erykah Blackburn and her mother, Pauline, were not alone in feeling they had moved on significantly. Six months after talking to us, Pauline wrote that she had completely redecorated her house, including the living room which, at the time of the interview, had the air of a shrine to her son. 'Maybe this is a cleansing process,' she said. 'It now does not look like the house where Zennen used to come.' And Erykah said:

> You should do a follow-up now because, when I read what I'd said, it felt like a totally different person. I've moved on so much. It's amazing to see the growth and how far I've come. I can see where I was, but I'm somewhere else now.

The accounts in this book are highly personal and moving. At times they are harrowing, at times heart-rending, at times poignant, but in each one there is something positive: a touch of humour, a revelation, an unexpected insight. We hope they will help others who have had, or who are having, similar experiences to recognise that they are not alone.

CHAPTER 1

Mothers

Pauline Blackburn's son Zennen was shot dead in the Moston area of Manchester in 2002. He was 27. When she did this interview, in her front room, his ashes were in two gold-coloured pots on either side of the fireplace. Pauline has two other children, Erykah and Lyndon, who is 13. Erykah's story is told in Chapter 5: Sisters.

Zennen and his girlfriend Lorna had been living in Oldham for five years, but he still used to call in to see me every day. They'd been house-hunting that day, then they'd been to get some food and bring it back here to eat it. He'd left his car with a lad who used to wash it, so she'd dropped him off just down the road to pick it up, and she walked in with the food and said, 'Zennen's following behind.'

She was just undoing the food when his friend's girlfriend came running in hysterical. She wasn't speaking so we couldn't tell what it was. Lorna runs to her and she's like, 'What's the matter?' And she said, 'It's Zennen, he's been shot!' It was like a nightmare. You can't imagine someone running in and saying something like that and it be true – you hear it but it doesn't register, not for a second. So we ran outside and another friend of his who'd heard about it comes flying down, headlights on, beep-beep, to get us. We fly in the car, we're round there in one second and there's people there pumping his chest and stuff – but you could see he'd already gone. When I got out of that car and looked at him, I said, 'It's too late.' I knew immediately.

The ambulance was on the corner, but it wouldn't come. It was parked 100 yards up the road and I remember people screaming at the ambulance – but they can't come till the police come. The next minute I saw a police paramedic come over and he was a nervous wreck. I think he was just frightened to death of the scene, because there were loads of people there. It was a bright sunny afternoon.

Then the police arrived. It probably took 15 minutes, but you know what it's like when you're waiting, it seems ages. Then finally the ambulance came, and I remember it was a tall fellow with grey hair and he got out, got the trolley, stood there and said, 'We're too late.' Mind you, he were too late – because if I'd thought for one minute that they could have done anything…

The police cordoned off the area, covered him up eventually, then about six o'clock they put a tent up, but he was there until gone 12 o'clock at night, because they were combing the area for ages and ages. I stood beside him, for about half an hour.

They said it would have been instantaneous – he could never have survived it – which again is good. Because if they'd said, 'If the ambulance had come…' Oh, my God, imagine that. So no one could have done anything. Another friend of his had heard the shooting, ran out and Zennen shouted out, 'Help me!' That must have been the last words. He ran over to get him into the car and take him to hospital but it was too late.

It was like a madhouse here for three or four days, packed out. Two police liaison officers used to come every day, sometimes twice, just to talk to us: 'Has anyone said anything, do you know anything more?' and to go over the story with us – again and again and again.

They said, 'Don't worry – it won't go on for long, because we've got at least 250 witness statements, it happened in broad daylight, somebody somewhere has seen the car.' But after a month – brick wall. They've got all the witness statements, but no one can identify anybody, no one can come up with a reason for why it was done. To this day, no one's got a clue.

Whoever did it had a mask on. When it first happens, you're looking at everybody, because you don't know who's who. So we're no further on now than we were 16 months ago.

Everyone asks, 'How do you cope with it? How do you go on day after day?' I've no idea. I always thought if anything drastic happened to me, I'd go berserk, but not at all – in fact, I was the complete opposite. It's not some-thing you can put into words. I don't know how I coped with seeing him lying there. It took some time to get over that picture. But you just have to get on with your life. What else can you do?

It happened 500 yards away. I've got to drive past the place every day. For the first 12 months there were lots of flowers there. We took all the flowers from the funeral round there, three carloads. Then for Christmas we all took flowers down and had a drink round there, and for his birthday we all went out for a meal and put flowers there again. But since Christmas I've said, 'I don't want to do this any more, let's leave it.' So we don't go any more, and we've removed all the flowers.

His ashes are there – in that gold pot and that gold pot [pointing them out in the fireplace]. I'm not into graves and I don't see the point of putting flowers on them – you're no longer there. He felt the same. He wouldn't want to have been buried. He never liked being dirty, he couldn't bear to be dirty. I don't want his ashes to be buried. I'm more comfortable that they're there.

I've always gone to mediums – just out of curiosity – and I've been to one or two that are really good. A lady I've been to four or five times since it happened, when I first went, she described everything that had happened to him.

I didn't tell her anything, but she said, 'I've got someone coming through', and, 'Oh, my God, calm down!' She said to me, 'My God, doesn't he talk fast?' and he did. It does make you feel better, whether it's true or not.

She said when it happened to him, he didn't know it had happened – like in that film Ghost. According to her, when you die, your spirit leaves your body and someone in the family comes to collect you. But when you go like that and no one's expecting it, then for two days you're in limbo. Hence the reason you sense things straight after.

Like, we used to smell his aftershave. Now, you could put that down to imagination or what, but it did happen a lot. On one occasion – he used to have a shop in Oldham, the girl across the road used to work in it, and I'd taken her to work one night. We were driving down the road and this smell came over me so much so that I couldn't breathe. I had to stop the car and wind down the windows – and the same had happened to her.

I've had a couple of funny things happen as well. I've got this book a medium wrote about when you have a child that died, and how they let you know they're there. It may take a long time to come through physically, but children will move stuff. Like, you put a pen down and they move it to another room. I'm still experiencing little things now and again, which let me know that he is still there. So that bond between you – it's got to carry on, hasn't it? If there is an afterlife, it can't stop, can it?

We've always been close, always talked, talked for hours, right from him being small. He used to come round every day. I'd come home from work and he'd be sat there, where your bag is – and if he missed one day, he'd ring me. Sometimes he'd be here in the morning, or before or after he'd been to the gym. I miss that a lot.

I've sometimes wondered if he didn't have an insight into his death, because the week before he died, he was a different person. Him and Lorna went away for the weekend to London, and she said it was the nicest weekend she'd ever had but she felt a bit weird about it. They came back from London on the Monday and he went to someone's funeral on the Wednesday, and he said, 'I hate funerals, they're depressing', but he felt he had to go. And the next one was his.

As a mother, you never get over something like that. You learn to live with it but you never get over it, it's not possible – no matter how many mediums you go to – you never get over it, no, no.

I wouldn't have thought I could cope with something like this happening to him, but you've got to. You never forget it, but as each day goes by, you take a deep breath and try and put it out of your mind and go about your business. But then a record comes on or something like that – but you have to learn to live with it because you have no choice.

Rose Dixon's eldest daughter, Avril, died aged 22 in 1991. Rose has a younger daughter, Penny, who lost her third child shortly after birth. Rose gives her account of her grandson's death in Chapter 10: Grandparents.

I walked into the kitchen one Friday evening and my husband, Larry, was on the phone. He was saying, 'No, please God, no!' I snatched the telephone from him and said, 'Who is it?' Larry ran out of the room and into what was then a little sitting room and he just locked himself inside.

I asked who it was on the telephone and it was somebody we know in Yorkshire where Avril was living at the time. She said that she'd collapsed about half past one that lunchtime and they'd called the paramedics. I was waiting for her to say, 'She's in such-and-such a hospital. How quickly can you get there?' Then she said, 'Mrs Dixon, I'm so sorry, but Avril's dead.'

I went to the sitting room, but the door was locked and Larry wouldn't let me in. I could just hear him crying and wailing. I went back into the kitchen and telephoned a friend. I screamed down the phone at her that Avril was dead. She was in the middle of cooking her tea, but she downed tools and came round straight away.

While I was waiting for her, I just paced up and down in the hall and I couldn't believe what I'd been told. I didn't want to believe it and when my friend knocked at the door, I opened it and fell into her arms and started crying. She kept saying, 'Who's dead?' I was just hysterical. In the end she shook me and said, 'Rose, who is dead?' I'd been incoherent on the phone and the only word she had picked up was 'dead'. I told her it was Avril. Much later this friend said she thought it was Larry, because she thought, if anybody was going be dead in the family, it would be Larry of a heart attack.

That was the beginning of a nightmare. Larry still wouldn't come out of the other room. I contacted our other daughter, Penny, who was at university in Birmingham and told her to come home immediately. Eventually Larry came out of the room and he became the tea man. He made pot after pot of tea and lots of cups of coffee.

Larry and I went to bed about two o'clock in the morning and I think we lay there talking till about four. We both slept, but I remember waking up at about ten past six and my first thought was, 'Oh, my God! What an awful nightmare!' and I turned to Larry and started to shake him to say, 'I've had a terrible nightmare about Avril', then the realisation hit me that this was true. It wasn't a nightmare. I think, in a sense, that was the worst moment. We just lay there and cried together.

Avril had literally got out of bed and dropped dead. She hadn't been too well. She'd had a very heavy cold and it had gone onto her chest. When she went to see the GP saying she was tired and lethargic, he said, 'That's depression.' He gave her a prescription for anti-depression tablets, but at her post-mortem it turned out that she'd had pneumonia.

I think the hardest thing I had to do in the early days after Avril died was kissing my other daughter goodbye and letting her go back to university. I wanted her here with me and I wanted her wrapped in cotton wool, never out of my sight for one minute. When you have lost one child, you are terrified of losing your surviving child or children. Absolutely terrified.

It was better for Penny that she did go back to university, because if she'd been living at home, I'd have made her life a misery. But it was interesting that her attitude changed. Before Avril died, Penny was going off to clubs and pubs and all sorts of things. I don't even know a tenth of what she was getting up to. I used to say to her, 'When will you ring me?' She'd say, 'Oh, some time. There's always queues of people at the phone.' But this time when she was going back, she said, 'Will you ring me?' and 'When will you ring?' and 'What time?' So she obviously had fears about us and she needed reassurance. Looking back, I don't know that I was terribly supportive towards her. She suddenly went from being a child with a sister to being an only child and she lost a friend, too.

Penny eventually got married to Paul and they had a little boy called Joshua and, I have to say, in lots of ways he saved my sanity. It was going to be our first grandchild and we were thrilled to bits. This baby was in no way a replacement for Avril, because nobody could replace her. I do remember being exceedingly angry with a colleague. I told her Penny had had Joshua and she said, 'A little baby to replace Avril. Aren't you lucky?' I just looked at her and thought, 'The woman is so stupid and so insensitive, don't even waste your breath talking to her.' I just walked away.

When I saw the baby for the first time, I was numb. I felt nothing. Because Penny had had a post-partum haemorrhage and was very ill. When I went in to see her, she was pale and drawn, her eyes were sunken and she had these big shadows. I just looked at her and thought, 'My God, I'm going to lose her as well.' But the next day she was fine and once I saw she was OK I thought, 'This child is the best thing that has ever happened to us.'

Grief affects everything. It affects your mental faculties. I remember not very long after Avril died I'd been shopping and I came back home. A friend was coming. She'd said she wanted to go to the chapel of rest and see Avril and I'd said, 'Don't go on your own. Call for me and I'll come with you.' I'd kicked off my shoes and unloaded the shopping. Then the friend arrived and I put my coat back on. I went to the hall to get my shoes, but I couldn't find them and I got so angry with myself, because I couldn't remember where I'd put them.

In the end my friend said, 'Let's just calm down. We'll have a cup of coffee and have a think. Then you can decide whether you're going to find these shoes or wear a different pair.' She treated me like a child, but it was what I needed. We put the kettle on and I opened the fridge to get the milk out and my shoes were in the fridge. The milk was in the hall and the shoes were in the fridge. I felt quite frightened, because I thought, 'You're going mad, woman. You're going to be committed to the mental hospital very soon.'

Avril died on the Friday and on the Sunday my boss came. She had a box with two very large home-made fruitcakes in it and when she handed them to me – I am by nature a very polite person – I looked at them and said, 'Thank you very much. That's very kind of you.' I put them on the coffee table and I remember thinking, 'My child is dead and you bring me two cakes!' But I have to say that was one of the most useful things anybody ever did for me, because there were people in and out of this house like Grand Central Station for weeks on end and it was so good to have those cakes. I cut them, sliced them, and whenever anybody came it was 'a cup of tea or coffee and have a piece of cake.'

Larry took Avril's death very badly, but in a different way to me. I categorise people into 'feelers' and 'thinkers'. I'm definitely a feeler – he's a thinker. We heard about Avril's death on a Friday evening and the following Monday morning Larry went into the university and he gave a 9.30 lecture on thermodynamics. To me that's a typical thinker: 'If I concentrate on doing other things, normal things, I don't have to think about the death.' To save my life, I couldn't have done anything on that Monday morning, but he could. I suppose it's a different way of grieving.

Within a couple of months of Avril dying, Larry seemed back to normal. He was out cycling with the cycling club on a Sunday and I'm sitting here sobbing my heart out, wanting to talk to him about Avril. I felt he was over it, that he couldn't have loved her as much as I did, because he couldn't possibly be back to normal.

Then lots of resentment comes in and you start to get conflict. A lot of men go off and have affairs. They want everything to be normal, but every time they walk through that door they see this woman falling apart. I now realise that the only way a lot of men cope with it is to bury it and do ordinary things. 'If I go cycling on Sunday, I can pretend this hasn't happened.'

I do feel I failed to protect Avril. She was my responsibility. OK, she was 22 years old. She was an adult. But she's still my child. Intellectually I know it wasn't my fault, but in here – in my heart – it was.

K ate Hull Rodgers is director of HumourUs, a humour consultancy. Kate and her actor husband, Bill, already had one son, Harvey, when Kate gave birth to a stillborn son, Neil, in 1999. Bill gives his account in Chapter 2: Fathers.

I was 38 weeks pregnant – second pregnancy, perfect, everything absolutely fine. Then I went for my 38-week check-up, big as a barn and wide as a house, and the midwife couldn't find a heartbeat.

So we phoned my husband, and he came to get me, and we were off to the maternity hospital. There, the consultant found a heartbeat and everything was fine. Then the midwife couldn't find the heartbeat. So the consultant came back, couldn't find the heartbeat, called in the big consultant. And, as time is passing, it's getting worse. And when the two consultants started talking in polysyllabic doctor words and not talking to me, I knew that this was pretty bad. The heartbeat they'd found was mine. Because a baby's heartbeat is very fast and my heart, from anxiety, was rushing, they thought it was the baby's. But the baby was dead.

I just remember being cross at the head consultant. I said, 'Could you speak to me? Could you tell me what's going on?' Then he said, 'This is as difficult for me as it is for you.' At which point I could have punched him in his uterus.

You know something is going on when the midwife is not talking but is rubbing your hand, and when the consultants – who are all men – are talking amongst themselves. It was a gradual realisation. I can't remember the exact words they used. I do remember it wasn't until they brought Bill in. They told us together.

Then they left us alone and there was just silence. Bill broke the silence and said, 'We could always try again' and I said something like, 'Well, that might be fun' and then we started to laugh. I mean, what do you do at that moment, when you haven't absorbed the news? We laugh a lot, that's our way. I think that's why I married him, because he makes me laugh. That is probably the most comforting thing you can say when a baby dies – 'We can always try again.' And that is what has come to pass. We got pregnant about three months later and that heals you pretty quick.

Once the baby was discovered to be dead, they started to induce me, and because the baby was dead I could have any drugs I wanted. So I got very stoned for a couple of days on very pleasant morphine-like painkillers. The whole thing is a bit of a haze, but it took 72 hours and they let me go home to pack. Someone advised us to bring a baby outfit, because there's the saying goodbye, the mourning with the body. So we went and packed and got our little outfit – the Babygro and baby hat.

What they do is they ask you what you want to do. Do you want to give birth and then have the baby on your chest or do you want this or that? What we chose was to have him taken away and swaddled and then brought back. In retrospect, that was both the right decision and the wrong decision. I don't know how I would have done it differently, but what actually happened when I gave birth to him was his head flopped back and I felt total rejection, total rejection: 'That's a dead baby, get it out.' I didn't voice any of that but that's what I felt.

They took the baby away, swaddled him, brought him back and gave him to Bill. I didn't want to hold him. I've had to come to terms with it – but that's what was right for me at the time. We saw him later and I still didn't hold him. Afterwards I had these regrets, because people said, 'Well, at least you got to nurse him, you got to hold him and say goodbye' and I'm like, 'Well, actually I didn't.'

My girlfriend who came over from Canada to visit was really good about that. She said, 'Well, Bill did. You had him for eight months and Bill had him for eight minutes, and that's all his.' So Bill is actually the only person who held him.

He was born on Hallowe'en – the night of the living dead – and it was also the Sunday when the clocks go back. And all of a sudden it was dark at five. So it was the night the dead come alive, and he didn't. It was the night the world went black.

When I got pregnant with Dominic, my mother thought it was Neil's spirit, and I said no, Neil had been the generous baby who made room for his brother. Because we were only ever going to have two kids, so we wouldn't have had Dominic if Neil had survived.

You can put grieving up on a pedestal and worship it, which some people do. And some people tend to take a long process, and some people bury it. Everyone grieves differently. I was interested to see that I grieved really easily and well. The only self-recrimination was that I had a bit of guilt that I wasn't more devastated. People tend to project things onto you – like, 'Oh, you must be feeling awful, you'll never get over it.' And your inner brain is going, 'No, actually I'm OK.' I wasn't going to let anyone tell me I should be grieving more. Free advice is worth what you pay for it – nothing. But I was surprised by how OK I was about it – and still am.

Partly for the joy of our family – because he's a member of our family – we celebrate Hallowe'en as Hallowe'en. But on Bonfire Night, which is when he was due, one of the rockets is for Baby Neil, because Baby Neil is in the clouds. So we do celebrate his birthday. And it's funny, because Harvey, who's now five-and-a-half, will sometimes get sad and say, 'I miss Baby Neil.' And I think, 'Is that true?' But he's part of our mythology and part of the family.

After you've had a baby, you still look mightily pregnant and people say, 'Haven't you had him yet?' I was OK about it, it's the other people who are mortified. I did have one funny experience. There was one woman who was as pregnant as me, a few weeks later, I saw her cross the street to the other side with her little baby carriage. I don't blame her. She chose – either out of consideration for me or because she didn't want to go there – to cross the street. A lot of people say, 'I don't know what to say so I don't say anything', and that's unfortunate. Say the wrong thing, put your foot in your mouth, rather than go on the other side of the street.

When someone really close to you dies, it does brighten all the colours of the living. Grieving is about the living, it's something the living do. I don't think the dead grieve their loss or mourn for losing life. And I'm not upset that they're gone, because they're not. You feel them. You breathe them.

The hospital minister was very much a part of our death experience. He'd done the naming ceremony for Neil at the hospital, and he gave the eulogy at the funeral. Harvey [who was 18 months old at the time] was running around, with no concept of 'this is a chapel, we're all supposed to be upset now', and going up to sit with the minister because he wanted a piece of the attention. Bill spoke and I spoke – I spoke about Mother Courage. The most powerful moment for me in that play [by Brecht] is her silent scream, and that's what we were articulating. So it was a really good little funeral. And then we went for a pint.

I did talk to Neil for the first few weeks. I'd go to bed in the afternoon for a little nap and have a little conversation – 'I'll always hold you, I'm sorry I didn't hold you.' I didn't hold him in this life but I believe in some sort of afterlife, some sort of connection of souls, so I'll hold him then. It was a brief meeting on this particular cycle of life, but – saying goodbye? No. It's saying, 'See you later. Goodbye until we see each other again.'

Anandi Mehmood's 17-month-old daughter, Naseem, died in a drowning accident on a visit to Pakistan. Anandi was visiting the family of her husband, Tariq. He was still in England, sorting out the house they had just bought in Manchester. Anandi and Tariq's other daughter, Neelam, was three and a half. Since Naseem's death they have had two other children, Mishaal and Waris.

Naseem fell into a pond in her grandfather's house. I'd gone to Pakistan for a break because I'd just handed in my PhD thesis. I felt it was my fault. Why was I on my own? Why wasn't someone watching out for her when there were so many adults around in the courtyard at that time? Why was I so tired that day?

You're constantly evaluating everything that you've done because in a sense life is like a journey and when you lose a child it's almost like the path you're on takes a 180 degree turn and you're spiralling off in a completely different direction – one you never thought you'd go in – and you have to find a reason. But I couldn't find a reason and I had to accept that I wasn't in control of everything.

I was a well-educated woman and I was reasonably well off. Before Naseem died I always felt that I could control my environment. In a funny kind of way I was very different to all the people around me in Pakistan, many of whom didn't have the advantages I'd had.

To begin with people didn't know what to do because they had their rituals, but they weren't necessarily mine because I'm not Pakistani. My father's Indian and my mother's English and I'd been brought up in Bombay, so my background was a mixture of Hindu and Christian. In Pakistani villages, grief is a shared experience. I'd been to Pakistan before several times, but these weren't people I'd shared my life with. What I wanted was to be able to sit with my mum and my brother and with Tariq. I didn't want everyone else there.

There must've been hundreds of people in the courtyard and in the house just waiting for Tariq to arrive so we could have Naseem's funeral. Everybody stayed up the whole night sitting with her. There was one time I remember in the night I just walked out. My eldest daughter was sleeping and I got up and went out into the courtyard and I just started screaming. Nobody came over because I don't think they knew what to do. I was just lying on the floor screaming.

One of the things women there do, particularly in the first weeks, is come and sit on a mat to grieve and share memories of the person who's died. Women would come and they would sit and cry. But they weren't crying because they were missing Naseem. They didn't really know her that much. They were crying because of the tragedy of the loss and also they had known her grandparents and family. They were also crying for the grief in their own lives. But I felt so numb at the time that I asked Tariq to stop people crying, because I couldn't cry properly then and I couldn't bear listening to other people.

I just sat there for two weeks and I can remember the tension in my heart. It was like a knot. Although I wanted to be able to go and visit her grave every day, which I did, at the same time I wanted to come back to Britain, because this is where I'd lived with her and this was where she'd been born. It was only when I was back home that I could really cry.

I remember we came off the plane and we knew there were friends coming to meet us at the airport. I felt all right. Then we put the luggage on the trolley – I think I was holding Neelam's hand – and we walked through. There was this whole sea of people and I saw two of my friends. The moment I saw them I just turned round and I wanted to run back inside the aeroplane. I remember they ran and they grabbed me. I just cried and cried.

In the first few months – probably the first year – I wanted to be able to cry all the time. Every time I meet someone who I haven't seen since Naseem died, I will cry. Because it's almost like meeting every part of your life from before that moment and readjusting it to after that moment. It's like saying 'I am no longer the person that you knew'.

I hadn't thought very much about death until Naseem died, but the trauma of her loss has altered every part of me. Looking back I think I was quite an arrogant person and I've had to rethink everything. It made me realise how human I was. How vulnerable.

The first year was definitely the most difficult. Mishaal being born was a tremendous new beginning for us. Mishaal was born about nine-and-a-half months after Naseem died. When Tariq came to Pakistan I said, 'I want another child.' He said to me, 'We will fill our house with children', which was the best thing he could've said at that time.

All the way through the pregnancy and after she was born I would talk about Naseem. What I wanted was Naseem. I was having a baby but what I wanted was Naseem. I can remember friends saying, 'You'll always remember Naseem, but this is a different child.' I'd say, 'Yes, I know.' Rationally you can know that, but it's understanding it emotionally and accepting it that's difficult. If I'm really, truly honest, I couldn't accept it – at least not until I was forced to when Mishaal outgrew the age that Naseem was when she died. It was when she became nearly 17 months old. I can remember the day and I thought I can't keep measuring her against Naseem. I can't keep thinking, 'Naseem crawled at this moment and she walked at this moment and she talked these words and she could climb out of her cot.' I have to love Mishaal and admire Mishaal for herself.

To begin with lots of people came and actually when you're in a state of great shock that's quite difficult. In a funny kind of way what you want is everyone to go away. Then when everyone's gone away you actually want everybody there. I suppose you're dealing with an emotion, which is so raw and the pain is so deep, that there isn't an answer, but at the same time the best thing is having lots of people to comfort you and I think unfortunately in the West that's exactly what doesn't happen most of the time. People come and do their formal visit, but what you need is actually people to keep coming back and say, 'How are you today? Is this a good day or a bad day?'

On one level time is a healer. But when Naseem first died, people said this to me repeatedly. In many ways it's a stupid thing to say because when you have just lost a child the idea of healing is incomprehensible, although, when you reflect back, there is no doubt that life has become more bearable. At the same time a counsellor I went to for a short while would talk about letting go and I couldn't make any sense of the notion of letting go, because I didn't want to let go of my daughter. I wanted her to be with me all the time.

I think holding on to physical things which were hers is about not letting her go. When I was in Pakistan, I gave away a lot of her clothes because there are people in the village that are very poor, but when we came back to England all her clothes were in her drawers and her wardrobe and I couldn't give them away. They're still hanging in this little wardrobe on their own and even Mishaal, who doesn't really know who Naseem was, knows that these clothes are Naseem's. I just can't get rid of them.

It must've taken me a year to put all the condolence cards away. I used to have them all out with the flowers and I would light a candle. My mum kept saying, 'Anandi, put them away, that's enough.' But I couldn't. It was just before Mishaal was born and I felt it was almost like saying, 'Well, I've got another baby now. I can put Naseem away.' So I left them probably until after her first death anniversary or birthday.

I remember there was a calendar that Naseem had made at nursery and it had her handprints on it. It was on July, because during July and the beginning of August I'd been finishing off my PhD so I hadn't been thinking about tearing the pages of the calendar off before we left for Pakistan. We came back in September and it must've been around November when my mum came and saw the calendar. It was still on July. She tore off all the bits on the calendar to get it to the right month and I was absolutely devastated. I didn't want to accept that Naseem had gone. It was almost like trying to preserve everything in the house to that moment when she was still there and in July she was still alive. So I phoned up my mother and gave her a mouthful down the phone and of course she was really upset, because she'd lost a grandchild. It was just she was dealing with it in a different way.

I can talk about Naseem. You know, she was here and she was a beautiful – and she *is* – a beautiful part of my life. The spirit of her – because she was a very tough and vibrant child – exists somewhere in this world, you know. The forces of her are there and can't be forgotten. There's no physical thing that needs to exist in order to remember that.

R achel Osorio's second son, Jethro, was born with the incurable and life-limiting Tay Sachs disease, a rare condition found most commonly among Ashkenazy Jews. He died in 1999, aged just over three. Rachel and her husband, Tim Whewell, have had five children in all – Leo, who was stillborn; Esther, who is now ten; Jethro; Shifra, who is five; and Boaz, who is three. Tim's account is in Chapter 2: Fathers.

I think I had a sense there was something odd or different about him from quite early on – an instinct that something was not quite right. But to all intents and purposes he was perfectly fine. The first intimation we had that something was wrong was at the eight-month check. The doctors seemed very, very slightly concerned that his development was a little bit slow, and said we should go back in a month and see how things were.

It wasn't until he was 18 months old that we had an official diagnosis. He had Tay Sachs disease, a condition carried by a recessive gene, so if both parents are carriers, there is a one in four chance that the baby will be affected. I'd never heard of a child with the illness before, though I'd seen a television programme about it when I was pregnant with him, which is one of those strange coincidences.

Children with Tay Sachs develop normally but slowly until about 11 months or a year, then they gradually lose skills and die – the very longest they would live would be five years old. And there's no medical treatment at all.

One of the very early recognisable symptoms is that babies have a very exaggerated startle reflex. All babies jump at things, but babies with Tay

Sachs fling their arms out much more to very slight stimulae. So, for example, if you coughed with Jethro, even when he was newborn, he'd jump out of his skin. I remember being aware that there were these oddities about him as a baby.

In the immediate aftermath of being given the diagnosis, we went into a state of shock. Having said that – it's very difficult to describe these things without sounding perverse, but we'd been living with huge uncertainty about what was wrong with him, and having to deal with the idea that we had a baby that might have severe learning difficulties or a physical handicap, and with no idea of whether he would live to adulthood, or what he might be able to learn. That had been building up over a period of eight months which, when you're going through it, is an extraordinary amount of time.

There'd been all these thoughts in my mind which we didn't really communicate to each other very much, about what impact this might have on our family, on Esther. I was studying at the time, so the thought was – 'Am I going to stop studying, give over my life to this particular child?'

Then suddenly we were presented with a diagnosis where there was no hopefulness at all, nothing whatsoever that medicine could do. So in a very strange way there was a kind of relief around to know what we were dealing with, and suddenly to have permission to be with the child as he was and who he was, and trust our own responses and reactions, and not have to be surrounded by experts and medical interventions.

We were signed off by Guy's Hospital, though they kept in contact, and we were handed over to people like dieticians and special needs health visitors. Having said that, it was a totally isolating experience. All the places we found ourselves, I'd fondly imagine we'd find other people in the same situation and be able to make contact with them, and in fact that never really happened.

The thing that I felt very, very strongly actually was – and this will sound really mad – this sort of zeal that people of our age and education and social class, I felt, had. A kind of illusion that they were in control of their lives. They could have a child when they wanted to have a child, the baby would be born, it would be OK. If you play your cards right, you'll have a house, a baby and a husband – we seemed to be surrounded by people who still believed that. And I just wanted the whole world to know that we're out of control and there's all kinds of things that can happen to you, that will throw you back onto level pegging with a caveman.

When I knew that Jethro was going to be very sick and not be able to learn anything or perform or be a marvellous child, the biggest fear was that I wouldn't be able to love him. The discovery that he was still totally lovable and – I'm going to cry – and that we were able to look after him and respond to him and that he could respond to us, and that I could get to a stage where I could forgive myself for all the awful thoughts and fears that I had had around him, I feel it's given me something very large in relation to the other children. Because Esther is a very clever girl, very bright and sparkly and pretty and everyone loves her, and I might have feared that I could only love a child who would be a lovely reflection of what great parents we were. Discovering that that wasn't true was something really wonderful to find out.

Jethro didn't get as far as speaking. By the end, communication was very much at the level of a baby. His ability to hold things, to sit up, all the things he'd learnt to do, gradually disappeared. So there was just physical closeness and a sense of knowing whether or not he was comfortable.

He almost died in the hospice. It was a bad situation really. I'd left him in the hospice because Tim was in Romania for quite a long time, and there was a family wedding in Switzerland that I'd decided to go to. I left him in the hospice and went off to the wedding. I kind of knew that we were getting pretty close to him dying, because of how much presence he had – he was kind of disappearing. And I went off against my better judgement, and the hospice were trying to contact me.

So Tim came back and arrived at the hospice to discover this very, very fast-fading child. He was completely on his own with a baby who was about to die. He didn't know whether to stay in the hospice, or try and bring him home. In the end, he brought Jethro home, and I got back with the other children, six hours before he died. I phoned Tim from Luton Airport and he was completely distraught, obviously. We got home and spent a few hours together and Jethro died that evening.

I feel, in a very strange way, privileged – well, not privileged but there are big taboos around death in the world we inhabit, and I know I've held two of my babies who have died, while they were dead, and it's fine – well, it's not fine at all, but it's something you can do as a human being.

The griefs, though, were completely different. With a stillbirth, there's a very powerful sense of having disappointed other people's expectations, particularly because Leo was the first grandchild in the family, and there was all this excitement – and excitement in me. Also I felt very isolated, because when you have carried a baby for nine months, I felt as though I knew him, and nobody else did. For everyone else, including Tim, he was just something that never happened. So it is different. It's more like a gap, than missing a known person.

Every anniversary of Jethro's death, Tim puts a notice in *The Guardian*. It feels to me as if Leo's death is pretty much only marked by me, but with Jethro, Tim feels it very important to put something in the paper, and we do something as a family, like releasing balloons or making a cake.

Particularly with a stillbirth, people shut up about it very quick. There's a huge amount of embarrassment. In terms of meeting people casually – when you're sitting in the park or school playground – there's this sense of automatically exchanging information with other women about how many children you've got. There's always this dilemma of – am I going to lay something enormous on them at the first encounter, of two dead babies, or am I just going to shut up about it? One feels like a huge social gaffe, behaving in a way that's unkind to other people, and the other feels like a constant betrayal of reality. So I make decisions depending on the situation.

It still catches me out when I'm not expecting it. For example, when Boaz turned three, I suddenly became aware that he was getting to the stage where he was too big for all Jethro's clothes – he's nearly older than Jethro ever was. And it's the first time in ten years we haven't had a baby in the house, and I spent a month or two really feeling very desperate about that. It felt like the last link with Jethro was going and it hadn't occurred to me that I would mind so much at that particular juncture.

I think everyone who has babies reaches that last baby thing. But it's notched up another ten degrees of loss and poignancy, because he was so like a little baby when he died. It sounds awful when you say, 'The child loses all its skills, they've got dementia.' But it was almost as if we'd gone back to that closeness that you have when a baby is absolutely new and dependent. So there's some real strong nostalgia for that kind of intimacy with someone very helpless.

I don't think you ever get over it. It still feels like a huge missing thing. No, I don't think you get over it.

Maureen Pardoe's son, Matthew, died in his first year at university. He had taken LSD at a party and jumped out of an eighth floor window. Maureen and her husband, Edward, have two other sons, Mark and Michael. Edward talks about Matthew's death in Chapter 2: Fathers.

We have three children. I still like to say we have three, because we had Matthew for 20 years. There were guilt feelings, because when someone dies you put them on a pedestal and you forget that you both had faults. He could be quite aggressive at times and I could be quite aggressive back. The teenage years were hell. He was an experimenter, which I think was why, when he was at university, he had a dabble in drugs.

He was at London University studying Physics and he'd taken his first-year exams. He went to an end-of-year party and two third-year students brought some drugs to the party. So, of course, Matthew had a go. Most of the students took some cannabis at this party. But then he tried the LSD. He was found wandering about on the eighth floor by a girl who thought he was drunk. According to the inquest he'd had hallucinations. He thought he could fly and he jumped out of this eighth floor window.

This happened in the early hours of Friday and about six o'clock in the morning the police came to the front door and knocked us up. I thought it was Mark, because our eldest son was in Northern Ireland in the army. He was in the Intelligence Corps and involved when any bombs went off. This was in the early 1980s, when it was still bad in Ireland. I thought Matthew was safe at university and Mark was the one in danger.

Until the funeral, you're like a robot really. His friends all came down and slept in the lounge on sleeping bags. It was wonderful to see them. I hugged all Matthew's friends. They must've been very embarrassed, but they were lovely and let me hug them. But the day after the funeral, when they left, that's when the grieving really began.

For instance, he died in the June and in the August we got Matthew's first-year exam results. They were brilliant and we were so proud, but you think 'He could've had a career, he could've had a good degree, he could've got married, he could've had children'. It's all his future that goes and it's a part of our future, looking at his future. That all goes.

My husband and I grieved very differently. I'm very much into feelings and talking – and wanting to talk about how I feel, and he's more reserved. For ages he wouldn't really talk about Matthew at all. It was his way of coping. He would go to badminton or he'd mow the lawn. That would be his way of getting rid of his stress, but I think one of the reasons why he wouldn't talk was because he would break down and he didn't like breaking down. I didn't care if I cried.

During the first two or three weeks he did break down, but after that it was as though he wanted to keep going and it was his way of coping. But I resented it. I felt quite bitter about it. I wanted him to break down as well, I suppose. For me it was such a relief, because I would cry and it would all come out and I'd feel better. Not for long. It would all start to build up again.

We still go to the cemetery occasionally and there's a bench where we sit down on the anniversary of his death, sometimes at Christmas, sometimes on his birthday. Then not very long ago my husband broke down while we were there. I mean, I was upset because he was upset, but he sobbed and sobbed for ages. And this was more than 20 years after it happened.

When Matthew died I went right off flowers. People used to come round with bunches of flowers and I hadn't got the energy to put them in a vase. I think the memory of the flowers from the funeral means I'm still not very keen on flowers. I think it was the energy of arranging them.

I tell you what I did appreciate – and it probably sounds awful – but some people brought me a casserole. One or two people actually brought me food and that was wonderful, because I hadn't got the energy. We lived on soup for a few days. I just couldn't get myself together to cook, so anybody that brought food I thought was wonderful – or a few cakes or something. It's people's time and people allowing me to talk, coming and having a cup of tea with me. I had one friend that came one day and she wouldn't know, but I was feeling particularly bad and she whisked me off for lunch, and do you know – we only had an omelette or something, but it was just the fact that she cared enough to do that.

People would say, 'Oh, I see you're coping now.' But inside I was bleeding to death. I remember the lady over the way, she said something about me coping and I got quite cross. I said, 'Well, I'm not coping!' I was very bitter – why me? Why is this happening? There was a real bitterness and an anger there, which eventually went.

One stage that is really, really bad and that's at the end of the first year, when you go into the second year and you feel yourself that you should be a lot better. There's a real low feeling – God, it's just not going to get any better. It's not going to be any different. And you almost feel as though you're sort of leaving that person behind as well. It's really peculiar.

You don't get over it – you learn to live with it. I don't have to go to the cemetery now. We do go, but if we moved now, it wouldn't matter, because wherever we go Matthew will always be with me. It would've mattered earlier on. I don't know whether it's part of a ritual, but it did matter earlier on.

About 18 months after Matthew died, my younger son, Michael, was going off to Cambridge University, so it was the last son leaving home. That was horrendous for me, because I didn't want him to leave home. I was wanting to cling on. Halfway to Cambridge we stopped overnight at a close friend's in Leicester, then we dropped him off at the university and drove back to Leicester and – I remember to this day – I was just so upset. I didn't want to come back to the empty house and my friend got really impatient with me. She said, 'Oh, you'll see him again at Christmas.' Christmas! This was September. I can't remember exactly what I said, but I just went berserk. Even to this day I don't think she really understands. Unless you've actually lost a child, it's very, very difficult to understand.

At that time I really felt suicidal. When we got home I remember going up to Michael's room to change his sheets. I think I just wanted to give up then. I remember I snuggled on his bed and sensed a faint trace of him. I knew I wouldn't see him till Christmas and my husband had just got promotion. Edward was away a lot and I just felt as though I couldn't go on. I didn't do anything, but I certainly thought about it.

Those thoughts stayed for a few weeks. I suppose the only reason I didn't do anything is because you get this guilt. I'd ruin the start of Michael's career at Cambridge, I'd ruin things for Mark, I'd ruin things for Edward. That's the sort of thing you think about. It's like you're emotionally blackmailing yourself, in a way. You mustn't do it!

After Matthew died I used to go and see my mum. She was always there for me. She was my biggest comfort and support, because she would talk about Matthew. I felt as though I could go over there and flop and nothing was expected of me. It was super, it really was.

Afterwards, when you look back, you can see things from different people's point of view and I realise just how much she was suffering, because she was seeing me suffering and she must've gone through hell. It's very, very selfish. I just didn't realise how much she suffered until later on.

My mother died 18 months after Matthew and I felt my sister grieved a lot more than I did. It was a big bereavement to her, whereas for me, although I missed my mum – I really did, I loved her – but it just wasn't the same as the loss of Matthew. Maybe I hadn't much left – I don't know – but I think my sister felt that in some ways perhaps I wasn't grieving as much as I should do.

The last time I saw my mother I said, 'I'm really looking forward to coming over for a few days when Michael goes back to university' and I also said, 'Thanks for all you've done.' I'm just so pleased I said that, because that's the last time I saw her. You take and take, and you don't always think to say thank you.

When somebody dies you think of the times you've said horrible things to them or the rows you've had. I mean when Matthew was 17 or 18 and in the sixth form, he went through a real punk stage. He dyed his hair and then he went down to Brighton and had an earring put in. I had the headmaster ringing up saying, 'Matthew's come into school. He looks an absolute scruff.' And all I was concerned about was what the neighbours thought. I thought, they'll see Matthew going out, looking a real scruff and you think it reflects on you. Later I thought, 'Oh, God! I wish I'd been more understanding.'

I can only speak for myself, but I think losing a child is the worst bereavement.

Glenis Stott's daughter, Catherine, died in 1999. She was 22 and had just graduated from Lampeter University with a 2:1 honours degree in Religious Studies and French. The whole family – Glenis, her husband Jeff, son Andrew and Catherine – travelled from Burnley to Lampeter for the graduation. But the night before the ceremony Catherine collapsed and the next day, as the graduation ceremony was taking place, they were at Catherine's bedside. She was unconscious and never recovered.

It was going to be her day. She was full of it. We went down to Wales the day before because there was a 'do' at night. We were driving along and she teased, 'Don't you show me up at that graduation or I will reject you!' She was just so excited, so totally thrilled.

We got to the university and found our rooms while Catherine went to check her results, because she was a great worrier and she thought they might've made a mistake about the 2:1. Then she and Andrew went off to meet some friends in the Students' Union.

A bit later I heard Andrew knocking on the door. He said, 'Mum, you need to come. Catherine's ill.' She was on this bridge on the campus, lying on the ground. She'd just collapsed, but she was coming round when I got there. Then she was sick and someone said they'd sent for an ambulance.

By the time the ambulance came she was fully conscious. My husband, Jeff, is an ambulance man and he'd checked her over. He was fantastic.

Catherine had gone flat down and she'd smashed her teeth, which she was very upset about, but she seemed fine.

I went with her in the ambulance and I was just talking to the ambulance woman when Catherine muttered something and just screamed that her head was hurting and she started fitting. The ambulance pulled to the side and the driver came in. They were both working her. Jeff was following us and he stopped, flung the ambulance doors open and said, 'What's wrong?' I said, 'She's just been sick.' Catherine was unconscious now. From that moment in the ambulance she didn't come round again.

When we got to the hospital they took her away. One of the ambulance men came out and couldn't meet Jeff's eyes because he knew he was an ambulance man, too. He couldn't look at him. The doctor said, 'It's really bad.' He told Jeff it was a sub-arachnoid haemorrhage. It's a bleeding in part of your brain and that's where the thing that controls your breathing and your heart is.

Then I heard this noise – this horrible noise – and I realised it was me. It was like an animal howling. They put me in this corner because I was crying, but I came out because I didn't see why anyone should hide me because I was crying. They kept pushing me in corners and I kept coming out because I was entitled to cry. I didn't care. Then we went in to see her and she looked beautiful to me. She'd got all the machines and everything. Jeff – when he saw her – he just started to shake and I was holding his hand.

We didn't want to go back to the university so they found us a room in the hospital. We had a single bed and a mattress on the floor between the three of us. In the morning Andrew said, 'I can't take this. I have to go home.' So Jeff took him to Aberystwyth to catch a train back to Burnley.

Jeff was gone for five hours and I just sat by the bedside holding her hand and talking to her. It was Friday now – the day of the graduation ceremony – and I was saying things like, 'You'd be putting your gown and your hat on now. You'd be going into graduation. We'd be having the tea with strawberries and cream afterwards.'

Then the doctor said, 'We're going to test her for brain death.' I remember when Jeff came back, he was walking up the corridor and I just ran towards him and said, 'She's not going to get better. She's not going to get better.' They did the brain scan on the Saturday morning and they said, 'We're sorry. She's brain dead.'

The haemorrhage is something that's just waiting to happen. They did say perhaps the excitement had added to it a little bit. Apparently it was just classic – the drop, then you come round and seem fine and then you go again.

Now all her friends had gone to this graduation and they had no idea what had happened. Jeff had called in at Lampeter to get our things and he'd seen one of her friends, but he didn't want to upset her, so he said, 'She fell and broke her teeth. She's not coming to the ceremony because her teeth are bad and they're very painful.' But another friend rang the hospital and I spoke to her. This girl said, 'Hiya, how's Catherine?' So I said, 'I'm sorry. She's dead.' She was just hysterical.

Jeff and I talked about transplants and we said that we'd like them to use her organs, but I wouldn't let them take her eyes. I said, 'You can have anything else, but not her eyes.' Because of the transplants it was 12 hours from her being declared dead to when they took her to theatre. So for 12 hours she was breathing with everything working and yet we knew she was dead. That was really strange.

She'd got a position at Merchant Taylors' public school, so she'd got this fantastic job to go to, and she'd won the French Literature Prize, which she didn't know about because they announced it at the graduation. On the lid of her coffin they put BA Hons after her name. It was the only time it was ever used.

The funeral was exactly a week after the graduation. Even the time was the same. People say how terrible funerals are, but quite honestly it wasn't. It was a great comfort. It was a lovely occasion. The flowers cost us an awful lot of money. She was doing Religious Studies, although she wasn't religious herself, and we got flowers done with a Hindu, a Sikh symbol and a Muslim symbol and a birth sign. We did that because you would never ever see those all together anywhere else. They were just special for her.

Me and Andrew both spoke at the funeral. I wrote it at the beginning of the week and then I kept reading it out loud until I could read it without crying. We had a humanist minister and he said to me, 'Give me a copy and if you break down, I'll take over and I'll say it.' But I was determined. No way!

I went to the front and looked at all the people. If you'd wanted an ambulance in Burnley that day, you wouldn't have got one because they were all at the crematorium. It was full. I looked at all the friendly faces, but then I saw somebody who was upset and I thought, 'If I look at him, I'm going to cry.' So I didn't. I just read the words I'd written and then Andrew made them laugh, because he talked about him and Catherine having burping competitions on the phone and things like that. Jeff just put his head on one shoulder and Andrew put his head on the other, and it was just such a comfort.

Then I was stood with a man with my arms round him and I looked up at him – because he was about two foot taller than me – and I said, 'I haven't the foggiest idea who you are!' But that was a comfort, too.

There couldn't be anything worse than this. There couldn't. Because she was part of me. I used to search for her. I don't mean physically. But I'd close my eyes and I'd look through the house and then look through Burnley, then through Wales and then everywhere she'd been – America and Turkey and France. Then it was as if I was above an empty globe. There was just me floating above this empty globe. But there was just nothing there.

As time went on it got worse, because she got further away. The Millennium was bad, but the year after it got to New Year's Eve and I thought I was fine. Then just after midnight I thought, 'She's another year away from me and going further and further away.'

One thing I've learnt is that life is special. I've been depressed on and off all my life and I'm not saying I'm happy, but I think life's more important to me now. It's fragile and you can lose it so easily.

Death's this big secret. People used to bring cards and they'd run down the path and push them through the letterbox and run away again so they wouldn't have to meet us. Also my sister-in-law said something that really annoyed me. We had Catherine's voice on the answer-phone and even before we got home from the hospital she said to Andrew, 'You need to take that message off. It's upsetting people.' Andrew said, 'I'm not.' Then at the funeral I said to Andrew something like, 'Anyone who wants us to remove that answer-phone message can just fuck off.' I presume she heard that.

Oh, and I'll tell you what else makes me mad – people who don't appreciate their grandchildren. Andrew came out as gay, which meant I mourned the loss of the grandchildren I wouldn't have, but I thought I had Catherine. Then she died and I went through it again. So when people complain about their grandchildren and say, 'Oh, I don't want to look after them. They're not coming round wrecking my house', I think, 'Oh, shut up! Bloody give 'em me.'

CHAPTER 2

Fathers

Arthur Bickerstaffe is now in his seventies. Almost 50 years ago his first child, Janet, just 21 months old, was killed in a freak accident. He and his wife went on to have three other children: two daughters and a son.

Memory plays tricks on you, but she was a beautiful child – a little blonde-haired beauty – and she'd just started talking. I remember perhaps a day or two before she was killed, she was standing on the table, looking out of the window at the snow, and I can remember her saying it was 'nowsing'. It wasn't 'snowing' – it was 'nowsing'.

My wife was wheeling her into the village in the pram and a man was chopping a tree down and it fell the wrong way. It didn't injure my wife, but it so badly injured my little girl that she died. We went to hospital and I can remember my wife and I sitting there. I was so shocked I wanted a drink of water and I walked into a room to look for one, and there was this little tiny girl. Nurses were holding her down, because she'd been brain damaged, and that was my daughter.

This was almost 50 years ago. We had no car, no telephone and we walked home from the hospital. These are the dreadful thoughts: I can remember thinking, 'My God, if she's brain damaged, they'll probably take her to Manchester or Birmingham and I'll have to travel every day to see her', which is a most uncharitable thought, but nevertheless it's a real thought.

They called us back the same day. I think a neighbour got the telephone call and when we got there they told us that she'd died. I had to formally identify her and these images are burned into your mind. You can't shift them. There was this tiny little thing lying on the slab and they'd put some snowdrops in her hands.

I think one of the big things that helped us both was the clergyman, whose name I can't even remember. People had said to us, 'Poor little thing. Only 21 months. She hadn't lived. Think of all the things she's going to miss.' But he said, 'She won't miss anything. That was a complete life.' And I thought, 'Yes, anything beyond 21 months is imagination. The 21 months is reality.'

Just days after Janet's death, we discovered that my wife was pregnant with what is now my eldest daughter and I really didn't want that child. Until she was born, of course, and then it all changed. It's these selfish, evil little thoughts. I wanted to be looked after. I didn't want to have my wife bothering about a baby.

When the children started to toddle I struggled with being overprotective. If there were steps or anything, I used to be like a mother hen. I was a damned nuisance, I really was.

Later on – it's now 27 years ago – my wife died and she was only 48. She died of lung cancer and those memories are in a strange way clearer. I remember she said, 'I don't think I'm going to make it.' I took her hand and not long after that she died. I remember a nurse came into the room and she burst into tears. So I went and put my arm round the nurse and said, 'It's all right.' I found that helped.

Losing my wife was very different from losing my daughter. I'd got a 14-year-old son at home and people would say, 'Come round for your tea, love, and bring your washing.' And I can remember talking to Ian and saying, 'Ian, we'll manage for three months. If in three months they're still asking, we'll go.' But of course in three months they'd forgotten. Not forgotten, but put it down.

I sometimes think I've got no heart, because if it's a friend that I don't see very often that dies, in one sense it is no different right now to what it was before, because they're not there. With a child or a wife or somebody very close to you that you see every day, there is an enormous, immediate gap in your life. Yesterday she was here and today she isn't.

When Janet died, people did allow you to grieve, but they didn't wallow in it. I'm not very fond of seeing the railings at the school where a child's died covered in flowers. It strikes me as being slightly affected.

I had a very good friend and he's still a very good friend, and whenever anything's gone wrong, I've always gone to Bill. And Bill has gone straight to the nub of the thing. He was tremendous. He made no demands on me, expected nothing, offered nothing in terms of advice, but was always there, just there. And I could cry with him, I could swear about it and he was wonderful.

I've been a Samaritan and the one big thing that I got out of it is to be able to talk to somebody who's suffering from grief or a terminal illness. Before Samaritans I could never have done that. Their tears are their tears and I'm not going to say, 'Stop crying. I can't stand your crying.' Because that's me that I'm worrying about, not them.

For me, your grief is unique. Don't try to compare it with anybody else's. Don't think, 'I should be doing this or I should be doing that.' Accept your grief as it feels in your heart, because it's not a head thing, it's a heart thing.

Joe Lawley's son, Kenneth, died in an accident on his way to school in 1968. He was 12 and his sister, Angela, was 14. Shortly after Kenneth's death, Joe and his wife, Iris, became founding members of The Compassionate Friends, an organisation for bereaved parents. Another daughter, Lisa, was born almost two years after Kenneth's death. Lisa's first daughter was stillborn. Both Joe and Iris talk about that experience in Chapter 10: Grandparents.

Kenneth left home with his sister, Angela, to cycle to school. About a quarter of a mile down the road Angela branched off to her school and Kenneth continued down past a tractor factory, then he stopped at a T-junction. He was sitting astride his bike and a council van swept round the corner and knocked him down.

We received a call about 8.30 from his house master. He said, 'Kenneth's been knocked down. I don't know any details of the accident, but he's in the Coventry and Warwickshire Hospital.' So, of course, Iris and I dashed down there. We thought maybe he'd just broken a leg, but the dread fear, of course, was already there that it wasn't that and he might be dead already.

We were shown into the room where he lay. He was stripped to the waist and breathing naturally. He simply looked asleep. The young doctor said, 'He's got a cracked skull, but I've seen worse than this.' But Iris said, 'We're going to lose him, Joe.'

They operated, but he never regained consciousness. I remember the chaplain, Simon Stephens, came up and said, 'I don't want to intrude, but if I can be of any help, I'll be here night and day.' I said, 'Well, you can say a prayer, please.' In the course of this prayer he said, '…and we pray for Billy…' We waited till he'd finished and asked, 'Who's Billy?' He said, 'Well, there's a boy in another ward of the children's hospital dying of cancer. He's also 12 years old.' So for that brief moment our thoughts went to the other parents, envisaging them with a dying child for all of six or nine months, every day, every night. We were only a day into Kenneth's – if you like – period of dying and the grief and the pain and the anguish was unbelievable. [A later meeting with Billy's parents led to the founding of The Compassionate Friends.]

The surgeon would come, the consultant would come, they reach over and do things like feeling his heart and say, 'Fine strong heart there.' But we knew he was going downhill. They were doing all the tests for his reactions and they were just non-existent. Eventually they just closed the machine down and he died.

Your friends and relatives want to be as helpful and as supportive as they can, but there is inevitably, on their part, some sort of timetable: 'You should be a bit along the road now', 'You should be a bit better now.' At the doctor's: 'Take these pills. Is it six weeks? You should be over it by now.' Whereas we were – and I believe all bereaved parents are – absolutely crushed with the pain. It's with you day and night. It never gives up.

We discovered quite early on that we had to say to people, 'If you've ever read anything about bereaved parents, forget it. This is what it's like and, if you can't live with that, you can't be our friends, because we can't change. We're going to flood you forever till we stop. We don't know when that will be.'

You wake in the morning and for ten seconds you think it's different, but it's not. Back it comes. You can't stop talking about your child. Anybody could start any conversation and in about ten seconds we'd turn it round to talking about Kenneth.

Now this puts a terrible load on almost everybody – except another bereaved parent. They will listen to you and let you exhaust yourself. Then you will probably be kind enough to say, 'And what happened to you?' They will tell you their story and they will cry and the wavelength between you is so strong.

Another bereaved parent knows exactly how you're feeling. Their circumstances might have been different, but the grief they're experiencing is exactly the same. The same intensity, the same order of things. And when they say to you, 'I know how you feel', you accept it. If another person says it, you will immediately say, 'You don't know how we're feeling. Have you lost a child?'

In the early days we were almost missionaries. We knocked on people's doors, stood there with a bunch of flowers and said, 'We're from The Compassionate Friends.' They might've been bereaved for just two weeks and they'd look at you after a bit and think, 'They're not as bad as me' and we'd look at them and think, 'We're not as bad as them.' Because the grief is difficult for you to gauge. You wonder, 'Am I getting better?' You still felt as if the world was over, but here was an example of how you had been in the very early days. You knew it was worse for them.

In your mind's eye you begin to see your son at that stage between a child and a man, and you think 'in the future we will do this together and we will do that together and one of these days he'll marry and there'll be other children – grandchildren.'

Also he was our only son. We've lost the future as well and that's the end of our name. You lose a future daughter-in-law. You lose future grandchildren. My daughters have lost nieces and nephews. It's like ripples in the water: it spreads, because your children are affected by this death, too.

After Kenneth died we had a third child, Lisa, and she would say, 'I wouldn't be here if Kenneth hadn't died', and there was a measure of truth in that, because we hadn't planned to have any more than two children. Who knows whether we would have had. I believe we would and that's what we have to say to her.

In the course of anyone's life they will, in the sequence of events, lose parents and grandparents, and then maybe sadly a brother or sister. All of which we've experienced and they were all people we desperately and dearly loved, but none of these deaths have brought the pain and the grief and the anguish of losing our son.

I often feel that if there's a worse pain than losing a child then don't let me experience it, because I wasn't very good at handling this one. The immensity of it absolutely surprised me.

Parents know they love their children, but you cannot quantify it till your child dies. Then you know just how much. But you've got to be careful, because overnight we elevate our child to the greatest person that's ever walked on the earth, but Kenneth was possessed of quite outstanding athletic ability.

You cannot believe that anything good has come of the death of your child, but that might not be quite true. First of all, you find you are able to talk to another bereaved parent – a completely unknown person to you – and listen to them. You can put your arm around them, man or woman, and you can hug them and comfort them.

Later, I gave this a rather glorious name. I labelled it 'the gift', because this is what all bereaved parents have. They didn't want it. They would say, 'Give me back my child. Never mind about the gift.' But this was something we did, in fact, inherit and we learnt to use this.

I've been a soldier and I don't remember being particularly cowardly, but when my son died, I cried. And when they buried him, I really cried. People might say, 'That's a very unmanly thing to do. You should've been there, being the rock of the family that everybody leant on.' But I couldn't, and later on I thought, 'Well, that's how I am. I've got to live with this and if another man sees me crying, then perhaps it's helpful, because somebody else has shown him it's quite normal. It's acceptable that a man can cry.'

E dward Pardoe's son, Matthew, died in his first year at university after taking LSD at an end-of-year party. He jumped from an eighth floor window. Edward and his wife, Maureen, have two other sons, Mark and Michael. Maureen talks about Matthew's death in Chapter 1: Mothers.

I was the one who let the police in at six in the morning and the next thing I can remember is us all being upstairs around our bed – me, Maureen and our youngest son, Michael – just hugging and crying. At that time it was just sheer shock.

Maureen and Michael didn't go to the inquest, because Michael was coming up to his A level exams. So I went with our other son Mark. I've never told Maureen the full story of when he fell, flew or jumped off the eighth floor. It was a nightmare. I took in every word.

After the inquest it was in the evening paper. There were headlines about a 'drugs den'. They had got it way out and so exaggerated. On the day when these headlines came out, it was the first day of Michael's A level exams and he saw the headlines on the billboards as he was walking home. How he managed to cope with his A levels and get five grade As, I don't know.

I think I coped differently from Maureen. I had the advantage that I went back to work and that to me was an absolute godsend, particularly because something big blew up where I had to prepare a lengthy report and my boss was away on holiday, so I had to step in and take over. I just threw myself into it. That really was a lifesaver.

I don't think it's that men don't grieve properly. We grieve differently. I think Maureen felt that the loss was much more to her than it was to me, because I wasn't talking about it as much, and that I was suppressing my feelings – the stiff upper lip, you know. I was not trying to keep a stiff upper lip. I just wanted to escape from the pain. I was grieving, but I didn't want to spend all my time grieving, and I can't see the point of reliving it over and over again. The pain was huge and tremendous, so I didn't want to keep on bringing it all back.

I remember going to the office one morning, sitting at the traffic lights – I had the radio on – and Bob Marley's 'No Woman No Cry' came on. One of Matthew's favourite records. I've still got his LP upstairs. I just broke down. That really caught me. And once I went to the crematorium to clean Matthew's plaque. I think I was on my own – I was probably on my way to badminton – I was cleaning away and I broke down then. After more than 20 years I am still emotional on these occasions, even if I don't show it the way Maureen does.

Matthew was just 20 and doing well at university. It was such a waste. He might've had 50 or 60 years to go – and didn't have the chance to live life. I still have feelings of guilt about not being a better father. I often wish I could've done things differently.

Bill Rodgers is a Sheffield-based actor. He and his wife, Kate Hull Rodgers, already had one son, Harvey, when Kate gave birth to a stillborn son, Neil, in 1999. Kate talks about Neil in Chapter 1: Mothers.

I was actually in a café with my eldest son when Kate went to the midwife. She phoned me on the mobile – 'We can't find the heartbeat' – so I quickly ran Harvey to the babysitter and I ran Kate to hospital for a super-scan.

The doctor that put the ultrasound in found a heartbeat and we all breathed a sigh of relief for five or ten minutes until someone else came in and said that was Kate's heartbeat, not the baby's. That was a real kick in the guts for me, because we'd tried so hard to have a baby, which was Harvey.

We'd tried for four years – fertility treatment and all that – to be told that our second baby could potentially be dead was a real kick in the guts.

But also the caring instinct in me fires up. The dad, the man hunter – the adrenalin and testosterone kick in and you have to be strong, you have to be brave for the sake of the woman, the mother of the baby. So I became protective of Kate, and had to think of Harvey and protecting him.

So we quickly got Kate back home to pack her bag, because they wanted to do a Caesarean section, but when we went back she wanted to deliver naturally, so you go along with it. The carer kicks in again and you say, 'Do what she wants.' So they gave her a lot of drugs and she gave birth without fear – I don't know if she said that. But there was no fear of hurting the baby or of hurting herself, because she had so many drugs inside her. And for me, I could relax a bit.

I cut the umbilical cord, which I did for all three of my boys – because I was and always will be the father of three children, even though one of them isn't here. I still sired, if you like, three children, and Kate gave birth to three children. So I cut the umbilical cord and they wrapped him up and they gave him to me.

I wanted to hold him and Kate didn't want to hold him, because he was slightly decayed. But he was the spitting image of Harvey when Harvey was born, and he was also the spitting image of me when I was born, because I've got pictures of me with little sideburns and long curly hair and he looked just like that. He was beautiful, a perfectly formed child who looked as though he was fast asleep. I welcomed him into the planet.

I'm so glad they didn't just take him away, do what they do, find out why he died, wrap him up, box him up then send it to us in a box. I'm glad I spent some time with him, which I think is very important for mums and dads of stillborn children. Because at the end of the day it's still your son or daughter.

Some people might not be able to face it, some people might create false emotions, where they feel they have to cry because their baby has just died, but how can you do that unless you've had a relationship with them? Yes, the mother's had a nine-month relationship with carrying this thing inside her, but I defy anybody to feel sad or sentimental, especially a dad, about a child they never even saw. 'What did it look like?' 'I don't know, I didn't see it.' You've got to have had a relationship with that child before you can say hello or goodbye to it.

So I'm glad they gave him to me, because at least it creates some kind of relationship. I was holding my son, my Baby Neil. I don't want to over-sentimentalise things, but if there's any way you can have a relationship with a stillborn baby, I would recommend to anybody that they hold it. Or caress it, or name it. With Neil, no matter how long or short it was, I had a relationship with him. I'm his dad.

We had a naming ceremony for him. Neil is Gaelic for 'champion' and Niall is North American for 'cloud'. So he's 'champion cloud'. We called him Neil because my own mother lost her first baby who was also Neil and also full-term stillborn, so I wanted to name him after his Uncle Neil. That was important, to give him an identity and history. So they now have a history, an identity – uncle and nephew – and that's very important as well.

For me, one of the worst things was going to the register office, because I did all the running around, was registering the birth and the death at the same time. They give you a special certificate, and it says 'Registration of Birth' and, in brackets, 'Death of a Stillborn Baby'. That's something they don't tell you about at the hospital: to register the birth and death of a child at the same time.

Because I organised my parents' funerals, I knew what to do. Then when my grandfather died, I knew what to do. Even the undertaker said, 'Have you got a season ticket here, or what?' So when my baby died, I knew what to do. And it's not bravado, it's knowing where the phone number is for the under-taker, for the florist. It became a very practical thing.

We had a full cremation service with music and a very nice vicar, who came to me and said, 'Dog collar or flowery tie?' So we said put your tie on, and his flower was sunflowers, which is a sign of rebirth and regeneration. And it was a child-friendly funeral, so anyone who wanted to bring their child could, because we didn't want to hide the fact of death from our kids. Harvey sat on the pulpit, and there was a little white coffin, and I carried the coffin in, and we put a photograph and a teddy bear on the coffin, and the photograph was of me, Kate and Harvey.

It was a lot easier to tell people than I thought, for me. What tends to happen when men have had a tragedy is that other men will rally round – not for long, but they will rally round each other and be supportive. When women have tragedy, the women rally round and that support will be ongoing. So for me, and for a lot of men, I find that the sooner you tell people and get it out into the open, the quicker you can do the bonding and the 'let me buy you a beer' and then it's gone. It's get it in, get it done, get it over with and get it out – a bit like sex.

So I told my pals and they were great, very supportive – 'How do you feel? How's Kate?' That was the main topic. 'How are you feeling, Bill?' came and went. But 'How's Kate?' that carried on. And it was good for me – quite cathartic – talking about how well Kate was doing, because she wasn't sad, she wasn't depressed, and I was ever so proud of Kate, the way she kept it together.

You mourn or grieve in your own way. When I go out on the park with my boys to kick a ball round, it would be great to have three of them. They'd all be under six. And sometimes when I'm here, reading the paper and wanting to be quiet, I think, 'Thank goodness I've only got two'. So I don't think I would have wanted more support, because you can overkill with it.

If this hadn't happened to Neil, would we have had Dominic? I think not. And he's adorable. He's a great bonus, and he was born one year and one week after his brother's death. Every Hallowe'en, the three men in the house go down the garden and we have a big rocket, Neil's rocket, and we set it off. And it's always the biggest rocket in the shop.

Harvey talks about him as though he was real. And we've still got his ashes, in a little green velvet bag. We planted a willow tree in the garden and we may put them round there. We just haven't found the right place or the right time. We're not hanging onto it through remorse or grief.

Because of Neil I started to 'over-parent' on Harvey. Because it took us so long to get him in the first place, you get really overprotective – 'I'm not losing this one!' I remember the first time he ran across that road by himself – he was three or four – and anyone would think he'd committed murder the way I reacted. And it's only about six and a half feet from here to the park. So it's like, 'You *will* hold my hand while we're walking from the kitchen to the living room!'

A lot of my peers would be the last people in the world to admit that they've lost a child, whereas I do. I've heard people chatting at the shops – 'Mrs So-and-So has lost a baby' – and I'll openly say, 'So did I. Give her our phone number if she needs to talk.' I'll talk openly about it, but a lot of men won't, because it's a woman thing: a man will say, 'Oh, my wife lost a baby.' I'll say, 'I lost a boy, one of my sons died.' And men should. There is someone out there who'll listen.

J ohn Suffield's son, also called John, was the eldest of six children. He was 23 and he worked as the manager of a betting office in Liverpool. On Friday 13 March 1981 he was murdered in the course of a robbery. Two men were given life imprisonment for his murder.

John was tortured and stabbed 19 times as these men tried to get the combination of a safe from him. What they didn't know is he couldn't open the safe. He couldn't explain to them that there was a time lock mechanism on it.

The problem is that John had had a stammer since the age of six and, although he found ways of coping with it, stress and anxiety would bring it back. I'm sure that the trauma of the violence and the torture he experienced that day would have made him unable to explain about the safe to his attackers.

The first I knew about what had happened was when a colleague of John's from another betting office knocked at the front door. He told me I had to go as soon as possible to the police station in Toxteth where the betting shop was. I noticed he was extremely agitated and I said, 'Is John all right?' He wouldn't say, but I persisted and he broke down. I knew then that John was not all right and eventually he told me he was dead.

Now I wouldn't go to the police station. My wife was at work and even though I didn't know any details about how John had died, I needed to be with my wife. I had to be the one to tell her about John. So instead of going to the police station, I went to my wife's work. On the way there, I rehearsed what I was going to say to her. How can you tell a mother that her son has died? I went into the office and she looked up and saw me. She must've known by my manner – the look on my face – that I was bringing bad news and despite what I'd rehearsed I could just say, 'Betty, John's dead.' And I put my arms round her.

We went together to the police station and they confirmed that John had died as a result of an incident at the place where he worked. At the time they weren't giving us any other information, but I just knew from the number of police officers, from the atmosphere at the police station, that a major incident had occurred. I just assumed it was an act of violence. I can remember considering it was a shotgun and, on reflection, I wish it had been. It would've been an instantaneous death and I could've accepted that more.

Betty and I were separated. I was taken immediately to a large room and I was questioned for two-and-a-half or three hours by this detective, who wanted to know everything about John's life – the time he was born, childhood illnesses, what sort of school he went to, his success at school, the type of friends he had at school, did he bring them home, could he fight, did he have any enemies, had he seriously hurt somebody?

All the time I was constantly thinking of my wife and my children. Two of my children were at school, one was at college and two more at work. I didn't want them coming home on public transport, knowing their brother was dead. I kept thinking, 'Who was holding them? Who was giving them support?' It was my duty as a husband and a father to do that, but I couldn't get away from the police station.

When the questioning finally finished about two o'clock in the afternoon – remember I'd been there from about 11 o'clock in the morning and had been offered no cups of tea and wasn't asked if I wanted to use the toilet – I was asked if I could go and identify John's body.

So I was taken to a Victorian mortuary. I remember there was a terrible smell of disinfectant and there were marks where the trolleys had hit the walls and plaster had fallen off. There was no dignity there – absolutely no dignity whatsoever. It appeared to me to be a sort of dumping ground for bodies that nobody had claimed and I didn't want my son kept there.

In the middle of the room was the sole trolley and there was a body on it covered by a sheet. I was then asked to identify this body as my son. The sheet was withdrawn from the face and I got a shock. It was my son all right, but I saw the injury to his face alone and I couldn't understand how anybody could inflict such violence on another person, just to rob them. I felt so much anger. For the first time the reality had hit me that there'd been no mistake. My son was dead.

I tried to say a silent prayer, but I couldn't pray. I just couldn't pray. I couldn't make the sign of the cross. It would be acknowledging in a way that this was God's will and I felt contempt for God. You know, my perception was a loving, caring God and my son was dead. The two didn't match up.

As I was leaving, I turned to the people in white coats and I asked them how soon John would've died. This was important to me. This might be the one bit of good news I could take home to my wife. They reassured me he would've died within five seconds of a stab wound.

We returned to the police station and I was told that my brother had been waiting for me for the last two hours. We went off in his car and found a telephone box to ring my wife. Later I thought, 'Why didn't I ask the police – can I ring home? Why didn't they offer me that?' She told me that four of my children were at home.

My son, Peter, was still at work and hadn't been told. He worked for the City Council in the Treasurer's Department, so I went there to tell him myself. There was a queue of people making various enquiries, but I ignored them. I went straight up to the counter and in a loud voice I said, 'I want to see Peter Suffield, please.' I could tell that they all knew what had happened, because one said, 'I'll get him' and another said, 'No, I'll go and get him.' Two minutes later, Peter came out and he said, 'Hiya, Pop.' He didn't know. All the staff knew, but Peter didn't.

So I said, 'Get your coat, Peter, we're going home.' As we were walking through that hall, he said, 'I know there's something wrong. In the lunch hour we normally have a laugh and a joke, but there's an atmosphere there today and people won't talk to me.' I said, 'John's dead.' And I remember as we came out into the street, opposite the building there was a newsagent with a billboard of the *Liverpool Echo*. It said, 'Betting shop manager killed.' I thought he merely had to look out the window and he'd have seen it.

I kept thinking I couldn't break down, I must not cry. I would now have to hold myself together for the others. I accepted that the future was finished for us, but somebody had to take charge and that fell on me as the father. It's your role to protect. We came home and all the family were here. I just wanted to hold Betty and have the children round me, but we were denied that, because everybody was here – neighbours and police officers. This would be about four o'clock in the afternoon and it went on till late evening.

The police sent for the doctor and he wasn't very compassionate. I can remember him saying something like, 'These things are sent to us and we've just got to get over them.' At that stage I hadn't even exchanged words with my children and my wife.

The doctor left us each with two pills. I can remember saying to my brother, 'I don't want sleeping tablets.' The others took them without question, but I said, 'No.' I didn't want to go to sleep, because I couldn't face the awakening and the realisation of what had happened. I knew I'd have to go through all this again and I couldn't face it. But he insisted I take them, so I put the tablets under my tongue, but at the first opportunity I took them out and disposed of them. I didn't sleep that night. I sat on the chair and I thought, 'What are we going to do? Just what are we going to do?'

During the night I made notes about things that I must do for the children. The next day, the Saturday, was my daughter Kathy's twenty-first birthday and we had a dinner arranged for all the family, so I thought, 'I'll have to do something about that.' And I can remember thinking, 'Thank

God my mum and dad are dead', because I don't know how they would've coped with this. Then I wrote down 'church' and I remember crossing that out and I put 'priest' and I crossed that out. I think I was sort of divorcing myself from my religion. In those first few days my views about God and the church had completely changed.

My perception of a loving and caring God had been completely shattered. Why had he allowed this to happen to us? We had harmed nobody. We had always lived our lives according to the standards and principles demanded by our society. Was this the reward?

On the Sunday morning, for the first time in my life, I had no intention of going to Mass. When my wife had asked me to go with her I'd said, 'I can't. I really can't.' Then I remember Kathy came and put her arms out to me, and said, 'Dad, how are we going to get over this? I don't want to live.' And despite what I felt about God, I said to her, 'I don't know, Kath, but I promise you this, some way or other, with God's help, we'll get through this.'

In those early days I was in desperate need of advice and I remember deciding that on Monday morning the children who were at college and school would go back. Get them away from this environment. How wrong that was. I'd never considered that they were grieving as much as me and my wife. Never gave that a thought. I just felt that they should not be in a house where grief was everywhere and it was best to get them back into their normal routine as soon as possible.

It was a long time later I realised it was the wrong thing to do, but I insisted they went and they obeyed me. I can now visualise them standing in the school playground, having to give people explanations and it was the cruellest thing I could've done. They needed to be at home with their mother and father and brothers and sisters. But we were all going through a crisis that we'd never anticipated and we'd never been trained for.

Two days after John died, the priest sent the curate to be with us and he had the greatest compassion of all, because he never said a word. He was a young priest, 26 or 27, and he admitted, 'I don't know what to say. The boss has sent me over. I just feel so much sorrow for you, but I'm here. I'm here.' That was marvellous, because I didn't know how to handle it either and I didn't want somebody to come in and say, 'I know what to do on these occasions.' He became one of the family. If visitors came in, he made them welcome and offered them cups of tea. He went round to the chip shop for us. The man who admitted he didn't know what to do for us, did everything.

For the first week we didn't move out of this house. We had constant streams of visitors and at times some of these people were, not a nuisance, but it was inconvenient. You could well have 40 to 60 people here and they all needed catering for – cups of tea, a ham sandwich and biscuits – it cost us a fortune. It really did.

After about a week we had to go out of the house and I saw that the buses were running and the shops were open, but John's dead. Life hadn't changed and that made me angry. I know it's a selfish attitude, but I couldn't see how it didn't affect them. A massive thing had happened to our family. Surely the ripples would affect them?

John's death affects my relationship with my family to this day. I have a tremendous concern for their safety and that increases as I lose control of them. My children are adults, but when they go on holiday they have to ring me from the airport before they board the flight and again when they land, and while they're on holiday they have to ring me every day. That is without a doubt a legacy of John's death.

I know it's being overprotective and they laugh at me. My daughter says, 'Dad, I'm 44 years of age. Let me grow up.' Their husbands look at me and say, 'Thank God I wasn't born into your family.' We laugh and joke about it, but they know I'm very serious.

At one time John's death stopped me having goals and ambitions, because the reality is they can all collapse, but now I'd say we have a lot of fun in this family and that's as a result of John. It might sound strange, but we feel that life is there for the taking – because we have an understanding of what it's like to be without – the ultimate 'without.'

Tim Whewell and his wife, Rachel Osorio, had a stillborn son, Leo, and a daughter, Esther, before their next son, Jethro, was born in 1996. When Jethro was 18 months old, he was found to have the incurable Tay Sachs disease. He died two years later. Rachel's account is in Chapter 1: Mothers.

I've never really talked about this to anyone, actually. It's to do with, in general, the difference in kinds of friendships that women have compared to the friendships men have. Or maybe I just imagine women would find it easier to talk, but I certainly haven't.

I've never really talked to my father about this, either. When Jethro died, he sent a very nice card – he wasn't up to coming to the funeral – and something that he'd written, which we read out, about what we've learnt from Jethro. So he'd thought about it quite a lot, more than I'd thought, but he put it in writing, and certainly never said it to me face to face.

You have to force yourself to make some kind of sense of it, just because you inevitably, desperately, desperately need some kind of sense. Because in itself it seems so totally absurd, particularly when you're talking about children, who haven't tasted life. You keep thinking, 'I just wish he could have done this, could have lived long enough.'

The image I could never ever get away from is the idea of him never having run across a beach barefoot and feeling sand squeeze up between his toes. He never got to the point of standing, and certainly not walking. I got obsessed with the idea that he was going to die, and then that he died, without ever having done that. As though just to have done that would somehow have been enough.

So, for my own mental peace of mind, I had to be able to say, yes, this was the moment when he actually had a sensation, an experience, a flash of light, and that's enough for me. But I wanted him to have more and more of them. I never got to the point of thinking he could grow up and go to school and be a mathematician or anything like that. But it was these sensations, like standing where the water laps between the sand and the sea – to have felt he could at least have felt that.

Because of never ever having spoken to him, because of only half knowing ever what he experienced and what he didn't experience – what you continually search back for is occasions when he smiled. And there *were* things that he smiled at. The only way you can make sense of it is by absolutely forcing yourself to remember those – 'I remember he smiled then, and he smiled then.'

Towards the end, maybe nine months before the end, when already he was failing in other ways, he went through this strange period of laughing – giggling in a very sweet and charming way. We couldn't necessarily say what it was. Lying in his buggy and suddenly laughing. We don't even know if it was an internal sensation or an external sensation. I don't know how well he could see by that point. We could see by the reaction on his face, by some of the smiling, that he responded to patterns of light and sparkling colours – that's why we made all sorts of mobiles made of silver paper and things to play patterns off the ceiling.

And he seemed to get pleasure from hearing the sound of a lot of high-pitched voices. If he was somewhere like a swimming pool where you hear a lot of laughter and shouting in an echoey environment, that seemed to quite excite him. So I made up a tape of sounds like that, which I recorded – we've still got it somewhere, 'Jethro's Tape' – and I got him headphones and we used to play it to him. I wanted him to have had a minimum of those experiences, so I could feel his life had been worthwhile.

The formulation we came up with afterwards – because you do need to have something like that – was that it was a small life but that it was a life nonetheless. And it was a life that contained all kinds of things. Everybody's life contains some things and not others, some sensations and experiences, some good and some bad. And his life was also a mixture of those things.

So that's one way in which you make sense of it. The other way is he was good for other people. You have to justify it in both those ways. That he got something out of it – and that the people around him got a great deal out of him as well.

I got a sense of proportion, an ability to value the smallness of things. That's what I mean by a small life. Lives can be big or lives can be small. But they're as interesting and as full in their way if they're small lives as if they're big lives.

What it taught me was about patience and about quiet and about differ-ent forms of communication which aren't verbal communication, which may be something difficult for me, because I am a very verbal person and I probably find communication without words is not something that comes that naturally to me. But Jethro did partly enable me to understand that. That there are means of being close without speaking. And there is some kind of spark that goes between people – maybe it's incredibly obvious and banal to say that – but I held him in my arms and our hearts beat next to one another. I felt his heart beating and I suppose he felt my heart beating.

In many deaths there is a very heavy element of guilt – and there was quite a lot with this – that I wasn't around as much as I could have been.

As Rachel has probably told you, she wasn't around for the last day or so, and the way things fell out, I was. I spent the last night with him, and then drove him back from Oxford, not knowing whether he was going to die halfway down the M40.

I couldn't contact Rachel – she was at this wedding in Switzerland – and I knew she was coming back with the children the following day, and I had no means at all of contacting her. And, without saying so, the people at

Helen House [the children's hospice in Oxford] had given me to understand he wasn't going to survive – they'd given up feeding him, so it was quite plain. But I hoped against hope that Rachel would have some way of coaxing food down him that they wouldn't have, that she would have some kind of touch that they didn't have, by virtue of being his mother.

So there he was in Oxford – and these things always come down to terrible, terrible practicalities. Should I keep him there and go myself to the airport and bring Rachel straight back to see him? Which would remove the danger of moving him – which I thought might itself finish him off – but which might also mean possibly me and her missing his final moments, which we would feel awful about. Or should I put him in the car and go back down the motorway so that he would be there when she came back, then at least I would have been with him in case he did die? At least one of us would have been there at that moment. But then I had this appalling nightmare that I would have to live for the rest of my life with the fact that Jethro died at Junction 5 of the M40. All these awful, awful things.

In the end, she came back and he died two or three hours after, and it was very, very nice in the end, because she sat out with him on that bench in the garden for the last hour or so, and actually in that sense it worked out quite well.

I was angry with Rachel, yes, for putting me in that situation. I was so overwhelmed by grief at that time that I wasn't *very* angry, but yes I was angry. But then, who am I, in a sense, to be angry? Because, as things worked out, I'd been away on a very long work trip immediately before that and we just didn't cross over.

What I was most angry about was I was totally, totally unprepared psychologically for the fact that this was the end. I just hadn't realised. I planned to come back home to have some lunch, and then go to Oxford, and literally the minute I rang the hospice, they said come absolutely immediately, and I could tell that something was terribly wrong. When I got there, I could see at once – even though you tell yourself this isn't the case – you can tell when death is approaching. And they know, and they know you know, but no one says it because it's too difficult to say. That's what I was cross about, not that she wasn't there, but about not having been warned or psychologically prepared for what kind of stage it had reached.

[At this point, Tim gets up to find the journal he wrote around the time of Jethro's death.] Saturday 26 June – the day before he died. Shall I read you this? It's probably more interesting than anything I'm saying. There's pages and pages of this. I'll start at random.

In the morning, I had a shower and then I tried to feed him myself, sitting in an armchair opposite the kitchen door. But he could hardly take any of it before he started coughing ever so weakly. At least he'd had a peaceful night, apparently his first for a while, but now I could see things are really bad, with him not having eaten properly since Thursday, with it now clear I couldn't feed him either. Even in the morning when he should have been at his strongest. So I decided to take him home, so at least he'd be there, though I wasn't even sure he'd survive the journey, and the nurses obviously thought that was the right thing, so they offered to come with me. I must have seemed in a real state, but for some reason they seemed to want to delay me, maybe in case Jethro didn't survive the journey, so we'd get a little more time together. So I carried him well out of sight and earshot into the convent garden – it was really really beautiful there, actually – and sat on a bench with him, and cried and cried.

Downstairs this same night, it goes on:

Jethro was breathing very quietly but calmly and I sat next to him for a long time, holding his hand and stroking his hair. Then I turned on the radio and there was a poetry programme about fathers and sons, including John Silkin's *Death of a Son*.

That's one of the ways you try and make sense of it – those weird coincidences that have great importance.

Has Rachel given you a copy of the funeral service? This is interesting. [Retrieves a copy from the filing cabinet.] To me, the compiling of this was incredibly important, and I channelled an awful lot of my energy into it. Getting it right was incredibly important to me, and I wrote a poem, 'All the girls will be after him with eyes that blue'. I'd been in the post office with him and a woman had said that. It's what I said before – I wanted him to run along the beach, that's what I wanted him to do.

The other memory I have – he died late at night on the Sunday, and nothing was going to happen until the next morning, so what do we do? We put him on the sofa – and we sat up with him all night, until the morning. Then Esther had a child over to play, and Esther says, 'This is my brother, he died yesterday' or whatever. And the other child's probably never seen a dead person before, so there's a bit of silence – and then they played, in front of a corpse. This image stuck with me for a long time, a very powerful image, of children playing in front of the corpse of another child. But what can they do? How long can they stand around? After that, they're going to play, aren't they? Because (a) it's what children do and (b) it's for their own self-defence. So they played.

A lot of what helped afterwards, for me, was the organising of the funeral. I've become an enormous believer in funerals and the value of funerals and the point of going to funerals. I feel incredibly strongly about that.

Like, I've got an aunt who lives up the road in an old age home – she's got dementia – and effectively, when she dies, I don't know how many people will come to the funeral but even if no one came – if there were nobody there but me – I would write and give an address. And somehow, even to give an address to the air has an enormous value. Literally to be speaking to nobody but to be speaking out loud is a form of monument. It doesn't matter how much or little happened in her life. The address is for her, and it makes sense of a life even if nobody hears it. There may be no visible practical benefit, and yet actually there is an enormous benefit.

Most deaths are messy and don't end nicely. But the point previous to that is there were moments of togetherness, frozen in time as it were, little bubbles that you can store in your memory. And you need that. There was a garden and you sat in it behind a table and there was a shaft of sunlight and you shared that. It happened.

And whether you have a whole lifetime of them – like partners who've lived together all their lives – or you have a child who dies at three-and-a -half, and there have just been a few – well, frankly, even if there is only one, so what? There's been one. And that's the sense in which it's a small life but it's a life. It's a life all the same.

Daughters

Linda Arstall's mother, Annie, died in 1965 when Linda was just 16. She has a younger sister, Eileen.

I remember walking home from school happily chatting with my cousin and I said, 'How's Mum today?' She said, 'Oh, Linda, you know your mum's very poorly, don't you? You know she's dying?' I knew she was ill, but I'd no idea until then that she was dying.

After that I didn't want to leave her side. She was being nursed in the front room downstairs and I remember that night Dad calling me through to have my meal and I didn't want to go. I can even remember exactly what we ate. It was a Wednesday, so it was steak pudding, chips and peas.

The following day I didn't want to go to school, but I was made to go. I'd always thought of the deputy headmistress, Miss Dugdale, as a real ogre – a very stern 'miss' – but that day she was so sweet to me. I started crying in class and my friend took me to see her and she said, 'My dear, you come with me and have a chat.' I've never forgotten that. All the way through school I'd really disliked her, but I'll never forget her kindness that day.

For the funeral my aunties made me wear this black, furry bonnet. Remember, this was 1965. It fastened under the chin with a button at the side. I hated that hat. I was a bit of a tomboy and to have to wear a hat was a punishment to me, but to wear a black hat! For years I couldn't wear black. Wearing black meant my mum's funeral.

We lived on a farm and death was a normality, so I wondered why nobody ever talked to me and my sister. Even my aunties, who I'm still very close to and who are still alive in their nineties, didn't talk about death. I think it would have helped if somebody had explained that the pain would get better and that I would be sad, but it wouldn't hurt as much. Nobody ever did.

I felt very different at school. I remember people talking about me and going quiet when I went past. There was this sense of isolation. In those days there were very few single-parent families because of separation or divorce, so I didn't know anybody who didn't live with both their parents.

I felt responsible for my dad. I had to be the housekeeper and I would have to go to the market and buy the food. I had to go to a certain stall on the market to buy Mum's favourite biscuits, which were Chocolate Viennas. Even after Mum died, Dad still bought them.

I went to do my nurse training when I was 17 and I remember having a medical the first week. This was almost a year after my mum had died. The doctor was asking me about my family history and I started crying when I told him about my mum. He was very offhand and abrupt. He said, 'What are you crying for? It's almost a year since she died. You've got to get on with life. You're going to be no good as a nurse if you don't learn to deal with this. Emotions are just no good in nursing.'

I think I was so wrapped up in my own grief that I don't think talking to my sister even occurred to me. It was only when I went to do my nurse training that I talked to people there about my feelings. It did help to be able to talk to people who weren't involved, so I could say what I wanted and not have to try to protect other people's feelings.

I really missed my mum when I was expecting my first child. I wanted to ask her, 'What was I like as a baby? How did I feed? What was your labour like?' There was a tremendous sense of loss and I think the grief flooded back to the surface again then. I got close to another mother and we'd go to the child health clinic together. She'd say, 'I'm just going to my mum's today' or 'I'll just ask my mum about that', and sometimes I'd feel overwhelmed. I don't think my husband could understand that. Both his parents were still alive.

My father died in 1980 and I remember thinking, 'Gosh, we are the next ones.' Friends did come round, but my very best friend who I'd known from primary school stayed away. She didn't speak, she didn't phone, she didn't send a card. I remember feeling that so vividly and being so hurt by it. It took me probably about ten years to tell her how hurt I'd felt. She said, 'I didn't know what to say. I was so devastated that you'd lost both your parents.' I think that's one reason we drifted apart. She let me down when I needed her most.

Just recently I've started to think about death again, because one of my aunties has just died at the age of 92 and the other two aunties are quite frail. My Auntie Elsie has been my surrogate mum for all these years and I shall be devastated when she dies, because that really will be the end of my family.

I do think it could be my turn soon, but I also think, as a Christian, I should be celebrating my life and I shouldn't be worrying about death. I think it's just recognising your own mortality. I don't dwell on it and when I'm surrounded by a mountain of paperwork, I think it might be quite a blessed relief in one sense!

Ellie Bennett is now in her fifties. Her father died just before her seventeenth birthday.

[The name in this interview has been changed.]

I used to pray my father would drop dead and he did. My father and mother did nothing but argue when I was little. I used to ask my mum why they married one another. They did try separating, but she was a Catholic and they've got this thing about you can't divorce and you really shouldn't separate.

My father kept his money to himself, he went out drinking and he didn't really have a lot to do with us. I'd wake up in the night and hear people shouting and I'd go to the top of the stairs and listen. And I'd cry because I didn't want them to argue.

I felt the only solution to this problem was if he died. It was very simple. There was no emotion involved in that. It was almost mathematical. You know, there's four of us and there's one 'baddy'. There's no use him just leaving, because Mum can never marry again – she's a Catholic.

I was brought up such a good Catholic that I thought if you wanted something you had to go to church and pray for it. So I prayed that my father would die. 'Please God, let him drop dead.'

He went to work one Saturday morning on overtime and he literally dropped dead. I think it was either a heart attack or a stroke. It was very early and I hadn't got out of bed yet. A policeman knocked at the door. My mother came upstairs and said, 'It's your father. He's in hospital. They're probably pumping out his stomach again.' That's drunkenness, isn't it?

She was getting her coat on as she said it and I remember thinking, 'What's she going for? After the way they are with one another, what does it matter if he's in hospital?' But I said, 'Oh, I'll come with you.' I thought it was so generous of me. I was going with her for her sake. I thought, 'She absolutely hates him, yet she's getting her coat on and going up there – on her own. If she can be kind then I can, too.'

Then somebody from his work knocked on the door to say he was dead and I thought, 'This is what we've always wanted. It's the solution to everything. It's absolutely wonderful!' But it's sad that a person should be happy that their father's dropped dead.

I was very surprised at my mother. She was saying, 'Jesus, Mary and Joseph! He's dead! He's dead!' And I thought, 'What's the matter? This is OK, isn't it?' She was behaving like it was the end of the world and it was the beginning really.

The doctor came round and took me outside into the front garden and he put his arm round my shoulder. But I was thinking, 'There's nothing wrong. You're trying to comfort me and I don't need it.' But this is what he did: he gave tranquillisers to the mother and took the children outside, pointed to flowers and said, 'It's all right. Things die and things get born again.'

My father was buried on my seventeenth birthday. I left home when I was 18 and never went back. There was nothing for me there. And the further away I got and the more time passed and the more I looked back on it, the more I realised I was stood on and walked on and used as a child.

About five or six years ago my mother died. I'd decided that, when she did die, I probably wouldn't go to the funeral, because my stepfather was almost a stranger and my brother is just a cold fish. So I thought, 'If I go to her funeral, I'll have nothing but misery'. I would only be going for her and she's the one that's dead. Also it would cost a fortune to get there.

But when she did die, I'd already changed my mind, because I realised it would be my last visit there and I'd probably never see my brother or my stepfather again. Having given myself the freedom to make the choice, I thought, 'I'm going to make it an adventure and have some fun out of this! I'm going to fly there.' So I booked an aeroplane from Heathrow to Manchester and I started to look forward to it. You get a whisky and a cup of coffee and a sandwich on the plane. And I didn't have to be respectful really – just a darkish jacket – and I didn't have to wear a hat in church any more either.

I've missed my mother slightly. I think that's because she's not here to argue with. But I've never missed my father at all. I can't think that there's anything to miss. I cannot ever hear the sound of his voice, I can't actually recall a conversation with him and I cannot remember anything that he ever said, so I suppose there isn't anything to miss.

Abigail Harrison is six. She was just ten months old when her father, Bob, who was 39, died of a heart attack at home. She is the sister of Oliver, whose story is in Chapter 4: Sons, and the daughter of Karen, whose story is in Chapter 7: Wives.

I remember people saying my dad was kind. I ask Mum questions like, 'Did Dad have curly hair?' and I know that's yes. I ask her all different questions. Sometimes we look at photos. There's a photo of me there with Oliver and my dad. If you look at pictures you can know who you're missing.

If Dad was here it would be easier for Mum, because Mum could cook and I could play with Dad, because I always end up playing with Mum all the time. Oliver doesn't really want to play with me, because he's a brother, you know.

I feel a bit the odd one out. It's not very nice feeling different. I think, 'I wish my dad could be alive.' Mum's not got that much strength to pick me up, but Dad would have because boys are really strong. And dads tickle you and dads are really fun.

I know people are sad about it because they always talk about it and they never stop. That's how I know they're sad. Sometimes they cry a little bit.

I miss Dad on Father's Day. Father's Day is probably one of our 'specialest' days. We think about how good he was. For tea, we put a candle in the middle and we all blow it out and say, 'Dad! Dad!' It makes me feel quite happy, because I'm thinking about him. But I always think about Dad. It pops into my mind each day. I don't know why it does.

Loads of people are mentioning it. I don't like people talking about it, because it's not really their business. What happens is, someone I know comes along and then tells someone else. I'd rather they didn't know. Someone's teased me about my dad. They said, 'Your dad was never alive.' I felt a bit upset, because I didn't know if my dad *was* alive or not.

I have to be very, very sensible. It's really, really hard. If you're playing with a jigsaw and you've just finished the end of one hundred million pieces, you want to go, 'Whee!' and bounce all over the place, but you have to be sensible. You can't jump all over the place. It feels a bit unfair. I feel a bit older.

I feel like nine or something, because I'm always sensible, not hyperactive and everything. That's what people expect.

Val Hough's mother, Dorothy, died in 2002 at the age of 81. She had met Val's father when she was just 14 and they married at 21. Val's father died in 1972.

I thought my mother's death was fantastic. I've always said that if there's such a thing as a good death, then she had it. She didn't want to be in hospital or a nursing home. She was determined to stay at home.

She'd had her hair done the day before. She was going to have streaks, but she was a bit too weak for that. My brother and I went down in the evening. When we did say we'd get her into bed, she said, 'You die in bed.' And I said, 'You'll be a bit stiffer in the chair', and she laughed. She really giggled. My mum had a good giggle, sometimes her teeth would start to wobble. She would laugh a lot. Her hands and feet were very cold and I used to wrap her up in a thermal blanket and she said, 'What do you think I am, an old lady?'

She was really interested in life right to the end. She was driving up to the age of 79 and she got a newspaper every day. The week before she died, she was watching the snooker. In fact the Saturday before, she was watching football on the television and she said, 'If Blackburn Rovers don't get themselves sorted out, I'm going to go down there and sort them out myself!'

I just felt my mum was at peace. My brother, Peter, and I were there. We sat with her during the night and told her we loved her. And my daughter, Katy, came home that weekend and Mum was so pleased to see her. She wasn't in any pain, she had all her faculties up to six or seven hours before she died and then she literally drifted off to sleep.

I just feel grateful to have had a mum like her, even though at times I got very frustrated. I'll be honest, I've closed that door sometimes on a Sunday night and heaved a sigh of relief and I'm sure she did, too. Because mothers always think they can say what they like to daughters, whereas sons are perfect and so if there was anything wrong I got it in the neck. I think that's the closeness of mothers and daughters – you can say anything to each other.

It gave me a lot of comfort that she went in the way she wanted to go: her hair was beautifully done, she adored clothes and the day she died she was immaculately dressed in a pale blue jumper and navy blue cord trousers – colour co-ordinated.

I think she chose her time. She thought, 'Everybody's quite happy. Everybody's quite settled. I'll drift off now.' She couldn't have planned it better if she'd tried. If she was looking down, I think she'd have been quite pleased with herself that she'd organised it so well.

Bernadette McConnell's mother, Bridget, died at the age of 77. She had been ill for nine years and eventually she had to have her leg amputated. This interview was done just two months after she died. Bernadette has two brothers, Martin and John.

I was desperately close to my mum. She was very good-looking with blonde hair and blue eyes. A feisty character, very Irish, loyal to the family and strong-minded.

She died on a Monday. It used to take me up to two hours to get to her house and I went to see her most weekends, but that particular one I didn't go. Perhaps it was because she didn't want me there, because she knows I'd be the most hurt. Apparently she breathed two breaths and then she just went and that was it.

I just feel very raw at the minute. I want blankets and blankets of affection. I cry on my own. Yesterday it was hard, because I was trying to write out memorial cards and send them off to people and my brother phoned and I was just in floods of tears.

I used to work in Switzerland and still have very good friends there so I decided to go over straight after the funeral for a few days. I thought if I go there everything will be fixed, but it wasn't. I was worse than I am now. You need time. It's not about being able to get over it, it's about being able to deal with it. You've not got to be cruel to yourself.

My closest friend in Switzerland didn't know how to deal with it, because she's never had to live through this. She's never ever lost anybody in her life. We'd go out for a glass of wine and I'd just end up sitting there like some zombie. She just could not cope with it and she was quite cold. She probably didn't want me hurting and I'm sure she thought, 'What if that was me?' because, like me, she's very close to her mother. So it wasn't her fault, but it was quite hard on me.

I've not been numb at all. I've really felt it. I remember going skiing with some friends a few years ago and one friend cut her leg open on the ski. The back of her leg was just like a piece of beef. That's how I felt after my mother died – like a piece of raw meat. I just felt so exposed.

She was a really elegant lady, a real classy chick. I used to cut and colour her hair, because obviously she couldn't get to the hairdressers'. When she was in the coffin I put her lipstick on and I also dressed her up in a really expensive brown and cream suit, and I put a cream silk blouse on her. She looked 'drop dead gorgeous'. And I sprayed her with Coco Chanel perfume. Then I put two shoes in the coffin, even though she only had one leg. I thought, 'Bugger it! You're going out in style!'

I cleared out the florists. I got beautiful lilies for the top of the coffin and I also bought lots of white roses and yellow roses. Yellow apparently symbolises friendship and white is for family. I distributed them amongst everybody at the funeral and we threw them into the coffin when it was in the ground. Neither of my brothers could have done that.

I feel the same about sorting through all her stuff. There's only me can do that. Well, I don't want anybody else doing it and she wouldn't have wanted anyone else going through her things.

She was a lot closer to one of my brothers than me in the end. After my dad died, she depended on him and she moved to be nearer to him. That was so hurtful. When Mum moved over there, it nearly killed me and her death has nearly killed me.

There is absolutely nothing that can compare to a mother–daughter relationship. She was always there for me, fighting for me. She was there for me getting into the grammar school. I wasn't in the right catchment area, but she went to see the right people and got me a place. She rooted for me at university, when I failed some exams. And I remember when I first went over to Switzerland, I had a really rough time the first six weeks, but she came over to see me. When we went up on a ski lift, she sprained her bloody ankle. Stupid woman! And she was so proud of herself, because she used to order croissants, even though she didn't speak any French.

She did love me a lot. Apparently she was always worried about me. I don't know why. Her presence everywhere I go is really strong. I feel she's here now. I want her here. I need her. Stupid old tart! She's here to stay.

Dorothy Rowe is an Australian-born psychologist and writer, now based in London. Her father, Jack Conn, died in Newcastle, New South Wales, in 1964.

My father had always been a very strong, healthy person. He never got ill. But then he developed late onset diabetes and he found it extremely difficult to keep to his diet, but he was still working as a commercial traveller – he was 70. Then there was a little recession and the firm he worked for asked him if he would mind leaving because the manager had to lay somebody off and he didn't want to lay off a young man with small children. That was just the kind of thing to appeal to my father, so he left.

He was home with my mother for a year and then he died. Being with my mother was a considerable strain – she was a very difficult woman – but while he was working he was out of the house and with people. So I would say that that year was very stressful. From what we know now about the effect of stress on the immune system, I think it's not surprising that he developed severe pancreatitis, and that's what he died of, within six weeks. But nobody expected him to die. We just thought he was ill.

When people talk in detail about the circumstances of death, no one seems to manage it easily and organised. It's always chaotic, even when people know they're dying or that their loved one is dying. It all gets messy and confusing, and all your plans go awry. It's never what you expect, it's never what you think it's going to be.

There was a whole lot of not talking – of people not asking questions. My parents lived in Newcastle in New South Wales, and I lived in Sydney, 100 miles away, and I was working, married, had a small child. So when my father took ill and was taken into hospital, it was several days before I could get up there to see him. I couldn't get any account from my mother about what was happening except that he was in hospital.

We went into hospital to see him and I was still thinking, 'Oh, my father's ill', and my mother said to me, 'I want you to speak to the nurse.' This was a usual trick of my mother's – if she could get someone else to do what she should be doing, she'd do it. And if I was around, I'd be the one to carry out the task. My sister, who's six years older than me, was married, with children, and lived about 15 miles away from where my parents lived. She wasn't there that afternoon, she was working – she was a teacher.

So, still thinking Father was just ill, I went over to the sister in charge on the ward and said, 'Could I ask you how my father is and how long is he going to be ill?' And her face went very still, and she said, 'He's very seriously ill, you know.' And I realised that this wasn't just him being ill.

A little bit later, I was at my father's bedside, and he just said to me, 'I'm dying, you know.' I said, 'Oh no, no.' And he said, 'Yes I am, I'm dying.' So it was my father who told me he was dying. Not long after that he went into a heavy sleep, a sort of a coma.

I'd spoken to my sister on the phone and she said she was too upset to come to the hospital. A day or so later my father was still in this coma, and developing pneumonia. I was sitting beside him and there was no contact. The nurse said something about, 'Well, if there's anything you need to fix up, perhaps you should go.' So I drove home and I rang my brother-in-law, and I asked him if he'd arrange the funeral – I'd never even been to a funeral. My brother-in-law said he couldn't do that, he was too upset. My Uncle George was at the house so I asked him, and he said he couldn't do that, he was too upset. So I knew whose job it was to arrange the funeral.

I remember stopping at the garage to get some petrol, and as I was standing there in the sun, I thought, 'Oh, God, I wish this was all over.' Then I thought, 'I'm wishing my father dead. This is terrible.'

My mother and I went into the hospital and sat at his bedside from evening onwards. At about 11 o'clock at night, he seemed to come out of the coma, looked at me, took my hand – he had this special way of holding my hand – and smiled at me, and then gave that funny sound and died.

Now in Australia, funerals are held very quickly, so it was a matter of arranging the funeral that night. So there we were, at midnight, and I had to ring the paper and put a death notice in, and then ring the funeral people and make an appointment to see someone the next morning, because the funeral would be the day after. And I spoke to my sister – she and my brother-in-law were still at home, being upset.

Next morning, Mother and I were both up early and I went to the funeral director's and all I could think of was that all the relatives, particularly Dad's sisters, would all be there, so it had better be a grand affair. So, without asking the cost, I ordered the best coffin, with silver handles. And he was an old soldier, so he had to have a flag and all of that.

The next day was the funeral and we were having a service at a Presbyterian church, and the funeral cortège would go all the way out to the crematorium where there would be another service. It was quite a big service and, considering that my father was an atheist, he got the full works from the minister. I sat in the church and, when I saw the coffin come in, all I could think was that it was a splendid coffin, but my aunts couldn't see the silver handles because the flag covered them.

The service over, we went to the crematorium at Berrisfield, and I was looking back and I couldn't see the end of the long line of cars, and I was really pleased about that. My father had been a commercial traveller, and everybody knew him and he knew everybody. He lived his social life outside home. So it seemed like everybody had turned up. He would have been really touched by the number of people who came.

When we arrived at the crematorium, something happened that I've often puzzled over. Obviously I didn't know everyone at the funeral, but I knew by sight all the relatives and Dad's closest friends. But there was a woman about my mother's age and a young woman, standing off to one side, not talking to anyone, and both of them were crying, very upset. I asked my mother who they were and she didn't know, she'd never seen them. I don't know what happened to them afterwards, but it made me puzzle.

For many years while Dad was working for one of the firms he worked for, every month he drove up the north coast to a place called Coff's Harbour – that was part of his beat. It's a beautiful place. It was a fishing village then, and Dad would be away for three days every month. As I got older, I'd wondered what he'd done on those three days, because he was a very good-looking man. So when I saw these two women, I thought, 'I wonder if that's part of Dad's past that no one is going to tell me about?' I shall never know, but it certainly gave me something to think about.

Then we went back to the family home. Those wakes are terrible things. I remember feeling terribly angry with my father's closest friend because he was a man a bit older than my father who had been a soldier in the First World War and been gassed, and always been an invalid and on the point of dying. At the wake I was furious that my father was dead and this chap, a real bossy Scotsman whom I didn't much like, was alive.

My father and I talked all the time. I would always listen to him because he was a great storyteller. Things about politics that I was far too young to understand, yet in lots of ways I did understand. And lots of his war stories. I liked him talking about politics and about what was happening during the Second World War, whereas my mother didn't want to hear about that.

After he died, there was a realisation that no one would ever love me the way my father did, because he loved without expectations. He loved you because you existed. That was an enormous help to me in my work as a clinical psychologist, because I could see that so many of my clients were suffering because their parents would say that they loved them, but the love was conditional. The child had to be a credit to the parents or whatever. Whereas my father – he didn't want me to live my life according to what he wanted, or to be a credit to him. So I realised then that there are people in our lives who are irreplaceable and so you grieve their loss for the rest of your life.

The other thing I felt was – because he'd died, when my marriage became impossible I was free to leave Australia, whereas if he'd still been alive, I wouldn't have felt I could have done that and that would have been disastrous for me. It was only by coming over here that a whole swathe of dismal thoughts and feelings and repetitive actions just fell away, and I could be myself. So I felt in a curious way grateful that he wasn't there. And that's a mixed emotion.

I couldn't have left Australia before, because I couldn't have left him with my mother. That wouldn't have been fair at all. He had to have some support. He'd managed to marry a woman who didn't let strangers into the house, and a stranger was anyone who wasn't immediate family. She just didn't like people coming into her house. I would have felt terribly guilty about going.

What did I miss about him? He was just warm and loving and accepting and entertaining. He was never boring. Oh, God, the world is full of boring people! As he got older, he got sadder, but he could still be entertaining. That's what I missed.

I didn't turn to my father in my adult life as he had enough coping with my mother. But just his presence – just to know he was there and on my side.

In the house where we lived, you went through a door from the dining room into the living room and Dad had a chair where he always sat. And within a week or so of him dying, I was going into the living room and thought I saw him sitting there. But that's very common. He wasn't a ghost. We always see what we expect to see. But once I looked, the chair was empty. People call that a ghost, but psychologists who study perception would say it's not.

People talk to me about the death of their parents, and a thing that comes up again and again – particularly people in their late twenties or thirties when their parent dies – it's that feeling of being right on the cliff edge. There isn't that barrier there any more, the older generation that you'd always seen as a sort of protector.

When Elisabeth Kübler-Ross wrote about the stages that we go through when we're bereaved, she was writing about death at a time when nobody was writing about it. She had noticed that people went through those stages, but she noticed that different people went through the stages at different speeds, and some people got stuck at a stage or took a long time over one stage and then went through another stage fairly quickly.

But all the stuff that goes on now about training of bereavement counsellors and so on – what Elisabeth Kübler-Ross had simply noted as observations has now hardened into dogma, and you're supposed to go through these stages like you're doing it properly.

It's analogous to teaching women how to give birth, and all these women trying to do everything perfectly then feeling upset afterwards because they haven't done it properly. They've got a live, healthy baby, but they didn't do it the way they were taught to do it. That's just silly. We grieve at our own pace and in our own way and that's it.

CHAPTER 4

Sons

Tim Bentinck is an actor best known for playing David Archer in Radio 4's *The Archers*. He is also the 12th Earl of Portland. In 1967, when he was 13, his mother, Pauline, committed suicide. It happened during the holidays after his first term at Harrow School.

I was having breakfast and my father came downstairs. He walked through the door and said, 'Tim, I've got some terrible news. Mum's dead.' I said, 'You're kidding.' He said, 'Why would I joke about something like that?'

So I went and hugged him. His shoulders were going up and down and I thought he was laughing, because I'd never seen him cry. I said, 'You beast!' and pushed him away, because I thought it was just a silly joke. Then he looked at me with these absolutely dreadful eyes and said, 'Why me?' That was when I realised he meant it.

We never spoke about that conversation until a few years before he died – this was about 30 or 35 years later – and I said, 'You know when you told me that Mum died? You didn't think that I blamed you for Mum's death, did you?' He said, 'Yes.' I'd always thought he'd realised that I thought he was laughing. All those years he had thought I blamed him for my mother's death. He felt it was his fault and he'd held that inside him all those years.

Because I was 13, I thought I was the only person who'd lost their mother. It didn't occur to me till many, many years later that my elder sisters were grieving too. Sorrel is 12 years older than I am and Anna six years older. They were grown up and I thought that grown-ups can cope with it, that they are used to death and it was because I was a child that it must be hurting me more than it was hurting them. I thought I was the only one who deserved comfort.

The only time in my life I've ever kept a diary was when my mother died and it says:

> When I was doing my breakfast Papa came down and told me that
> Mummy was dead. I don't really want to think about it. Papa rang the
> doctor and the police came and we rang people etc. At 10.28 I caught
> the train to London to stay with Nan [Anna]. When I arrived they were
> all v. cheerful thank God, and we went to see 'A Countess From Hong
> Kong'... I still can't really believe it, but I'm happy that Mum's happy
> now, since she was so mis [miserable] when she was alive.

When I was back at school, I wrote, 'Went to sleep feeling mis.' I shared a room with my best friend, Noel, and he was great, because he did that blokey thing of laying off. He didn't tease. But he wasn't going round saying, 'You all right, mate?' None of that. But he defended me against other people. He was on my side.

My mother's death was my ammunition against the teachers, because there I was, at boarding school, where they were all-powerful and they could beat you. They could punish you and you were this minion. But I had grief as my weapon. I remember once a teacher said, 'What would your mother say about that, Bentinck?' and I said, 'I haven't got a mother, sir. She's dead.' And I felt great, because he went, 'Oh, I'm terribly sorry. I'm so sorry.' To have a teacher say 'I'm terribly sorry' is brilliant. Massive power.

I certainly remember how the grieving process went. I went into a process of complete denial really, total denial. Because I couldn't take on board the finality of it, I did subconsciously think they were all wrong and that Mum was going to come back one day. She wouldn't have just left me like that.

The analogy would be like a door or a window where you could open the door to the horror and see the horror, and then shut the door very, very quickly, and then cry. Be allowed to grieve a bit. Just a little, little bit. Just to go, 'Christ Almighty! She's dead!' Cry and then shut it again and block. Then over the years one would be able to open the door for a little bit longer next time, have the same amount of hurt and shut the door again. And slowly, slowly, slowly you would open it until you were actually able as an adult to leave the door open and allow the full finality of the horror in.

For me her death came out of the blue, but Pa knew, because she'd tried, I think, twice before to kill herself. It was pills. I did know there were times when Mum was unhappy. I came home one day from school and found her crying. I said, 'What's the matter, Mum?' and she said, 'I can't explain' or 'You wouldn't understand.' But I've read her diaries since my father died [in 1997]. Every single day of her life, she kept a diary. What's absolutely clear from them is that she was clinically depressed and, if they'd had Prozac in those days, I would still have a mother.

In *The Archers* just recently there's been a suicide, so of course it's been discussed left, right and centre. Lots of people don't know about my mum, so they're sitting chatting away about suicide and I'm sitting in the corner going, 'I don't want to hear this very much.' People were saying, 'It's well known that you can't be sane if you commit suicide. You have to be mad.' I think that's very true, particularly if you've got children. I mean, how can a mother possibly leave her children behind in a normal state of mind?

I've also been asked, 'Aren't you angry with your mother? Three children and she kills herself. How could she possibly do that?' Any outsider says, 'You've got to look at this, Tim, and say your mother let you down. She deserted you. She was horrible. She was a bad mother.' My wife, Judy, has said, 'Don't you think that might be true? Haven't you considered that?'

You have to say, 'If she was sane, it was a dreadful thing to do. If she was sane, she didn't love me, she didn't care about me. So she must've been mad.' That's the only way to look at it, because she was a good mother. She did love me.

She wrote a letter. I found it after my father died and I thought it was written either to him or to her lover. It said, 'My darling, how can I possibly leave you, but I must.' Then I worked out that it was me, because it said, 'my darling fair-haired boy with your beautiful blue eyes'. I wish somebody had bloody well shown that to me before. Why didn't somebody say, 'This is what she thought about you'?

My father was a very strong person, whom I admired enormously, and he was fantastically loving and caring and thoughtful. He did make up for the loss of my mother in a lot of ways. I don't know whether or not I'd have had such a close relationship with my father if my mother had still been alive. I think it would've been dissipated, because he was being Mum as well. But he was very huggy, Pa. I'd always kiss him hello and have big hugs a lot.

My parents had a very open marriage when they met. They were very sexy people. My father was fantastically good-looking. She was completely beautiful. But then what happened was, as they got older, Pa kept on having affairs and she didn't. She was having a long-term affair, but then he had affairs and wasn't telling her about them, so there was an imbalance. That's why the girls, I think, blamed Pa quite a lot.

But there were other reasons. She was stuck in the countryside and she was drinking. She'd drink in the afternoon and then get maudlin. She'd drink to make it feel better, but it made it worse, I think. I don't know whether my mother was getting distant before she died. I do remember a lot of 'tidy your room' and 'do this and do that' and being told what to do. And a lot of her not being there. Mum didn't cook much and if she did it was fish fingers and frozen peas. That's what I lived on.

I do fear death. I'm just convinced that I'm going to drop dead from a heart attack or get cancer. When I leave the family, I always think that this could be the last time I'll ever see them. Every time I walk out the door to go away for three days I think to myself, 'The boys will say, "The last time I ever saw my father he waved his normal cheery goodbye and he went off into the distance and I never saw him again."' Every single time I go to bed at night I think, 'This is the T-shirt they'll find me in.'

Also we always say goodnight to each other – always – wherever I am in the world, whatever I'm doing. That's because I didn't say goodnight to Mum on that night and I usually did.

I am absolutely so terrified that my children are going to die. I can't tell you how terrified I am when they go off at night into London and they come back at one o'clock in the morning on the night bus. All parents must feel like that, but if anything did happen to them, that I could not cope with. I could not deal with that. I really, really think that I would lose it totally, because it does feel like in my life things have been taken away from me.

I was very lucky in having two sisters, because they turned into my mum. They were just fantastic. They were just so loving and caring and tender and looked after me. In a way, if your mother represents the female loving presence at home, then in some ways that wasn't taken away from me, because it was substituted by my sisters.

I remember them being cheerful. That was the extraordinary thing. I think that's why I never realised they'd lost their mother, too. Because they were putting on a brave face, I believed their act. 'Hello Timmy! Come on, let's go and have fun today.' 'Oh, OK,' says the 13-year-old, 'We're all going to have fun.' Much better than being at school where everyone was horrible to you. They would take me on days out all the time. Masses of cinemas and I wrote down in my diary all the films I went to see: *The Return of the Gunfighter*, *Laurel and Hardy*, *Warning Shot*, *The Quiller Memorandum*.

They did that for about the first six months, up to the point where you stop going bonkers. Then the reality hits and you can kind of talk about it. But there is a hell of a lot that I still block. There is a hell of a lot that I have on purpose not remembered.

O liver Harrison was six when his father, Bob, collapsed with a heart attack, aged 39. Oliver is now 12. His sister, Abigail, was just a baby at the time and her story is in Chapter 3: Daughters. His mother is Karen and her story is in Chapter 7: Wives.

I went upstairs and I heard him shout, 'Karen! Karen!' and it just shocked me a bit. I found my dad. He was like in a bundle on the floor. He'd knocked the lamp over onto his head. My mum said, 'Where's Dad?' and I went, 'He's there. He's on the floor.' I just was shocked. I wanted to go to the hospital with my dad, but my mum sent me to the people next door.

When my dad left to go to hospital, I came back. I woke up in the middle of the night and half the street were in the house, but my mum and dad weren't. I didn't really think he was going to die. I remember I came downstairs and I said, 'Is Dad here?' and then my mum arrived and she told me he'd died.

I went to the funeral. I didn't want to say goodbye. At the time I wasn't that upset. It still hadn't hit me. It was kind of like a celebration in a way, because the whole family – we don't get together a lot – everybody got together, but everybody was sad. I didn't really know what had happened, so I was really happy. I remember we were sat on the front row and Nana was there and my dad's sister was there and they never really lifted their heads out of their handkerchiefs. I wonder why I didn't feel more.

The day after it happened, I went back to school. The teachers said, 'You come and play with the toys.' You only got to do that on a Friday afternoon and I thought, 'Why?' I understand now why they did that, because they thought I must've felt different, but it doesn't really hit you till afterwards.

Everybody felt sorry for me. People looked at me in a different way. It was nice the first couple of days, but after the first week or so it got really annoying. Because I didn't really feel it. You feel they're coming back, but they never do. It's hard to explain, really.

He liked doing the things that I like to do – like football. We used to go to Manchester United a lot and when they scored he used to lift me up. I took that for granted, but now I don't. I think that was something special. I just think of the things we could've done together.

Also I collect these things called Warhammer and my dad used to collect them. They're really expensive, the models, and he'd buy a box for just me. My mum didn't really know anything about Warhammer.

I used to be quite naughty and now it's made me into a kinder person, a bit slower, sensible really. It's given me more of a desire to do well. This drive to do well helps me a lot. It's like I'm doing something for him. In a game of football I was taking a penalty and it was in a cup final. It was five minutes before the end and if I scored we would have won and it just made me think about him and I wished he could be watching me. It made me want to score. I thought of him before I'd taken it, then I took it and I scored. It was really weird. I saw his face smiling. It was weird.

They're like your whole world – your mum and dad – because you're with them all the time. It's terrible to lose one of them. It hit me a lot about a year and a half ago. I think that was when I was really old enough to understand – why he'd died and what he'd died of. I try to think of why – why he died. I think of so many different reasons. It's complicated.

You see people who are arguing with their dads. I never really argued with my dad and you think, 'Why couldn't they have lost their dad instead of me?' I get angry that other people's dads are still alive, but I try to disguise that.

When I was six, I couldn't find the right words to say. I still can't find the right words. It's a bit like you have the perfect image, but when you think about the right words to describe them, you can't. You do realise what's going on. You do. My mum says, 'He doesn't really understand', but that's not true. I can remember everything. Now I think about it, I wonder whether Abigail really does understand who Dad was. She wants to think she remembers him, but she doesn't.

I used to get really upset. I still do. People think, 'Oh, it's a really hard subject. I don't want to upset you.' But I am quite keen to talk about it – with the right people. My nana lets me talk about it. She understands a lot. I don't really like talking to children about it. I don't want to tell friends to their face. I'd rather if they read your book.

I'd like people to know what I'm going through. To understand what it's really like. Because about a year ago I watched a programme about people whose parents had separated and this person said, 'I suppose in a way it's better if people die.' And I thought, 'How could you say that? At least you've actually got a parent and it's what both parents wanted. It's maybe not what you wanted, but you can still find them. They're still out there and they can come back.' But when somebody dies, they can't come back.

I feel empty. I still feel empty. With my mum and dad it was like 100 per cent together and then 50 per cent of my world has been taken away. It's in some ways harder when you're a child, because they are your world – your mum and your dad. Then when you lose that person, it's like you lose some of yourself. I feel just as sad as my mum, if not worse. I have feelings. Just because I'm not an adult, I am still a person.

S ir John Harvey-Jones is the retired chairman of ICI. His mother died when he was in his thirties.

I wasn't expecting my mother to die, though she was obviously getting older. She died very peacefully – she had a lie down after lunch and didn't wake up.

It was a considerable shock. We were living a long way apart. I was in the North East and she was in Henley. We were in touch regularly – once or twice a week – but I was not linked in with her daily life, so I was totally surprised by how alone I felt, which was hurtful to my wife. I was very close to my mother and always had been.

When she died, I went down on my own. My wife stayed at home with our handicapped daughter, Gabrielle. I felt totally alone in the world. I'd always before had the certain knowledge that I could tell my mother things or ask her advice or whatever. Yet it really wasn't that way round at all. Mother had not been able to help much, physically or financially. In fact, it was the other way round.

It's the loss of someone on whom you had been totally reliant all your life – unconditional acceptance. Yet I was at prep school when she was still in India, I was at Dartmouth from the age of 12, at sea from 18, and when I was in the Navy I was away for two to three years at a time. So there was no daily support. We were close, but she was rather a 'proper' woman. There wasn't a great deal of emotional intelligence. We had a real feeling of affection towards each other, but no touchy-feely discussions. In the 1920s you would have been considered half-mad to discuss feelings.

I was the only child. I had been a twin, but he had died before I knew him. My parents had a non-marriage for years. They barely cohabited. Father made his life in India. The only years we spent together as a family were from my birth until I was five or six. Father and Mother were bringing up a Maharajah. Father was a great rider and shooter and played the violin. They were all things he did on his own, not as a family. He wasn't involved in teaching me any of the sort of skills that were the hallmark of my class. I had a feeling of dislike and fear towards him.

Because I was on my own from the age of six onwards, there were no shared memories, only individual ones. Therefore my life was a very independent life. Which was a lack.

When my mother died, there was hardly anyone I could turn to. Yet my wife helped me work through the grief; my wife and my daughter, Gabrielle. My wife had not got on very well with my mother, who hadn't made her feel very welcome, so she had every right to feel unsympathetic. But she was splendid at supporting me.

For a long time I had a feeling that I wasn't as good a son as I should have been and hadn't given as much support as I could have done. But it's difficult to see how I could have done better. The prime feeling is one of emotional regret and neglect rather than physical actions.

I'm now 80 and I still think about my mother occasionally. It's not a regular thing. Sometimes something happens that makes me think of her, but we spent so much of our time apart. It wasn't a normal childhood. I had a very independent, almost orphan-like life. I didn't feel like an orphan when my father died, ten years later. I didn't feel anything, because he had done very little in terms of discussing my life and my future. I never managed to live up to what he expected. In a way, the driving force in me was to do things to impress my father and become the sort of man who was admirable in my father's eye: hunting, shooting, fishing, stiff upper lip. The sort of man I now feel is less admirable.

Nothing I did earned his approbation. I made a film in India for the BBC. During the course of that I met people who knew my father, and I asked them if he ever mentioned me. They said no. He'd never told them that I was sunk during the war, for instance. He was driven by an overwhelming thought of duty and appearance. Yet there are an awful lot of my mother's values and ideas that I still recognise.

I do believe in a soul. Not in an afterlife as such. I believe we leave an effect behind us. And you live on through the way you affect other people.

Gerald Jackson's mother died in her early seventies. She was widowed and lived near Gerald and his five children. The interview was done in Gerald's front room, which is covered in photographs of his family including many of his mother going back to the 1940s and 1950s. His son, Michael, tells his story in Chapter 11: Grandchildren.

It was the Jewish New Year and I was round at my mother's house for a meal with my youngest son, Michael, who was 14 at the time. It was a traditional Jewish meal: chicken. Now my mother burned most things, so you could smell that something had been overdone even before we got anywhere near this meal.

There's no Jewish community here, so probably for my mother it was more important than it was for me that we could share this festival with her. She was just standing in the kitchen talking to me about the meal and that it would be ready soon. Suddenly she said she was feeling dizzy and that was the last thing she said. I went to get her some water and when I turned round she'd already fallen to the floor.

We went to the hospital and she passed away in the early hours of the following morning. So the whole thing was something of a trauma. We were standing in the kitchen of her cottage one minute talking about the quality of the chicken and the next I was sitting in a room at the hospital waiting for them to pronounce her dead.

I'm sure it was a fantastic way for her to go, because she never suffered at all, but it was an unbelievable shock for me and Michael. It's interesting, but Michael and I have never discussed anything about it since then and I've no idea why.

The night she died we had the problem of the meal. Now my mother didn't waste anything and I was brought up not to waste anything. So I had a slightly overcooked meal and when she was pronounced dead, I went up to the cottage and I brought the whole meal here to the house and I said to the kids, 'Grandma would be absolutely furious if we wasted this.' So we all sat round and ate it.

It was really difficult, because you know you're eating the last meal your mother made you, but she only made it yesterday and now she's dead. I know she'd have been furious if we'd wasted a whole chicken and all those vegetables. And all overcooked! It was right: to sit down with the family, eat this meal and know that Grandma made you this.

Because she was Jewish, I had to solve the problem of how to do a Jewish funeral. I'm not very orthodox and I'd no idea. I really needed somebody to talk to and the person I would have talked to was my mother and I couldn't do that.

My father had died in 1970, so suddenly I was the oldest member of the family. That's actually a frightening experience – to discover there's no other adult to talk to. My mother was the last link to that generation.

I locked up her house and never went there for three years, which was a ridiculous thing to do. I didn't want to disturb it and it became a shrine. I can see that now. I still have a load of her paperwork I haven't been through yet. I've got her Marshall and Snelgrove box which she kept her hats in. I've got her glasses. Tell me why? I don't know. I think I should have dealt with it far more quickly – for my own good, apart from anything else.

My mother always looked beautiful to me. But I suppose mothers do, don't they? Her clothes were really nice. She bought some really beautiful things, but could I get rid of them? We tried to take them to charity shops. They didn't want them, because they weren't everyday clothes. Things were slightly over-embroidered and they were very bright colours – dramatic colours. I found that quite depressing, because I knew my mother had bought her clothes really carefully and spent a lot of money on them and I wanted them to go to a good home.

She has left a legacy – because she was so over-the-top. Some people would say she was slightly mad. I think that's grossly unfair, but she was melodramatic and massively outgoing. She once met a man on the train from Brighton and brought him back for dinner. That was my mother and that was the wonderful charm about her. Anybody who met her would never forget the experience and I still meet people today who don't know that she's died and they say, 'I'll never forget meeting your mother. How is she?'

It's nearly seven years since she died, but if I'm watching something on television I'll think, 'I'll just ring my mother and talk to her about that.' That never seems to go. Although I avoided seeing her on so many occasions, because she was so demanding. I made so many excuses not to go and see her. She'd say, 'Are you not coming round this week?' and I'd say, 'I will. I've been very busy.' I felt it was a duty and, of course, once that duty's no longer there, you know that you should've done a bit more.

My mother was unique. I don't think you can replace the relationship between a son and his mother.

Brian Lewis is an artist, writer and publisher based in Pontefract. His father Ernest [or Ernie], a poster-writer from Birmingham, died when Brian was in his late fifties.

His death wasn't particularly expected. He seemed quite fit. He had some sort of bladder problem, and I didn't associate it with cancer, but eventually he ended up in hospital and he died ten days later. He was 84.

I wouldn't have said I was particularly close to him. I now know that I have massive debts to him, and I've come to admire him much more after his death than I would have thought I did during his lifetime. I was very, very close to my mother. I loved my mother. But my father – I always felt that there was a tension between us, partly because I had taken opportunities and my father, partly because of his upbringing and his character, had not. I thought he resented the opportunities that I'd taken.

There was a lovely moment at the deathbed, actually, that illustrated this. We'd got about ten days to go, and I came down from Yorkshire so I could be close to him for that period. My brother came up from Cirencester. We were sitting by the bed, and by this time you knew he was coming towards his end. My father started to wander from reality, and he thought that he was talking to two gentlemen, for some reason, who lived on the outskirts of Birmingham.

My brother took the opportunity of saying, 'You had two sons.' And my father said, 'Yes, Brian and Malcolm.' Malcolm said, 'What were they like?' My father paused and he said, 'Well, Brian, he was clever but he could have done better for himself.' So I thought, 'Well, if that's his final blessing, I want to find out about Malcolm.' So I said, 'And what about the youngest son?' And he said, 'People said he was a good singer, but I just thought he sang loud.'

So that summed it up in one sense – he acknowledged my ability to think, and I have great debts to my father about that, massive debts, but he didn't actually think I'd done very well. Whereas I would have thought I wasn't all that good as a thinker, but I'd done all right doing things, so that was that. So were we close? Well, yes and no.

I owe him a debt of learning. Remember, he was a man who, when I was born, he was a poster-writer. Then, during the war, he went to work in a foundry as a labourer. And because his handwriting was so immaculate – beautiful handwriting – a managing director saw that and put him in the office. From then on, he became the man who ran the office. I learnt later in life that he'd never paid tax in his life, not because he was fiddling it, but because he'd never earned enough.

When I was 13, he bought me two books which were the foundation of everything I know and everything I believe in. One was *The Complete Plays of George Bernard Shaw* – it was one of the few serious books we had in the house – and the other was *The Complete Works of Shakespeare*.

Then in 1948, when I was probably 10 or 12, and he was still a man on about £4.50 a week, he bought the *Encyclopaedia Britannica* for me, and that was a marvellous thing to do. He would always say, 'Anything you want to know you can find in a book' and I later ended up publishing books, basically because of that.

The conflict between father and son was interesting in another way. When he retired, I bought him some paints because he was a poster-writer. After about six months, he hadn't painted anything other than pictures of cottages and he gave it up, and I said, 'What else can you do?' He said, 'I could write my life story.' And I said, 'Aye, you could, but you're too idle.' It was a wrong thing to say, because of course he wasn't idle. But I went on, 'If you reckon you can do it, I'll have a thousand words from you by Thursday.' By that Christmas I'd printed his life story in an edition of three and started my totally new career as a person who was interested in people's life stories.

He started his personal story by saying, 'Most people write their life stories to justify their existence. But this is the life story of a nobody.' And what he wasn't was a nobody. He was a dead impressive man in his own way. I've got to see that more as the years pass.

I didn't think he was going to die so quickly, and I had to do something back in Yorkshire, so I left Birmingham at about eight o'clock the night before he died, intending to come back on the eight o'clock in the morning train from Wakefield. And I had a phone call at seven o'clock that morning from a friend of his, Les, saying, 'Your father is very ill. I think he'll die within the hour.' I rushed back, didn't make it, got there an hour later.

I'd never seen a dead person before, so the first dead person I saw was my dad. That was a very odd thing. I thought I would be more afraid of a corpse than I was. I wasn't afraid at all really.

I sat with him for a little while and then I went outside and I cried. Probably I cried twice after that. Perhaps I would have liked to have cried more than I did cry. It's odd because I can cry and don't have problems with crying. But I didn't cry.

When my mother died, the funeral was at a Catholic church. I'm a committed atheist, so it dissolved into farce for me. My father had a massive celebration after his funeral. That was partly a change in my philosophy – I had become a more tolerant atheist – and a massive change of attitude in how you should celebrate death. I hadn't worked it out by my mother's death, but by my father's death I had.

So when my father was cremated I decided that, because a lot of people were in the Birmingham area, we would celebrate his life in an evening about my father. And the book I'd encouraged him to write – which was the first of two and I'd edited them together – was used.

In the week of his death I'd asked him who his friends were and he named 17 people. So I decided to give a book to each of his friends. I printed it out, got it bound, and on the night of the funeral, I had 17 copies. At the funeral, all of his grandchildren who wanted to read, read. I read and spoke about my father. Malcolm also spoke about him. One of my kids played the flute and my wife accompanied her on the piano, and one of my daughters sang, 'My Grandfather's Clock'. She was only five, so there was not a dry eye in the house. It was impressive to see this little girl celebrating her grandfather. We called the evening 'Celebrating Ernie'.

As the eldest son, I felt that I had obligations to bury my father with honour and to give him a dignified burial. So I conducted the service at the crematorium. I don't believe death should be left to professionals. I believe death should be ordered by the person when they're alive and fulfilled by the child. Bring back the cult of the dead!

What it's all taught me is that death is The End. Just as when the sperm hits the ovary – that's the beginning. The end is death. And my only obligation to anyone is to attempt to make a 'good death' – one in which I recognise death to be so natural and try to be dignified.

I used to think I'd like to die on Mercutio's line: ''Tis not as wide as a barn door nor as deep as a well, yet 'tis enough, 'twill do. Ask for me tomorrow and you will find me a grave man.' The Renaissance tradition of death, that's it. When it will come, it will come.

Jimmy Mulville is the co-founder of Hat Trick Productions, the television company responsible for the success of, among others, *Have I Got News for You* and *Room 101*. His father, also Jimmy, committed suicide in 1978 when his only son was 23.

Father was a boiler operator in Tate and Lyle's factory. Before that he worked at a power station on the Dock Road in Liverpool. He was very bright, my dad, and very hard-working. He always did well in any job he had. But he didn't have any opportunity to further himself in that sense so I suppose, like sons do, at some level I was living the unlived life of the father. Me going to university, going to Cambridge, and him coming down and seeing me, for him must have been a very bitter-sweet moment.

In my teenage years there was a lot of friction. They say that the closer you are in childhood the more bloody the separation is in adolescence, and we had a very bloody separation, terrible rows.

If I could relive one scene in my life, it would be the scene where – I was working at a cake factory in my gap year between school and university, to get some money, because I wanted to get married to a girl I'd fallen in love with when I was 14, which I did. Which pissed my father off – that I was so hell-bent on this romantic excursion, as he saw it, when I should have been concentrating on getting my life going.

Anyway, I'd just done my interview at Cambridge and we were now waiting for the letter to arrive. This was a period where we weren't speaking. And the post arrived. He climbed up the stairs, and he said, 'Jimmy, it's arrived.' My face was to the wall, and I said, 'Leave it there, I'll open it later.'

Now, aged 49, if I had my time again, I'd have turned round, opened it and we could have shared that moment. But the truth is, I was 18 and I was self-righteous, and he was wrong and I was right, and I was going to teach him a lesson.

On one level, he was incredibly proud of me – that was the overriding feeling. But in the mix somewhere, there was jealousy. Jealousy of the life I was going to have. But overridingly I knew that he was dead proud that I'd got to Cambridge.

I got married two days before I went to Cambridge. In my heart I knew I was doing something rather silly. That's slightly unfair on the person involved, but I could hear the voice of reason, that I was very young to get married. And the risk didn't pay off. The marriage didn't last – well, what a shock, eh?

But I would not be told. I was a very bright lad and I thought I knew everything. I thought education was the equivalent of intelligence, and now I know it's not at all. The kind of education I had inflated me beyond belief, really, and they found it quite hard to cope with.

It's a wonderful moment when your teacher tells you, 'If you put in extra work, you can get to Cambridge.' But what you don't realise is that there's a price to pay for that. And for a while I didn't know who I was, who I belonged to, whether I was really this boy from Liverpool, or whether I was now this young man at Cambridge.

I got the news that my dad had been struck down by illness just after my finals. I'd been ringing home during my finals and my mother had answered the phone each time and said, 'Oh, your dad's working', or 'He's out', or – and I thought, 'That's odd.' Then, after the last final exam I phoned her and she broke down: 'He's been in hospital these last three weeks but he insisted on me not telling you because he didn't want to worry you while you were doing your final exams.'

So I drove home that night and went to see him at Walton Hospital. He'd been struck down by an illness called transverse myelitis, which is an umbrella term for quite a few central nervous viral diseases. It affected his central nervous system, and when it came back it was completely damaged and impaired, so he had paralysis and pins and needles, poor circulation.

I suppose I was just too young, too immature, to bridge the gap and sit down with him and say, 'How are you feeling?' And we didn't come from a family or from a background or an area where people sat down and talked about their feelings.

I knew that my mum and dad loved each other intensely. And me in the middle, there was an intensity between the three of us. Yet when he got ill, no one talked about it. It lasted about a year, and then in the May of 1978 I got a phone call – I was sharing a house in Catford with people from university and I was still married, just about. We didn't have a phone in the house, and the two old ladies from next door came round and said, 'There's a phone call for you.' I went round and it was my father-in-law, and he said, 'I'm really sorry, Jimmy. It's your father. He's dead.'

I remember banging my head against the wall. Then getting on a train that night and going up with my wife. I was in the back of the car – my father-in-law had picked us up – and I said, 'How did he do it? Was it pills?' Hoping it was pills. And he said, 'No, he hanged himself.'

That shocked me. I rocked back, and I sort of took it like a punch. Even now – it's like that painting, *The Scream* by Munch – that frozen expression. Somewhere inside me is that frozen scream of disbelief.

We got back home, my mother was there – she had found my father's body – and I was very angry. I was very angry with the doctor – he'd said,

'Oh, you know, I've sometimes thought about whether Mr Mulville should see a counsellor or something.' Of course, I was just angry because my dad had died and I wanted to pin it on somebody.

On the day of his funeral, we all got drunk, as we always did. And my grandfather said something to me: 'Are you going to come back up now and look after me and your mother? Your father was very disappointed that you moved down south.' I didn't need to hear that. I grabbed him, banged his head against the wall, punched him – I was pulled off by my closest friend and his father. And that was the best attempt we got at grief, really. Grief plus alcohol.

So I never grieved for my father properly until I stopped drinking. The truth is, on the anniversary of his death, I'd get drunk and I'd get maudlin, or I'd get angry, or I'd try and get laid. I'd just get out of myself, try and obliterate the day. I'd get into a fight or into some girl's bed. My grief was frozen. I'd never really looked at it. I blamed the doctor, I blamed his circumstances, I blamed my mother, I blamed my grandfather, I blamed myself. Why didn't I ring him on that day? I usually rang him on a Tuesday – why didn't I do that?

Then when I stopped drinking [ten years later] and I began to look at some of the things that had gone in my life, one of them was this, my father's suicide. On the anniversary of his death, the first anniversary after I stopped drinking, I went up to the garden of remembrance where we'd scattered his ashes and I cried. I cried sober. It wasn't crocodile tears or maudlin, it was just – I missed my dad.

See, the thing is that I adored my dad. I felt extraordinarily close to him, even though we'd had these rows. We were very, very close. He was a very funny bloke, you know. We'd sit up to all hours and he'd go out into the back yard where we had an outside toilet and he'd look up at the stars and tears would form in his eyes and he'd say, 'Aren't we small, son? Aren't we so small?' And I'd think, 'I love this guy.' To me, he was so poetic. Then to see him in the last year, it was very painful to witness. And I suppose with his suicide, I just didn't want to open the box.

A friend of mine said to me, 'Every anniversary of his death, you get sad. Do you get angry with him?' I said, 'Why would I get angry with him?' 'Because he killed himself. Because he left you.' He said, 'Did he leave a note?' And yes, he did. At the inquest, they showed me the note for the first time. In his really meticulous handwriting – he was very proud of his handwriting, my father – he mentioned my mother and myself and expressed this desire not to live any more because the pain was too much. He didn't specify what pain it was, whether it was physical or emotional. And this friend said, 'Have you ever written it out?' I said, 'Why would I want to do that?' 'I don't know, try it.'

So I'm in my friend's office – he's quite a wise man, this guy – and I start to write out this note. I'm halfway through writing it out – it's emblazoned on my brain – and as I'm writing it, the pen is going through the paper, I'm so angry. I was furious with this man. I was so angry with him. How could he write my name down, and my mother's name down – the two most important people in his life – and then go and hang himself? How could he do that?

Once I'd got the anger out, I could then feel grief. So I would say it took me about 15 years before I really began to grieve for my dad.

Having children has brought me more into the present and the future. I've got three sons and when Joe [the eldest] popped out, I had this metaphysical moment when I looked at his face and I thought, 'I don't know you but I recognise you, I know you so well, but I've only just met you.' That moment in his face when I saw me, I saw Karen [his third wife], I saw my father, I saw all these people coalesce in his face. Then that moment went and he was himself. But it was an amazing moment. And the truth is, at any moment like that, any big moment in my life, I recall my father. Because he's the big absence, the big gap.

I often think, 'What would he make of it all? What would he make of me now?' I don't know really. The thing is, I love my family, I like my job. It's provided me with a fantastic way of living, and I really like the people here, it's a very nice thing to do, but I would never now dream of missing an event involving my children at school for a meeting here. Now I am awake, I am a tuned-in radio. I am 49 years of age, and I know how important these things are in life, much more important than doing a funny comedy programme or earning millions of pounds. This is the stuff that makes me live, that I feel alive doing.

My relationship with my father, I'm pleased to say, has changed more since he died than when he was alive, because I've changed, and I've changed the way I've seen him. I'm very proud of him. He worked so hard, and he was a very likeable man. If my sons wound up feeling about me the way I feel about my father, I'd be happy.

I still walk up those stairs sometimes and think, 'What was going through your mind the moment when you did this?' Because when you jump off there with the electric wire round your neck, there's no going back. Was it like Anna Karenina, when she jumps in front of the train and thinks, 'I've changed my mind, I didn't want to do this after all?'

J ohn Naish is a journalist and author, and writes for *The Times*. His mother lived with cancer for 25 years. She died when he was 35. John's brother, Chris, is three years older.

My father died when I was just coming up to four and it caused a huge physical shock to my mother. She went very short-sighted overnight and her kidneys went strange. She was instructed by the doctors to go and have a kidney removed, which she refused to do, because she had no one to look after me and my brother. Then when I was seven she had breast cancer. It was quite advanced. She had a radical mastectomy and lost two ribs.

She wasn't expected to live, but later she told me that, as she was going in for the operation, she suddenly realised she didn't have time to die. A lot of people had written her off and I think, if she'd believed them, she would have died. I think she was just being cussed. In fact she lived for another 25 years.

Not long before she died, she came back from a hospital appointment chortling, because some woman, who was probably her age when she first got cancer, was sitting next to her, being very worried, and said to her, 'How long have you been coming?' and my mum said, 'Well, I think it's about 1970.'

She didn't talk about death until towards the end. Then about three days before she died, she said, 'I think I've got about two days and people normally die at three in the morning.' She was about two hours out.

She'd been in hospital for so long, so many times and I knew what she really wanted was to die at home. So this was the deal I made with her: 'Look, you can die at home. I know you want to. But frankly, if it goes on for a long time, I'm not sure I could cope.' She was very happy with that.

In the past I had edited a nursing magazine, so I thought, 'Well, I can do it.' Then suddenly you realise you can't. You don't quite know when you're going to tip over the edge of the sea where all the dragons are. You're always on the brink of something terrible happening.

Although in retrospect I'd say it was easy, but that's because I hadn't done it before. One of the reasons it was easy was mere fortune. Mum wasn't messy. She had a peaceful death. She wasn't screaming; she wasn't fighting.

So all we really had was twice-hourly visits by two Macmillan nurses, hospice nurses, all these people turning up and standing with their arms folded saying, 'Isn't she peaceful?', checking her morphine injections and going off, which was fantastic because it was very reassuring.

The one thing I really wanted to do was give my mum a good death – at home, with her sons, not having lots of medical machinery around and not being told what to do. Not being regarded as a little old woman in hospital, which is what they would've thought she was. If the cancer wasn't going to get her, I think being patronised would have probably finished her off.

We weren't very physical, but the last two days we held hands. I think it was because, after my father died, she was informed by her family that she couldn't bring up two boys on her own, so she'd better get remarried. But she didn't do that. Then someone told her she was going to die and she didn't do that either. In a nice form of 'Lady Macbething', she had to 'unwoman' herself to get through a lot of these things. But towards the end – fine – she could become Mum again.

Both of us were very brave up to that point. Then we're at home rather than in hospital and I'm there and the GP's coming at her with a needle – and I think it's the first time she was allowed, or had allowed herself, to feel scared. So we held hands. It was a strange feeling. It was connecting in a way that was, for both of us, quite perilous, because it was admitting something.

Once the home nurses had her settled down on the morphine injections, it was really a matter of time and I just sat there, book in one hand, her hand in the other and every hour or so I'd just give her a nudge and say, 'Everything OK? Are you in pain?' And she'd say, 'Yes' and 'No.' That was it.

It was a beautiful mini-heatwave, so I had the window slightly open. It was peaceful, so you could sit and just do nothing. In a hospital, not only would you have people buzzing round you, you might also feel you were in the way or that you ought to be looking as if you were doing something. Certainly not reading the *Which? Guide to what to do when someone dies*. Mother was quite amused I was sitting reading that. She didn't mind at all. For her it was very useful to know that she could go off and her useless younger son was doing the proper things.

The local GP was very useful. He just turned up and told me that it was cancer-induced kidney failure, so he said, 'I'm not coming back. Cherish the time.' It was just being. That's all we needed to do.

After a day or so I really did need to go to the pub with a friend and just let the pressure out of my skull, so I asked my brother, Chris, to sit and hold her hand for an hour on his own with her while I went off and he agreed. I think that was very useful for both of them.

My brother and I are quite ying/yang. He can do very practical things perfectly. Emotional things, he's sometimes not too happy with. So when my mum was getting ill, if something practical happened – if the fence blew over – Chris would do that. Meanwhile I'd talk to her about life and things. So she was perfectly well covered.

The most amazing person that I encountered was one I hadn't asked for. She almost turned up like Mary Poppins. Part of me doubts that she ever existed. She was a night-sitter and as far as I can gather, she didn't have any nursing or medical qualifications. She turned up in a Mini Metro, which is sort of a modern version of the boat across the Styx really, because she turned up unannounced on the night that Mum was going to die. She was a rather plain-spoken woman from the estates, who just sat. She sat with people in their homes when they were dying. She was around to make tea, sit around when I was going to the loo. 'I'll call you if anything changes' – that sort of thing.

Anyway, her breathing changed and the night-sitter said, 'That's going into the final stage' which was useful and reassuring to know. A few hours later she said, 'This is going on quite a long time. Are you her youngest son?' 'Yes.' 'Well, she doesn't want to let go of her baby. Look, you've got to tell her it's all right. I'll go and make a cup of tea.' So I just said to Mum, 'It's time to go. We're all fine. You've done a marvellous job.' And she went.

It was a moment of extraordinary deep contact. The nurses and people had said, 'She is to all intents unconscious, but she knows what's going on. Be aware of that.' There did seem to be tears in her eyes, but she seemed happy that I'd said what I did.

The first thing I did when my mother died was go and do the washing-up. The night-sitter came out and smiled at me as I was doing this and I said, 'I expect you think this is an extremely crazy thing to do.' She said, 'People do everything different.' I think it was useful, having people around saying it's OK, whatever it is you're feeling.

There are two people dying if you're very close to someone who's dying, because a bit of you dies, too. And if it's a parent and you wish to continue being irresponsible, or – if you like – creative, you have to change your attitude about who you're being irresponsible to and for.

I think the death of your mother is the last snap of the umbilical cord for both of you. You've got no one to take your paintings home to.

Lemn Sissay is a poet and writer based in Manchester. He was fostered as a baby and did not discover his real name until he was 18. He found his natural mother when he was 21, then in 1995 he learnt that his father, an airline pilot, had been killed in a plane crash in 1975.

I lived with foster parents until I was 11 years old and I didn't really think about my natural father at all then. I viewed my foster parents as my real parents and I didn't even know my real name. My social worker gave me his name, Norman, and then my foster parents called me after Mark, the disciple, and their second name, Greenwood. So for the first 16 years of my life I thought my name was Norman Mark Greenwood.

I was the only black child in what was a very monocultural area and so I attracted a lot of attention. My foster mother used to have spit on her back when she came home. This is in deepest Lancashire in 1967 or 1968. She had to put up with all that because of me.

From 11 to 18 years old I lived in care. I lived in lots of different children's homes. When I left the last one at 18, I was given a birth certificate. It had the only truthful thing on it that I'd ever been told and that was my name, Lemn Sissay.

You talk about people who lose people and have grief. At 18 I had no mother, father, sisters, brothers, aunts, uncles, cousins, no birthdays, no Christmases, no Saturdays, Sundays, weekends. That was right until I was 32, when I'd found all the family.

At 18 I started to look for my mother. It took me three years to find her. She's Ethiopian and she was working in the Gambia at the time. I called her and went out to meet her, without realising that she was as frightened of me as I was of her, because she believed my father had used force in their relationship. He would've been about 22 the last time she saw him and I was 21 or 22 when I met her. She couldn't face me because when she was looking at me she was looking at his face.

For five years, she wouldn't tell me who he was. But eventually she gave me his name and told me he was a pilot for Ethiopian Airlines. So I flew to Ethiopia. She told me before I went that he was dead and in public I said, 'I've just found out my dad's dead, but I didn't know him, so it didn't matter.' But that's not how I really felt.

I went to Ethiopian Airlines and they told me when his plane crashed, where it crashed, how it crashed. Then I went to meet his wife – not my mother – his wife and all her sons and daughters and she said, 'I will not agree that this is his son until I see him.' So I go into the house and she says, 'It's him. Of course it's him. Our home is your home.' She shows me all the pictures of him and we look exactly the same.

My father has no grave. I actually went to the plane in the Simian Mountains. It took two days' travelling, one day on foot, one day sleeping in the mountains. The plane's still there, all scattered over the mountain. It was an accident. The plane went into the mountain and everybody on board died. There were only eight people on the flight. It was on New Year's Day.

His body is literally strewn over the side of that mountain and by the time I'd got there I felt I could let him rest. The plane was struck by lightning on the wing which sent it askew and into the mountain. He died – as he lived – in a hail of fire.

I feel I know what kind of relationship we would've had. It would've been very difficult and very volatile at first. I think in some ways I'm very like him. Everybody says so, because I like a bit of a laugh – a lot of a laugh – and he was the life and soul of the party. He was 'Mr Cool.'

My grief is not that my father's dead, but that my mother won't recognise me. In lots of senses, I'm the one that died. I grew up a lot of the time thinking that I shouldn't be alive. If nobody's there to acknowledge that you're alive, then are you alive? You see, this is what family does, it gives you reference points. The loss of self, that was true grief.

I spent all my twenties without a week going by when I didn't cry and I mean crying from the most deepest place, almost like an animal cry. Every week. Sometimes I'd just go out for walks and cry my eyes out. I found all these secret places to cry and I'd be thinking, 'It's not fair. I didn't do anything wrong.' Remember, my mother 'died' when I was born almost. My foster parents 'died' when I was 11 and I went into care. So my father's death was a compounding of all those things.

I wrote a poem about lots of different places where people cry. It goes like this:

Quiet Places

Some people on bus seats, shake at the shoulders
Stoned Elvises trying to dance after the gig

Some people walk into the rain and look like they're smiling
Running mascara writes sad bitter letters on their faces

Some people drive their cars into lay-bys or park edges
And cradle the steering wheel looking like headless drivers

Some sink their open mouths into feather pillows
And tremble on the bed like beach dolphins

Some people are bent as question marks when they weep
And some are straight as italic exclamation marks

Some are soaking in emotional dew when they wake
Salt street maps etched into their faces

Some find rooms and fall to the floor as if praying to Allah, noiseless
Faces contorted into that silent scream that seems like laughter

Why is there not a tissue-giver? A man who looks for tears
Who makes the finest silk tissues and offers them free?

It seems to me that around each corner beneath each stone
Are humans quietly looking for a place to cry on their own

CHAPTER 5

Sisters

Corrin Abbott was four when her older sister, Lisa, died. Lisa was born with a hole in the heart and was in and out of hospital till the age of six, when she had an operation. She did not survive. Their parents had separated when Corrin was 18 months old. Her mother died when Corrin was 18 and three months pregnant with her son, Callum.

On the day of Lisa's funeral, I was left with the childminder and I was taken to one of their family weddings. It was a grand affair in a big Catholic church. I can remember going to the church and the reception afterwards, wearing a yellow dress.

Lisa's death affected my life immensely, not because I was grieving for her, but because of how it affected my mum. She was in pieces and if anything I felt a great deal of responsibility towards her. I felt more sad for my mum than I did for losing a sister. I know I was incredibly frightened about what was going to happen.

I feel the family put a lot of responsibility on me, especially my mum's family. 'You must look after your mum. You must watch out for her. You be good.' If a four-year-old hears five times in one day, 'You must look after your mum', it's a big thing. It's worrying and frightening. I'm now a single parent and if I'm not so well, friends will pop round to help and I notice they'll say to my son, 'Now, you'll look after your mum, won't you?'

My childhood wasn't good. I don't know how it would have been if Lisa hadn't died, but it's fair to say that her death consumed my mum's life. Behind closed doors, you're the one that's seeing the raw grief. It was awful to witness and to be absolutely, utterly helpless. Uniforms not being ironed and meals not being prepared, that sort of thing.

I was constantly living in my sister's shadow. Everything revolved round the memory of Lisa: birthdays, Christmases, anniversaries of her illnesses, the anniversary of her death. December was a terrible month, because Lisa's birthday was in December and then there was Christmas. On Christmas Day my mum would sit crying, not sobbing uncontrollably, but she would sit watching me open my presents, presumably wishing Lisa was there opening hers. When my mum was drunk, she used to talk about it all the time. She'd say, 'You don't know what I went through, how difficult it was for me, how hard it is.' I used to think, 'How can I?'

She went to a psychiatric hospital for quite a while and they got her to make up this album of Lisa's life from the birth cards saying 'congratulations' to the sympathy cards and the death certificate, which I think is just completely and utterly crazy, but this was her therapy. She just used to pour over this bloody album and get drunk. I wanted to throw the bloody thing in the bin when I was growing up. I just think how bizarre.

She was an alcoholic and I resented her so much for that. I think eventually it killed her. But now, being a parent myself, I admire her, because she coped the best way she could and I can't imagine losing a child. I can't comprehend for one minute losing Callum and then having to go on for another child. It must be incredibly difficult.

My mum was on anti-depressants and sleeping tablets, and she was drinking. I can remember that from being five or six. And she frequently tried to take her life. I often came back and found she'd taken an overdose. It was awful. I could anticipate it happening. It would always happen at one point over Christmas time.

When I was coming home from school, I used to think, 'Right, what state is she going to be in tonight? How drunk is she going to be? Is she going to be asleep? I hope she's asleep.' Really, I became quite numb to it. Towards the end – the last two overdoses – I'd walk in and think, 'Oh, right, she's taken an overdose. Right, better phone an ambulance.'

She got a lot of sympathy at the hospital. I think I once made a remark to one of the nurses and she jumped on me and said, 'How dare you talk about your mother like that!' I thought, 'Do you know how many times I've been to this hospital in my life?'

When I was about six or seven, I felt guilty that I was still here and I was careful not to be seen and not to be heard, trying desperately to keep everything on an equilibrium. I gave her lots of cuddles and hugs, trying to make her feel I was still there and I still loved her. I tried not to add to any of the stresses she was already feeling. Sometimes I wished it was me, not Lisa, who'd died, because then Lisa would've had to deal with it, not me.

I wished somebody had intervened at some stage, because my mother needed help, but I never wanted to be taken away from her. Throughout my childhood I was terrified that somebody would split us up, so I tried to cover up. I genuinely thought, until very recently, that nobody knew my mum was an alcoholic and that our house didn't get tidied up and we didn't have meals on the table. I've since found out that everybody knew.

I ran away when I was nine or ten. It was a build-up of things at home. She was drinking heavily and when she went out to work I'd be left on my own. One day I was cooking something and I burnt all my arm, but I also burnt the work surface. She came home and went absolutely ballistic about the work surface. I felt really hard done by, so I packed a suitcase of dolls and dolls' clothes and got a taxi to take me to my dad's house, but I went back the next day. I don't know why. My mum didn't speak to me for about a week.

It's really sad to think you've had a sister and you've no longer got one. When I was a teenager I spent a lot of time dreaming about what it would be like to have a big sister, sharing clothes and a bedroom. That was quite hard to deal with. You felt something had been snatched away from you. It's different from being an only child, because I had a sister and I've got memories of her, and then to grow up as an only child is really hard. People say, 'You're an only child', and I say, 'No, I'm not. I had a sister.'

I left home when I was 16 because of the difficulties Mum and I were having. That was the best thing that I could have done, because she then sorted herself out, started to get her life together. She stopped drinking and we were having a really fantastic relationship, a proper mother–daughter relationship. She wasn't happy about me being pregnant, but she'd been supportive and we were getting on absolutely fantastically. I used to go and see her every day and I enjoyed her company.

It's almost ten years since she died. I was 18 and three months pregnant at the time. It was horrendous. She just dropped dead one night. She was going on holiday three days later. It was her first holiday abroad and I'd been round in the afternoon. She'd talked me into doing some ironing for her holiday, so I was at home ironing when people came round to tell me that she'd been found dead at home. It was an accidental overdose. All the years of taking anti-depressants and sleeping tablets had just built up.

Honestly, they say your heart breaks – it really does. You just have this constant feeling in your chest. It's a physical feeling, you know, pain. It gets better over time, but I still love my mum to bits.

My dad didn't contact me at all from when she died till I had Callum. I can remember standing in Maternity at Wythenshawe Hospital and them asking me my next of kin and I just broke down, because I didn't have one. It was an awful, awful time. I was 18, pregnant and I didn't have an older sister or a mum to discuss it with. You can't talk to other people the way you can with your mum.

Now I'm a mother, I make sure everything is right for Callum. Even down to making sure that his school uniform's ironed every Monday, every day he's clean and tidy and he's fed before he goes off to school. Little things like that are a big deal, because I didn't have anything like that.

Erykah Blackburn's younger brother Zennen was shot dead in the Moston area of Manchester in 2002. He was 27. Erykah is the daughter of Pauline Blackburn, whose story appears in Chapter 1: Mothers.

Zennen was my little brother. There was two-and-a-half years between us. We were very close, because it was just the two of us, growing up. So yes, we were very close – and we still are, I like to think.

Oh, gosh, he was great. He was six foot two and everybody fancied him. When we went to London, he got asked to model for Armani. He was very good-looking. He liked to be flash and he knew he was good-looking – he was a poser!

He liked his clothes to be immaculate, everything had to be immaculate – he was very tidy and really organised. And he liked jewellery – not big gold chains or anything like that – but he liked a good ring and things like that. And he was really fit. He'd always trained, he did weights, he was real big. He loved himself, he did.

He'd got a lot of friends, and he'd really settled down with his girlfriend – he lived with her and they were supposed to get married. He was a family man – he did lots of things with his two girls – and he had just opened up his takeaway in Oldham.

He and his girlfriend had been to buy some food from a Caribbean takeaway in Mosside – they'd been looking for a house that day. They came back here and he wanted to go and pick up his car – there's a guy round here who does valeting and Zen had left his car there all day. So he got his girl-friend to drop him off at his car. She came back here to put the food out, and two minutes later someone knocks on the door and tells us he's dead – just like that. His food was still warm on the side and he was dead.

He'd gone to pick up his car and the guy who was cleaning it for him was showing him some scratches on it, and a car came speeding round the corner and it came right up to where he was and someone got out the car and started firing. They had two guns. So he and the car valeter ran off, and Zennen was racing back here, but they chased him on foot and shot him several times. It was the back of the legs first – he fell onto his face – then they shot him in the neck while he was down on his face.

They shot after the car valeter as well, but he didn't get hit. It wasn't intentional for him – it was for my brother. We haven't got a clue who or what, but I don't think it was mistaken identity because they ran after him on foot, you know. And they made sure he was dead because they shot him while he was on the floor dying. I think he was shot nine times – my mum knows how many times – but they did remove 97 pieces of bullet out of him because the bullet had fragmented.

I was at work and I got a phone call. I came straight over and when I got here I tried to run to where it was but the road was all blocked off – it was the other side of the estate – so I got out of the car and started running, but they'd cordoned off the area, so I actually ran through someone's house and through the back and that would take me to where he was. He was covered up, but I could just see his trainer – it didn't even look like his body under it – it didn't look like him, the shape – and the next time I saw him was in Man-chester morgue.

When I walked into the morgue, I just could not believe my brother was dead. And as I walked into the room, it was spread with candles and it was supposed to be calming, but it was spooky – and he was just laying there, and I just couldn't believe it. I thought he was going to jump up and say he was alive. But then when I went to kiss him, my lips stuck to his skin because he was so damp and cold and he smelt – oh, my God, this smell! – and I thought, 'Oh, my God!' I couldn't believe that he was dead.

I don't think for a minute that the people who killed him were the ones who wanted him dead. I think someone was paid. It goes on a lot, especially with young lads – they want to earn easy money as well as selling drugs, so a lot of them are paid to kill someone. I don't know if the people who killed him even knew him – I haven't a clue. But even to this day, a year later, no one has an inkling – and that's unusual because on the street people tend to know who it is, but no one's got a clue. So we just live each day as it comes, because we're no further on now than when someone knocked on the front door. He wasn't involved in anything, he wasn't part of a gang. It just doesn't fit.

I do go to church – not religiously but I do – but my mum's not religious. I think this would test anyone's faith, but I still have faith. I just believe he's gone on to somewhere else and that's what keeps me going. My mum's big on the spiritualist thing – she's been to see people and had messages – and that keeps her going – but we do believe as a family that he's just gone to where we're all going to go. I don't believe that death is – that's it. If I believed that, I could never carry on.

Not long after he died, we went to a spiritualist church just down the road, and there were speakers from all over the country. They can't possibly know who you are, and he'd only been dead a few weeks, and the guy at the front kept looking over and he said, 'I've got a casket here and this person's shouting murder, and I can see a gun and the gun is pointing here', and that scared me to death. There was no way that person could have known that.

We talk about him every day, as though he's here – 'Oh, Zennen would have laughed at that' or whatever. His spirit is very much alive. We went out on his birthday and he's talked about daily, constantly. It's like he's somewhere else. And I think that's because he's just been took from us and next thing is seeing him dead.

I believe his life's been took short and that's why I joined Mothers Against Violence (MAV), because I've kind of pulled a positive from a negative and turned this experience round on its head. I drive up and down the country now for MAV and I speak to lots of people. I'm not sure how Mum carries on because I go to MAV and I'm with a lot of mums – to me it's like losing one of my children – and it helps, talking to them.

My coping mechanism is helping other people. I really want to help these youths. And, actually, I've just changed my job. I've just gone over to social services, working in children's homes. And this is all down to him dying, really. So it's been life-changing for me.

I never planned to have any more children. I'd already got two. But they say after a death there's a birth, and it wasn't long after the funeral I found I was pregnant. She's called Zennay after Zennen, but it's weird because she won't ever know him and I can't quite believe that.

I really loved him. I loved him deeply. And now even more. Love never changes. It's just like a longing for him now. I just wish I was brave enough to go to a medium. I'd just like to know he's fine – that would make it easier for me – just to take a little look into the door and then carry on with my life. At first I was very vengeful, wanted to know who'd done this and why. But – I just hope another family doesn't have to go through this. I would never wish this on my worst enemy, never.

How do I cope? Deep breaths… Some days are worse than others – like, I don't come here [to her mother Pauline's house] that often because it reminds me of my brother. It's literally round the corner from where it happened. We're quite a strong family and we believe in carrying on – that's our motto – but nothing will ever be the same again. If I wake up and I've got that awful feeling, like when they first told me, it's like my breath is took from underneath me, like a strong rush of panic – 'What if he really is dead and he hasn't gone on anywhere?' If I get that kind of panic, I say a prayer: 'Grant me the serenity to accept the things I cannot change, and to change the things I can.' That's how I try to lead my life, changing the things I can.

How would I want him to be remembered? As my brother, a caring brother, like a big brother to me, and caring towards his family. We all looked out for each other. He was a brilliant dad and he was a good friend to have – all his friends would say that. I loved him to death – and I still do.

J en Coldwell's twin brother Richard died in 1972, when they were 22. He was a computer programmer. Jen has a younger brother, John. For four years during the 1990s, Jen was press officer for the Lone Twin Network, the organisation for people whose twins have died.

On the day it happened, he was driving. We heard at the inquest that people behind had seen his brake lights keep coming on and they thought he was looking for somebody, for a house. Then he veered off the road and hit a lamp-post, and that was it. He was dead.

We didn't know this, but they found that he'd had an enlarged heart, and one valve had been gone for some time and then the other suddenly went.

In the small hours of that morning, the police went to my parents'. My mother got up and answered the door and he asked if she was on her own.

And she said, 'If it's bad news, just tell me. I don't want to wake my husband up.' She was being very protective already.

Then they rang me – I was staying with a friend – and they spoke to my friend. I'd gone to bed, not feeling very well. Afterwards, I wondered if somehow I knew.

My friend came and woke me up and said I had to go home, the police had rung up. I thought something must have happened to my father, because he was the oldest member of the family. So I drove like a bat out of hell and just before I reached their house, I turned up this lane, and a policeman was standing there with a torch, flagging me down. This would be the early hours of the morning and there was no other traffic around, so he must have known it was me.

He was very good actually, very clear. He first of all established who I was and then he said, 'Your brother, Richard –' and I thought afterwards he did that very well – 'Your brother – comma – Richard –' Quite right, because I'd got two brothers, so he was being quite specific. I can't remember his actual phrasing, but '– has died in a car accident', I think. So it left no room for hope, which was very good, because later on – I suppose the following day – I was there when my mother told my father and she said, 'Richard's been in an accident.' And I thought, 'No, no, no, you've got to tell him.' And I said, 'He's dead' – because she'd left it vague and open.

When the policeman told me, I think I howled straight away, absolutely howled. I managed to get to the house and my mother was there, and we hugged and cried all night – which was probably a very healthy response. She had lost a brother when she was 15, and her mother had cried every day for either six weeks or six months. So, because of this, I think my mother was determined not to do that. Well-meaning, but unrealistic really.

But then I do think that grief doesn't necessarily, or automatically, bring families together. People grieve at different paces and go through different stages at different times. So I might be feeling crap one day, but I'll try not to show it to the others, because they seem OK and I don't want to bring them down. So people don't always share their grief.

I remember on the day of the funeral, standing in the kitchen, leaning against the radiator, and my eyes started to leak. And my dad just said, 'What's the matter?' You know! We did a lot of that, skirting round one another – 'Don't mention Richard.'

I can even remember one phone call where an old school friend rang up – I was at my parents' house – and she'd not heard. She said, 'How's

Richard?' And I went: '[intake of breath] Er, I'll ring you back.' And I put the phone down and went down the village to a phone box to ring her from there and tell her. How bizarre is that? It was an untouchable subject.

Since then, my mother and I have talked about him, but not about how we didn't deal with it. With survivors, you go, 'Why didn't I see it coming? I wish I could have done something.' She was a nurse, and she's said, 'Sometimes he used to drive up from London and he'd look quite pale. Why didn't I recognise that?' Well, for crying out loud, none of us knew – there were no symptoms. He played rugby, he seemed perfectly fit.

Afterwards, I had an instinctive feel of 'Oh, my God, I haven't been anywhere, haven't done anything.' So about a year after his death, I went travelling. I look back and I think my parents were so generous to support me in doing that.

Perhaps all bereavement is unique, but when you lose a twin you reassess your whole identity, because you were born a twin and you expect to die a twin. You don't expect to be parted. Even if you're physically in different places, there's always that bond, that link, that there's always somebody there who is on your side. And being a twin was a very important part of my identity.

I remember saying to someone what a wonderful start to life it was, because wherever we went people would say, 'Twins – how wonderful.' We were a bit of a novelty. And it was a wonderful bond.

It can be difficult for same sex twins to find their own identity, much easier for boy–girl twins.

I looked up to him. He was clever, witty, well-read, iconoclastic. I knew he was more intelligent, he read much more than I did, was much more clued-up. I could always ring him and ask him things. I actually thought I'd discovered yoga and I rang up and said, 'I've started yoga classes.' 'Oh, are you doing hatha yoga?' Huh – smart-arse! But it was a great experience.

Afterwards, I used to go through all sorts of declensions: 'I was a twin', 'I used to be a twin', 'I am a twin', 'I'm not a twin any more.' How can you 'not be' a twin? How can you 'used to be' a twin? So when I heard of the Lone Twin Network, that was very useful in terms of grammatical terms. 'Oh, the Lone Twin, OK, yes that makes sense.'

So I coped almost by not coping really. By travelling. It took me years to get round to facing it really. Partly because of our culture. We live in a very unhealthy – in that respect – society. I think most of us are in denial in the West, and that's very unhealthy. Death is the last taboo. People like you are beginning to break that taboo down, Allelujah! And things have changed, definitely, since I was 22.

Clare Venables was very helpful. When she was running the Crucible [Theatre in Sheffield – Venables was its artistic director throughout the 1980s], she lent me a book by Dorothy Rowe called *Depression*. I read it and one of the exercises in the book was to write a letter to the person who'd died. That must have been 12 or 15 years after he died. It was an extremely helpful exercise. I just sat down and wrote, with a pen, which is important – as opposed to a computer or a typewriter – and I was absolutely gobsmacked and horrified to find I was angry with him, I was still angry with him.

The tears poured out, anger poured out onto the page: 'You bastard! How could you? Leaving like that?' I felt this huge sense of abandonment, which hadn't clicked. So of course I'd had all this displaced anger all these years and been going round like Jack-the-lad: 'Up yours! What the hell? Nobody's going to touch me, nothing's going to hurt me ever again.'

So that was a major breakthrough, that Dorothy Rowe exercise. The important thing was feeling it, expressing it and letting it go.

The Tibetan Buddhist classes were fantastic. It was so liberating to hear people talking about death and giggling. The very first Buddhist talk I went to, this monk got up and gave this wonderful talk about death, and about how stupid we are – though he phrased it better – about how really life is like staying in a hotel room and you book a room for a fortnight, then you leave. And he painted this vivid picture of people sunbathing on the beach, and you gather all these things around you – your radio, sun lotion, magazine, book, towel – and at the end of the day you pack everything up and walk away. And as you walk along the front, you look back and you can't even see where you've been. You know you've been there somewhere, but you haven't left any traces. I found it so exciting.

I believe in reincarnation. I do believe we'll meet again. There are things like – I wish my daughter could have met him. But then, I would have liked to have met Shakespeare.

I don't think I do still grieve for him. Again, there's a Buddhist belief that your worst enemies are your best teachers and your most difficult experiences are also your best. They're there as an opportunity to learn. And you can learn and grow, or you can not bother.

So his death was hellish and difficult and full of pain – very, very, very painful – but it has taught me a huge amount. It was a huge kick up the bum, and I regard it – and what's happened since – as being both creative and constructive.

I used to be envious of living twins. I used to long to say, 'I had one as well.' But then you feel like the spectre at the feast. For years I felt I was the only lone twin in the world. The Lone Twin Network was very helpful because you met up with people who were in the same or similar boats. People would come up to you at meetings and say, 'How did yours die?' Which was so amazing, having spent years denying it and avoiding the subject and tiptoeing around. Suddenly people – English people! – would be direct.

Nearly everything I've done since he died has been as a result of his death. The paths I've taken were probably prompted by his death. It's all been a growing, learning process. And I've come out the other end stronger and healthier.

Karen Rea's sister, Elaine, died from acute tracheobroncheolitis **and pneumonia when she was ten. Karen was only six at the time. She is now in her thirties and married with two daughters of her own. Karen was frequently ill as a child, whereas she cannot remember Elaine ever being unwell until that final illness.**

It was all very sudden. Totally unexpected. Elaine was really keen to go to school this particular Monday morning because she wanted to read in assembly, but she started coughing, so Mum told her she couldn't go. I was off school myself with a chest infection and I remember thinking, 'She just wants to stay off school because I am.' But over the next couple of days she got worse.

By the Wednesday she was having trouble breathing and I remember my mum got this bucket and Elaine had to put her head in it with a towel over her head. I thought this was hilarious at the time – my sister with her head in a bucket – but obviously this was to try and help her breathe.

Then I remember my mum screaming to my dad to get the ambulance. I walked out of the bedroom, nosey, and looked into Elaine's bedroom and I saw my mum had got hold of her like you'd hold a baby. I was just so confused, because – in my eyes – Elaine's gone from having a bit of a cold and having to smell that funny stuff to all of a sudden being limp and my mum, hysterical, screaming for the ambulance.

Elaine was taken to Walton Hospital in Liverpool, but they needed to put her on a special machine, so they transferred her with a police escort to Alder Hey Hospital. It was strange because my mum sat waiting at the hospital all day and she'd not asked the time or anything. Then all of a sudden she asked what time it was, because she got this terrible shiver and our vicar who was there at the time said, 'It's twenty-five past five.' Then about six o'clock the doctor came out to say that Elaine had died and Mum said, 'What time did she actually die?' He said, 'twenty-five past five.' My mum said it was as if something had left her at that time.

I'd been at school and when I came home I was taken to the next-door neighbours' house. My mum was in no fit state to look after me. Totally hysterical and out of it. The next-door neighbour's daughter was best friends with Elaine and I remember being in my pyjamas quite late at night and we were dancing – me and Elaine's friend – dancing in the living room. And in my mind I'm saying to Elaine, 'I've got Jean to myself. I'm playing with your best friend.'

That evening the vicar came round and he told me that Elaine had gone to heaven to live with Jesus. Because I was only six I didn't really understand what he meant. Our family went to church and it seemed an OK thing at the time to be told that my sister had gone to live with this person that I vaguely knew and I thought he was a good person so she would be OK. But what I couldn't understand was that every time I went into our house, all these people were there when I just wanted my mum and dad to myself. I found that very frustrating.

The main thing that I've realised now is that I felt I couldn't upset my mum and dad, because every time I looked at them they were crying. I got it into my head – being six – that I couldn't do anything now to upset them. They'd been through enough. So I turned into what you probably would call a bit of a 'goody two shoes'. Everything they asked me to do, I did, even if I didn't want to. And I did it with a smile.

I used to be a little rebel, but Elaine wasn't and when she died I felt I had to be good all the time and live my life the way Elaine would have lived it. From the age of six to now, I've done everything – absolutely everything – with this one thought in my mind: 'I mustn't do anything wrong and I mustn't be a rebel.'

Also, every time my parents asked me how I was, I told them I was fine, although I wasn't. I was really missing Elaine, but I thought, 'I don't want to burden them with that. They're burdened enough, so if I keep telling them

I'm fine, then that's something less for them for them to worry about.' Little did I know that they were upset because I wasn't talking about it. I bottled everything up for so long. Consequently I've gone through the whole of my life till very recently covering up, telling everybody I'm fine about all sorts of things, when I'm not.

My mum and dad bought me a dog because someone had said, 'A dog would be company for her.' My mum told me that one day she heard me talking to the dog and saying, 'Well, you're my sister now, Sandy, because I haven't got a sister any more.' That broke my mum's heart.

It was just so lonely because I'd known what it was like to have a sister, whereas if you've always been an only child you've lived with that and life's no different, but I'd had this sister and all of a sudden she was taken away and I was completely on my own. When we went on holiday I'd nobody to go into the swimming pool with. I used to feel so envious of other people who had brothers and sisters and I used to think, 'Why have they got theirs and I haven't got mine? It's not fair. Have I done something wrong that God's taken her away from me?'

I felt excluded at school. Just after Elaine died I used to go to the care-taker's room at break and dinner-time, because the children used to taunt me in school and say, 'Your sister's died. You haven't got a sister.' I felt like some outcast. I wanted to lash out and I became quite naughty at school. I wanted to lash out and push other children and do horrible things to them.

My school work suffered and I always remember the report coming home: 'Karen hasn't worked hard.' I think it's the first time my mum has ever been up to a school in a temper and she said to the teacher, 'Do you realise what she's been through?'

Early in bereavement you're terrified that one day you're going to forget them and you don't want that, so you want to keep talking about them to everybody. But nobody wants to talk to you because they think you're going to get upset. You might get upset, but it doesn't matter.

The other thing is that the outside world homes in on the parents and everyone forgets about you. They forget you've lost your sister. As well as coming to terms with that, you see your mum and dad in terrible grief. Your whole world has gone topsy-turvy.

It all happened over 30 years ago, but last year my mum went in hospital for a big operation and it must have triggered something off in me. I started worrying that, if something happened to Mum and Dad, I would be an orphan. They are my last link with Elaine and when they've gone I've got nobody who knows what we were like as a family beforehand. So I began to have these terrible panic attacks. I'd be driving along the road and I'd have to pull in, because I'd be sobbing. I didn't want them to go for a night out because they might have a crash in the car. When they were out I'd sit up all night worrying till I got a phone call the next morning to say, 'We're fine.'

Then I had some counselling and I realised through digging how deep-rooted it was, because I've spent 30 years keeping my feelings about Elaine pent in, not talking about her. So recently I've started opening up with Mum and Dad and now we talk to each other.

Mum said she was upset because I never talked about Elaine. She felt I'd just buried her and forgotten all about her. That was the last thing I'd done. I thought about her every minute of every day, but I didn't want to bring her up because I felt it was a taboo subject.

It's been brilliant since I've had the counselling, because now Mum and I will sit together and talk about the good times we had: 'Wasn't that funny?' and 'Remember when this happened?' Now if Mum gets upset I don't feel that it's me that's upset her.

But it has changed my life. It's all the big milestones when she's not there alongside me. When I got married, Elaine wasn't there: she would have been my bridesmaid. When I had the children, she wasn't there: she'd have been a godmother. My mum and dad's Ruby Wedding, she should have been giving the speech as the elder child, but she wasn't there. So it never ever goes away. Never. I miss her every day of my life.

Catherine Thompson's only sister, Judith Darby, was leading a night-time Territorial Army exercise in the Peak District when a car mowed into her line of soldiers in May 1986. Judy, a manager at an international city bank, died as a result of her injuries. She was 38.

When Judy was killed, my mother-in-law said, 'She will be forever young.' At the time, 38 didn't seem particularly young. Now, of course, it seems so absolutely unfulfilled. There was so much promise of life that was never given a chance.

The shock of her death – well, it was the day life changed irrevocably. Although life was never the same after my father collapsed and died six years before. And within eight years I'd lost all my family, all suddenly. Daddy died running for a train, then Judy was killed, run down by a car, and two years later Mummy died of a heart attack on the operating table after an operation to get her fit to enjoy my newborn twins.

My father died on 25 March, Judy died on 31 May, and Mummy died on 30 April. So it's a bad time of year. I see the spring flowers and I think of Mummy's funeral, and I see the summer roses and think of Judy's funeral, because they were all out.

The evening when Judy was killed, Miles [Catherine's husband] and I were waiting for some friends who were coming to stay for the weekend. They were late getting here from London, and I was watching television, and all of a sudden I suddenly felt this wham! in the side of my chest. I felt most peculiar. This bang! and then a darkness. Then it passed off and the friends arrived and I thought no more of it.

We didn't get the phone call until eight o'clock the following morning, when the Army rang and my husband took the call and they said, 'Can we speak to Mrs Thompson? I'm afraid we've got some very bad news.' And I knew, once he said that – and Miles put his hand out to hold mine and it was stone cold – that something awful had happened. It was like a tearing, a wrenching, like a part of me had gone, absolutely gone.

For people who haven't been through something like that – the gut-wrenching, the awfulness, totally unexpected – it's more than grief. It's the end. It is the end – the end of life as you know it. And it's almost like a solidarity of people who've been through that – and the people who haven't, who are on the other side.

But it's funny, because I felt Judy's presence, like a warmth. It felt like she was there, wrapping me in a warm blanket and helping me to get through all these things. All the time we were organising the funeral, I felt she was there. And then there was one time which was quite weird when she wasn't. It wasn't an emptiness but, when I mentioned it to a friend of hers, who had half-share of her horse, she said, 'Oh, that's because she was with me.' She'd been riding up on the Downs, where Judy always used to ride, and she said, 'I just felt she was there.'

Then, after the funeral, she went. She came back again three months later, when we were on holiday in Italy, and I was in the kitchen and I was almost frightened to turn round, because I felt she'd be there, so strongly. And sometimes, yes, I do feel that – that if I turn round, she'll be there.

When Judy went, because she was so much a part of my life, it was like part of me went. The other half of me being wrenched away. So as well as the grief of losing the person, you've also lost yourself. And, especially when my

mother died on top of that, my whole identity went, and it coincided ironi-
cally with a time when I needed a family identity stronger than ever because
I was the mother of newborn twins. The whole time, I kept thinking of how
Daddy would have been such a wonderful grandfather, how Judy would
have loved to be an aunt, how Mummy only went for this operation in order
to be able to enjoy being with them, because she doted on them for the three
months she was alive to see them.

So I have this grief for the loss of a family life, and the memories, and a
family voice, and people so close to me making me what I am and also, by
consequence, making my daughters what they are. My daughters will never
know them and I could never 'go home'. So yes, I am still grieving, not just
for the loss of Judy, but for everything that went with her.

Mummy always said how fortunate we were to be such a close and happy
family, and that we enjoyed each other's company. When you used to have a
family and you don't have a family any more, you're nothing. You are
nothing. Except what you build yourself back up to be or claw back from
your memory banks. So I have changed totally as well.

Now, I'm being a wife and a mother and a worker and all the rest of it,
but that gives a completely different picture of me to the Cathy that used to
be daughter and sister. And I often think this is where moments of grief are
so intense. With Judy, for example, how she would have been so proud of her
little nieces. How she would have spoiled them rotten. How we would have
had furious arguments about how I'd been bringing them up or what she'd
been doing with them on her day off, and I would have taken it utterly for
granted – I would have expected her to come up for the weekend and take
them to Manchester or take them to a horse show, and it would have been an
expectation – she's my sister. No one else can do that.

I would have loved her to marry. Judy would have loved to be married as
well. She had a succession of highly suitable boyfriends and a very good job
in the City – the first woman to be an executive for Saudi International Bank,
and this was in 1985 or 1986, so that was really crashing through several
glass barriers. But ideally I would have loved to see her married – to a farmer
perhaps – and with children of her own. So, by extension, I've lost the other
mythical family, the family of nephews and nieces, and a brother-in-law – all
that family that my husband has and thinks nothing of. And why should he?
It's the exception, after all, rather than the rule, to have it all wiped out.

I just have to look at my daughters and there they are – the family I've
lost and they'll never know. It's things like – as part of school, they both had

to be in the cadet corps last year and I have a photograph of them, which I took deliberately, because you have to hit yourself on the bruise so it doesn't hurt any more. And they're both in the same army camouflage uniform that I've got photographs of Judy in as well. And those are my daughters and they look so frighteningly like her.

It's so ironic that I have twin daughters, having lost my sister. I've always felt they were a gift from Judy, and they're so like her, and so like me. But of course I'm the only person who can see that, who can see that the way one of them behaves is exactly like Judy did.

We bought a house in the Lake District with the money from the sale of Judy's house in Balham. It's where all Judy's furniture is, and my parents' furniture – it's like a personal shrine, if you like, which means everything to me and nothing to anyone else. I can't bring myself to change certain things. Like Mummy's hat and all her scents are still in one of the bedside cabinets where she left them. But people walk in and they think, 'Wow! Aren't they lucky? What I'd give for a house in the Lakes.' But I would give anything to have my sister.

That's another thing – that everything I've done with them is now stale, it's old hat, and I've nothing new to bring out of the drawer to remind me of them, unless something suddenly catches me unawares. It might be a scent that Judy wore, or a song I'd forgotten she liked, or a song my father loved, or a joke he would have loved, or something my mother would have said – and I'll suddenly think, 'Crikey, it's Mummy!' And that's where the intensity of the grief comes back because it's new, and it's an area you haven't covered. I don't know which is worse – whether the grief becomes stale after a time because you've got nothing new to take out and examine and grieve over, or the shock of it hitting you again when something comes at you and you hadn't expected it.

I still sob a lot. This is where friends have helped so much, putting up with me going on so much about it. It's coming up and giving me a hug, or saying words of support, or just writing me a letter. It's loneliness that's the killer. Being in a place where nobody else can be. And you don't want anybody else there, but it's like hands touching through the bars, that there's still life out there. And Miles has always been a great support.

I take comfort where I can. I even take comfort from going to funerals because they are a family occasion and people are drawn together and it's in honour of someone we've all known and loved. I don't know if I'm a family seeker, but I relish family gatherings. I feel so fortunate to be invited into other people's families, whether it's christenings or funerals or whatever. There's a hunger in me for an extended family.

My faith helps. If I didn't believe there was more, something after death, I would find it very hard to carry on. And prayer. People say, 'I don't know how you can believe in God after what's happened to you.' But it gives me comfort. And where I live it's an active church, a very supportive church. And it gives me a legitimate arena of mourning. If we sing a hymn and something touches a chord – like *Jerusalem*, the hymn we had at Judy's funeral – I may find tears running down my face. But people have been very kind.

So any spiritual sustenance one can have, any emotional closeness helps – though now I've got to the stage where it can't be too overwhelming, because I've learnt the old cliché *Noli me tangere* – don't touch me, don't come near me – I've learnt I can't allow things to come too close. And that's actually the terror – I don't dare allow myself to adore the girls too much, in the light of past experience.

I try and live every day as though it were my last. I suppose that's why I'm so impatient – let's go on and do it and get on, make the most of it. All the certainties have gone, and it's looking down the abyss, the chasm, that hopefully not many people have to go through in their life – or they peer over, when they've lost a family member, and then retreat back. And most people can't take that on board – the chaos of the fact that there are absolutely no certainties, that everything is so frail.

I make a point, every day – the girls think I'm rather sloppy – of always kissing them as they go out of the door, because you never know what's going to happen that day. There's no reason why we should take anything for granted.

So – it's no comfort, but grief doesn't go away. Not if you truly love somebody and they are part of the fabric of your life. It doesn't ever go away, it can't go away. It's how you learn to cope with it that's important.

CHAPTER 6

Brothers

Jamie Bosworth and his older brother Wayne, both chefs, were running a highly successful restaurant in Sheffield in the late 1990s. They had plans to expand and Wayne was in the process of setting up a second restaurant when, in June 2000, he was killed in a road accident. He was 36.

We were very close. Wayne was eight years older than me, so obviously when I was eight he was 16, and by that age he'd left home. He worked in Scotland and London, then came back to Sheffield to work, and I was just finishing college, round about 17, as a chef, and that's when we linked up together again, really, and made up for lost time. That's when we got to know each other and work together and socialise together.

We were brothers, mates, business partners. We were very much mates. Like, when I was single and Wayne was single, we'd go out drinking on us nights off and socialising together, night clubbing it, football match – big Sheffield United fans – so yeah, big mates.

It was the Peacock Pub at Owler Bar – four or five miles from Sheffield city centre – that we were taking over. Now and again you'd get people ringing up and saying, 'Are you interested in doing this or that?' Because our restaurant, Rafters, was such a success. So Wayne went and looked up there and said, 'Yeah, there's potential.' And it was a success straightaway, and that's how he was drawn up there the night he died. So in one way you think, 'If we'd never had the phone call months before, he wouldn't have been up there', but you can't blame it on anything.

It was a Wednesday night. He was up at the Peacock and I was at Rafters. The last time I spoke to him was in the afternoon, about four o'clock. Then, about 11 o'clock at night, I was ready for going home, but for some reason I thought I'd left my car keys at home. So I said to me dad, 'Can we go home and fetch my keys to the car – I've left them at home.'

So we're on the way home and a police car passed us, with its flashing lights on, on its way to Owler Bar. I'd tried to ring Wayne on the mobile in me dad's car and there was no answer. I found that a bit strange because he always picked up his mobile phone. By this time, it was about twenty past eleven. Dad looked at me and I looked at him, and I felt a bit strange then. And he said, 'Oh, that's not good, someone's had an accident on Owler Bar.' So we got back to my house and I run in and then we're on the way back to Rafters and another police car passed us, and of course me dad says to me, 'God, it must be a real bad accident.' I think I knew something was wrong in my heart of hearts, subconsciously.

So we got back to Rafters, I got in my car and went back home. As soon as I stepped back into the house, the phone went and it was me mum at Rafters – she worked there as well. She said, 'Wayne's had an accident, the policemen have just come to Rafters.' Instantly, I could have broke down. I said to Jayne [Jamie's wife], 'God, that's what the police cars were on their way to Owler Bar for.' So I said to me mum, 'All right then, where is he now?' She said, 'He's on his way over to hospital apparently.' Just daftly, I said like, 'Well, give us a ring and let me know how he is.' Just thinking he'd be right as rain. But after a few seconds, I thought, 'Hang on a minute, no.' So I said to Jayne, 'I'll drive up to Owler Bar and see how bad it is, so I'll know whether I need to go to the hospital or not.'

As I got up there, the roads were closed – a good mile or so from where the accident was. I said to the policeman, 'There's been an accident, hasn't there? I think it's me brother. How is he?' And he said, 'He's not very well, I think you should go to the hospital straight away.'

So I went straight to the Northern General, but we never saw him, because they were trying to save him, until about three in the morning. Then they came in and told us the bad news, that he'd passed away.

We saw him as soon as they told us. They'd had to clean him up a lot before they'd let us see him – so probably half an hour or so after he'd died. The doctors looked devastated. They knew he'd got two kids and a wife and he was 30-odd. They'd really pulled the stops out to save him, but with the injuries he'd got it's probably better he never came round. I couldn't imagine Wayne being disabled, because he was such a full-on, grab-life-with-both-hands type of person. The only thing I can hope is that he didn't know anything about it, really. I wouldn't imagine he did, because we had to see the car and stuff, and with the impact, I think he'd been knocked unconscious straight away.

So it was a strange night really, almost surreal, being at the hospital, not doing anything, not being able to see him. It was almost like an unbelievable feeling, and numbness. It was a horrible night, raining, and I walked out of the Northern General – I had to ring Jayne and tell her and that's when I first broke down. I remember driving home with my sister and it was weird – about five o'clock in the morning, the start of a new day, and a weird silence, and we were just driving home not saying anything to each other. We were just devastated really.

We got a hell of a lot of support. On my answerphone there must have been about 30 messages – you know, people offering their sympathy. That helped. And at Rafters, there were lots of flowers, and we read the messages, and that helped. But it's just that overwhelming, gutted – I felt sick. I remember getting home to Jayne and breaking down. Just absolutely gutted, really.

My daughter Katie wasn't quite four weeks old. And it goes through your mind – she's not going to see her uncle and he's not going to see her, and he's not going to see his kids grow up, and how much he loved them, you know what I mean? And it was so tough for Joanne [Wayne's wife]. And when you see your mum and dad crying, you know, it's what they say – no parent ever expects their child to go before them.

I felt I had to keep myself together to help them – me mum and dad and Joanne. And I'd got to keep the business going, because after all we're all dependent on that. Joanne worked there, Jayne did, me mum and dad. I kept it closed until after the funeral – I didn't want to put customers in the position where they felt awkward coming in. A lot of customers came straight away, but to this day a few customers I've never seen again. I think they found it too hard to come back. But a lot gave us support and it was good to get back open. But it was like there was something missing.

I'd normally meet up with Wayne and have a coffee with him in the morning, talk over the day's business, go shopping for bits and bobs – obviously having to do that on my own was strange. Even now, sometimes I get lonely that way. I've got Jayne and the family, but it's a different type of lonely. Like, say a deal would come up, or something to do with football – someone had got sold to a different team – Wayne would always ring up or I'd ring him, even at half past ten or 12 at night: 'Wayne, guess what's happened?' Obviously I've lost that now. I miss that a hell of a lot. I still miss him, to this day.

Wayne would ring me up at all hours. You could be laid in bed at half past seven in the morning and he'd be up and doing things – he tried to cram as much as he could into the time he had here. And all of a sudden that had gone. You miss that.

Probably the day he died, he'd rung me up on the answerphone, and he was like, 'Jamie, Jamie, pick up the phone' – his normal excitable self. It took me a while to rub that off. Whenever I wanted to, I'd listen to it. But I did rub it off in the end because it was bugging me.

I've known people lost their loved ones, and you don't know what to say. But just a 'sorry' does help. You can't say, 'I know how it feels', because you don't. But at least you've acknowledged it. And most people did. They'd ring up and say they couldn't believe it. It made you realise how many people thought about him and what they did think about him.

The funeral itself was overwhelming, really. I expected it to be busy, but not as busy as it was. It was like the longest journey ever – all the way up the Chesterfield bypass at 30mph. Then we came to Hutcliffe Wood crematorium and it was a cracking summer's day, and there were probably about 1500 people there. It knocked me back a bit really, but it was good. It gave us a lot of strength, that so many people were supporting us.

It was hard, though – not having Wayne there as a friend. It's just myself and my sister now, and I did almost feel like I had to look after everybody else and take responsibility. But it did help me get through it, that I'd got something to think about, something to carry on for. Plus, obviously, having a newborn. So I had a lot to think about, a lot to keep me occupied.

Before that happened, I was a boy and all of a sudden I did grow up. I feel a lot more experienced in life. I matured very quickly, definitely. And one of the things that changed me, and why I've changed the hours I do – we all said, 'From now on, we're going to enjoy life to the full.' With Wayne, it was like he was always planning for the big day in the future when he was going to be completely sorted out – big house, nice cars, lots of money – these were dreams, working all these hours he did. Then it seemed such a shame – 36 years old and that's it.

So we said, 'Well, forget it.' We weren't going to work all hours, so we decided to get rid of Rafters, have a daytime place and perhaps have more family time. We thought we'd got to live for today, not for tomorrow. Sometimes you forget that, but then you have to stand back and think, 'Hang on a minute, enjoy today.'

Sometimes I've thought, 'I wonder if he can see us now?' So I think there's a bond there still. I would hope he knows what we're doing and I think he'd be happy. I don't think we've done anything he'd be unhappy about. And I hope he can see his kids growing up, because they're crackers, they're good kids.

A few times I've wished I could have seen him again. The odd thing is, I might not even have thought about him for a while, and I'll have a dream where he's come back and I've showed him round Sheffield, and how it's changed. Probably three or four times, that's happened. Or I've gone out for a drink with him and just before the dream's ended I've realised he's not here.

We still talk about him as a family. Like today, me mum and dad have been up there, to where it happened, and put some plants there because it's looking a bit bare after the winter. We'll go up there like at birthdays and anniversaries. I don't go up so much – I find it a bit of a sad place, really, so I don't like to go there. I remember him in my mind. But we all find it OK to talk about. And time does heal. You'll never, ever forget, and forget the grief that you had, but it's not as painful. Obviously you miss them still and think what they're missing.

We sprinkled his ashes at Bramall Lane. You're not supposed to do it, but Wayne's good pal at the time was the Sheffield United goalkeeper, so we split some of the ashes and I gave some of them to him. So the first game of the season, in August, the goalkeeper ran out, and it was quite comical in one bit, because he was sprinkling the ashes round the area in front of the Kop, and the linesman kept going over to him, apparently, and saying, 'What you doing?' And he just said, 'F... off, keep your nose out.'

The daft thing is, for about ten games, no one scored in that end of the ground and it was almost like Wayne was an extra pair of hands to him. He was such a big fan, Wayne.

Trying to imagine him old, I can't do it. Even before, like he's always been like he is in that picture up there [in his dining room]. That was taken not so long before he died. So Wayne will always be 36. He'll always look that age.

At times, I felt a bit sorry for my sister, because a lot of people didn't realise we'd got a sister, so a lot of support was coming through the restaurant to us and I almost felt they'd forgot Sarah. She's a hairdresser. She's got the same picture in her shop, and people would come in and not realise and say, 'Oh, that's that chef who died. Why have you got his picture on the wall?' And Sarah would get a bit angry like: 'Because he's my brother, why do you think?' People can be a bit thoughtless.

I mean, not long after, we went with Katie to the doctor's, and this doctor – he's a bit of a prat anyway – he says, 'Oh, you're Wayne Bosworth's brother, aren't you? I'm sorry to hear about your brother.' Fine. Then he says, 'My friends at the Northern General tell me he wasn't wearing his seatbelt.' I was like – I just didn't say anything. Just thoughtless, really.

I've never had problems talking to anyone about it. If anything, I find it easier to talk about it to people who don't know me, like you, because it's almost like telling a story. I said to myself, a bit after, I wouldn't always talk about it, because I didn't want to bore people about it. If people want to ask, you know, I'd tell them, because talking does help. I've got over it by talking to people.

We show Katie pictures now and she knows that's her Uncle Wayne. I'd say, 'This is my brother, one of the best chefs around', that type of thing. And he *was* the best one around. We've got loads of camcorder footage which, when his kids are old enough, they can watch. They do that already, bits, at their grandad's, so they can see what their dad was like, if they forget, which is bound to happen. If I look back to when I was three or five, I can't remember much. In a way, it's a godsend, that technology.

I still go to the football with me dad, but obviously I miss little things, like Wednesday aren't doing well and United are doing well, and I think he'd be loving it. So sometimes I wish I could grab hold of him and say, 'What do you think?' Or when we have this new little 'un [Jamies' wife was about to have their second child], he'd have been over the moon. We know it's a boy and Wayne would probably have took him under his wing: 'Come on, I'll show you how to play football, better than your dad.' So we'll miss that. We said if we had a boy, we'd call his middle name Wayne. William Wayne. So he's not forgot. Another Wayne Bosworth, really.

Rony Robinson is a presenter on BBC Radio Sheffield. He had two brothers, one of whom, Geth, his older brother, died during the night of 1 and 2 January 2003. He was 67.

I got the news in a phone call from Lorna, his ex-wife, saying something like, 'I can't think of any other way of telling you this, but Geth died this morning.'

She and my niece, Stephanie, had gone round to see him to take him shopping. They thought he might be asleep, so they went upstairs – not expecting the worst at all – and found the worst. He was in bed, dead.

He'd hung his clothes up in his meticulous way and gone to bed. There was no sign of pain or that anything unpleasant had happened to him. The house was just as meticulous as ever. He'd even filled in his diary, because he kept a daily diary, and he'd not only done the end of last year's, but I believe he'd done the start of this year's with the same entry in both diaries: 1 January. He'd done his diary, cleaned up and gone to bed and died.

He was a lifelong asthmatic and the final diagnosis was that he'd died of a lung infection, a colossal one that did for him.

We were very close, I would say. We'd been made closer over the last several years, what with the death of our dad, the death of our mother, his family crack-up with his wife, his health problems, my family crack-up. The children were very close to each other, mine and his, so it would be unusual for us not to meet each week, sometimes more than that. We went on holiday together and had continued to do so since childhood, so we always had a week's holiday if not two, in Wales or Scarborough. And we'd got used to meeting up for a drink, just the two of us, on a Thursday night. So I'd say we were very close, though very different. And he'd been an enormous support to me at the moments I'd been in trouble, over the years, and I hope I'd been that to him as well.

When Geth died, I became the oldest male in the family, and I certainly felt a bit of that – I wouldn't say responsibility – honour, really. Curious to find yourself at last being a patriarch or taken seriously in the family. I was the one who said, when we were sitting round in the afternoon, up at his ex-wife's house, feeling terribly sad, I suggested we should come down here and have fish and chips, and they listened to me. I was always the younger brother with Geth, so I lost a kind of authority figure – and became one.

He was also somebody who'd got a knowledge of my life from the moment I was born. I lost all the things that he and I had in common and that other people didn't. That included access to years, decades, of family history, from his first memory to his last. I lost access to that overnight, and that was grievous. But what do we do about it? We all know people who've learnt the lesson of that and start recording the life of somebody, to catch it before it goes. But I'd never done that with Geth, never ever thought that he would die.

In the times when we met, a great deal of the content of our conversations, especially after Lily [their mother] died, was in the past. He loved talking about it. He'd got quite a precise memory for two or three years of family life, and I'd got a very precise memory for about five years from 1945 to 1950, so we got delight from talking about that. And that – that wonderful pleasure of sharing memories – had gone overnight. The disc had gone. I found that very hurtful. I miss that enormously.

My mother kept a diary, a pretty humdrum page-a-day diary, from about 1954, when my younger brother went to sea, until she died, virtually. It dried up about a fortnight before she died. But even then I was writing it for her. So I've got this massive record of our family history there, which I read even today, occasionally. And I look at it with the kids. There's a tremendous consolation in that. Geth left me nothing. We found a box of photographs within the last two months, meticulously labelled, and they are a wonderful find, but they're not the same as remembering what it was like on this holiday at, say, Mrs Davis's in Colwyn Bay in 1952, and the people who were there, the anecdotes.

You've lost the self they knew when you were young. You lose a bit of yourself in the process of somebody dying.

When he died – well, you cry, don't you, and you hold the people you're with at the time. There are practical things to do, like on the day he died: 'Shall we go and have something to eat? Where shall we be for the rest of the day? Have we told everybody who needs to be told?' And I felt I was the leading man in the story for a bit, so I did that.

I went back on the radio the day after Geth died. Partly to get those moments when you can forget what's going on. Because while you're doing something like broadcasting, it can't prey on you and there's nothing you can do about it. So while I was a bit weepy on the radio, even more so than now – and that's saying something – I think I've become weepier by the week – nevertheless I went on working.

How did I feel? I felt part of it was a need to support the people he'd loved, in so far as I could, especially his daughter, Stephanie, through the worst of it. She was having a terrible time, experiencing all those feelings of going mad.

I felt a lot older. Yet they don't grow any older or whatever that biblical thing is. He will be perpetually 67 or whatever, and he wasn't old. I never saw him dead, which probably makes a difference. I resisted the temptation to go to the funeral parlour, though I was invited. I didn't want to see the caricature of somebody that they become after a bit. But it also left me with the feeling of him still being alive. For a long time, we all shared the experience that he might ring up again or pop in, as he'd popped in two or three days before he died.

I did the speech at his memorial, which was deeply comfortable to do and the most enjoyable piece of writing I've done for years. Trying to kind of accrue – in a version which was truthful and short enough – our childhoods and growing up together, and having a few jokes in there, and generally enjoying the business of writing, knowing it's for a function and it has to be performed, and hoping for the best when I did it. But I could never have written that *for* him, sent it to him when he was alive, something so elaborate and thoughtful and over the top. I don't know what you'd do with such a piece if you heard it in your own lifetime.

You can tell your children that you love them and they're marvellous, in a way maybe it's more difficult to do it for your parents and brothers. In the case of Geth, could I have written him a letter in advance and said that? We were men of a certain generation and those letters, how easy are they to write? I think he knew how important he was to me. But I'm not sure I knew myself really until he'd gone.

I've got a picture of him on my dad's shoulders as a two- or three-year-old, with blond hair. And I've got a picture of the three of us, the three boys, at a holiday camp in the 1940s or 1950s. So I've got those pictures and they're very helpful.

I talk to him. I look at the photograph of him. When people die – there's nothing else, of course there's nothing else, but you remember them and in that clichéd way they don't die. You can still laugh at them, you can still joke about them, you can still look at them if you've got photos, and you can still talk to them. So I do that. Out loud sometimes.

Telling people when someone's died is often the hardest part of it, though – whether it's because it makes it 'realer', or whether you don't want to see people collapse in a mess or say the clichés that aren't going to help, but that's not to say people don't try their best. Hugging people and crying is about all you can do. I know it's all right to have feelings, they're the most important things we've got, so I've no hang-ups about that any more: permission to grieve, to love people.

The consolations when someone's died take a bit of time to come back, but they do, and they include laughing again at the person who's dead, laughing at their peculiarities. We began to make a list of Geth's daft sayings in the family diary. So inside all the terrible sadness, you've got a consolation with the people who share the memory, which never goes until you've gone. They're myth, family myth. I've still got them, but I shall probably never mention them ever in my life again. Do I think about his death every day? Well, yeah.

There's a humiliation when someone dies. You realise that you weren't the only person who was important to them. They've got other lives which you know nothing about, so at Geth's funeral – his life was more fragmented than most – there were people who knew him from Jesus meetings, there were people who knew him from anti-alcohol meetings, people who knew him as a golfer. One of the disappointments is that you didn't really own the person who's gone. Other people owned them as well. So that's one of the 'un'consolations of it – that there were bits about him I didn't know or only knew bits about – but the consolation is that other people liked him. And he was clearly immensely popular. So the fact that he was liked, and as much as he was, that was a great consolation.

Of course, now I look at *The Guardian* obits and look on the years they were born and think, 'Oh, I've got another seven years.' I do the calculation – my dad died at 83, but my brother died at 67, has that brought forward the age at which I'll die? I do the calculation that says, 'It's this much time since I went to Oxford. I've not got that much time again. The time I started having children – I've not got that much time again.' Endless series of arithmetic calculations of a sort of Islamic magic quality – looking for the numbers, when are you going to go?

Every day you think, 'I'm going to die.' Arnold Wesker said he was 40 before he realised he was [going to die]. He knew other people were, but he didn't realise he was until he was 40. Well, by the time you're my age, you can't pretend otherwise. But you have to live as if that's not the case, otherwise you'd be doing a King Lear and giving everything away, throwing out incriminating stuff every day. And you would be going round telling everybody all the time that you loved them. You'd become impossible to live with long before you really died, wouldn't you?

Joshua Walsh is six years old. His older brother, Harry, was born
with a genetic disorder which meant that he had profound learning
difficulties. Harry died when he was nine and Joshua was five. Their
younger brother, Luke, is four and their sister, Lydia, is two.

Harry was a very nice person. He died when we went to France. He just died
in the morning when we woke up. I was sitting in my room and I heard the
ambulance and when I hear an ambulance now it reminds me of when Harry
died. I just feel sad. He was quite young to die.

The family did worry about Harry because he had fits. When he was in
France he had quite a bad fit. I just worried about him if he might die.

Harry went in a wheelchair. It was hard to get him round. Even though it
was hard to get him round, we liked him. It was good to ride him round and
we could take him for walks. We went to the beach and sometimes we went
out for a meal. We also played in the garden. Me and Grandad went on the
tractor that cut the lawn. Then Harry used to sit in the sunshine.

I remember when the men had to dig a hole and they had to put him in
the coffin and they had to bury him. I didn't like it really. It just felt a little bit
sad. Now it's changed and I just want him back. I used to think of what I'm
going to do for him. If he wanted a drink or something, I used to do it.

I liked him because he didn't shout when I put my tape on. He just sat
there. Even though he couldn't talk or walk I used to play with him.
We played 'tinkerboo'. You hide and then when you come out you say
'tinkerboo!'

I just like being a brother. Harry was older than me and he was bigger
than me, but sometimes I felt like his older brother even though I wasn't. It
just makes me feel like, if he's dead, I feel bigger. I just want to feel smaller. It
just feels different when you're older. I don't want it to feel different just
because Harry's died.

My brother, Luke, remembers Harry. Luke was born when Harry was,
but they're not the same size. Luke's younger than Harry, but it seems that
they're both the same size. When Harry died, Mummy had another baby
called Lydia. We've had her quite a long time. Lydia doesn't know Harry.

The grown-ups didn't like Harry dying. When people are upset, their
eyes turn red. I know they're feeling quite upset when people are hurt or die.
I just know they're upset.

Before he got died, when he was at Derian House [children's hospice], he made a little stone that reminded me of him as well, so we can keep that. It's got 'Harry' on it.

I don't talk about it very much, because it just upsets me. I just share the stone with my Mummy if she wants to remember Harry. I sit with my Mummy and we talk about it.

I just don't want my parents to cry. It makes me cry too.

S teve Williamson's younger brother, Mike, died of cancer 12 years ago at the age of 38.

Mike and I were very close. He was exceptionally healthy and even at primary school he was a very good sportsman. We used to play tennis most afternoons after school in the summer. For about the first six months I could beat him, because I was two-and-a-half years older, but after that he could always beat me.

He was in his mid-thirties and living on Anglesey with his first wife when he was diagnosed with some sort of gastric problem. In retrospect we think that it was obviously the first signs of the cancer. He told us that it was nothing to worry about. We don't know whether he knew from that point that he had a problem. He wasn't going to say.

I realised it was serious when I realised he had a swelling. Then one day we went out for a drink. I got two pints and he couldn't finish his. He said, 'Oh, it gives me a bit of a bloated feeling' and I started to think, 'No, there's more to this.' Anyway it was shortly after that he said, 'I've got cancer.' It was bowel cancer.

Then it was a seesaw. One month you think, yes, he's looking a lot better. But eventually it became obvious that they'd done all they could and the cancer wasn't going to go away. He said, 'It's just a matter of time, but what the hell! We've got to make the most of it however long it happens to be.'

I was very upset, but I didn't keep pumping him, because it's not what he wanted. I suppose it is a male trait, but it's our family, too. I mean, my mum won't open up about her feelings. She took it very hard, but you wouldn't have known. Nobody meeting her would know.

You keep the fiction going. We planned various things. We planned fishing trips. The one thing we did together – and always had done right from our early teens – was fishing and that's a thing I miss. Since he died I've only fished once and that was with a friend we both used to fish with. It just isn't the same. So I've got a shedful of gear that hasn't seen the light of day for years.

The day before he died he'd felt well enough to drive over to Mum and Dad's. Mike had remarried by then. Then he'd gone home and he more or less slipped into a coma during the night. In the early hours, his wife, Chris, had called the doctor and the doctor said, 'I think this is it.' So Dad rang me up at work and said, 'Can you get over?' So I shot out of work in the middle of the morning.

I was with him when he died. That's one thing I'll always remember. I was sitting on the bed with him, holding him. He'd been more or less semi-conscious, then suddenly he just went very calm and his eyes came into focus. I was just holding him and he looked straight at me and he knew – he knew me. You could see his eyes focus and then he went.

Of course, Mum was distraught and Chris, his wife, was hysterical. So you sort of switch into coping mode, I suppose, because you think to yourself, 'You've done everything you can for Mike. Now you've got to worry about the people who are here.' You have to put your grief on hold. I don't think it's a conscious thing.

I'd been estranged from my first wife for a long time and we hadn't spoken to each other since the divorce, but Mike had kept in touch with her and she came to see me. She just put her arms round me. It changed our relationship and now we do keep in touch.

I quietly curse Mike for dying, because now I've got to look after both ageing parents and we were supposed to share this burden between us. I don't mean looking after them is a burden, but it's a load that comes to us and he should be here to share it. They're both in their mid-eighties and they're remarkably well, but now is the time he and I would've been talking about what's going to happen. I feel the loss more keenly as they get older and older.

Mike's death has changed my attitude. Not long after, I knew redundancy was likely to be coming up. I was in accounts and I was being set up for interviews to find other jobs, but I thought, 'Do I really want to do this or shall I have a crack at something else that I might enjoy and actually want to get up and do in the morning? Life's too short to go on doing something you don't want to do, because you might be dead in two years.'

So I decided to do conservation work and that means I now work outside with my hands. It's a complete change of direction. No money, but I enjoy going to work. I might not have taken the plunge if Mike hadn't died. You only get one chance, so you might as well take it, because you don't know what tomorrow's going to bring, so don't waste any more time.

CHAPTER 7

Wives

Anne Bain's husband, Bill, died very suddenly at the age of 72. They had been married for 48 years and had six children.

It's two years ago now, but it feels recent to me. He died suddenly in the night. He sat up in bed and said, 'Oh, this damned indigestion of mine!' I called the ambulance and when I looked round to tell the girl what was wrong, he was dead.

It was an aneurysm. His aortic valve was consumed with cancer. They were going to tell him the following morning that he was a terminally ill man with cancer. So, whether I say, 'Thank God he didn't have to suffer', I don't know. It's the only way I'm coping with that: 'Thank God he didn't have to suffer and he never knew he had cancer.'

We didn't expect it at all and there was nothing I could do. I'm a nurse and I feel so guilty even now. Why could I not do anything? I've resuscitated many people before, but I couldn't do it for my Bill.

When I was actually in the funeral parlour on the day of the funeral, I couldn't believe that it was Bill lying there: he was so wax-like and pale. I just looked at him and touched his face and it was so cold. And I suddenly thought, 'It'll happen to me. I'm going to be like that and I don't want to be like that.' But there's nothing I can do.

I do think of my own death a lot now, though. Not with fear, I don't think. With age and maturity comes a sense of acceptance and a need to have things in order. I don't want to be a responsibility or a burden to the children. That's how I feel. So I'm calm in that way, because I know it's inevitable.

I think you go through stages in your life. When you're a child, you don't know what it's about and it's a bit frightening. Then when you're a teenager and a young adult you don't give it much thought, because you're busy doing. Then as you get older you think, 'Yes, it happens and it's not nice.' There's nothing I can do about it. No one knows if death's just round the corner and I think maybe that has a calming influence. If you knew, I think we'd all be full of fear. Wouldn't be able to cope. I think it's one of nature's calming ways: not letting you know too much.

One of my sons says, 'Mum, my dad is the only one who doesn't know he's dead.' And I thought, 'My God! How dark and how deep is that?' But yet it's true. Because you go to sleep every night, don't you? But when you're comfortable, when it's a lovely feeling, you're drifting off to sleep and then there's nothing until you wake up again – this drifting off is a really nice feeling.

Margaret Barraclough's husband, Bill, died six years ago, after attempting to kill himself. He was 74. He left behind a letter, which said, 'Goodbye, darling, it's been a wonderful life together. Things are getting worse for both of us, that's why I'm ending it. I only hope God will forgive. Make a life for yourself and don't grieve too much, love, you are the only woman I ever loved. I'll keep looking over my shoulder for you. If I don't die, but finish in a coma, tell them to turn the machine off. Please don't be mad at me for doing this. I know it's for the best.'

There it is, love. You read it. He wasn't very good at spelling or writing, though. I can't read it now. It's too upsetting. He was always telling me he loved me. Wasn't a day passed.

I was 12 when I first met Bill, but I was 16 when I joined the group he was in, The Lucky Stars. He was a fantastic tap dancer. I did tap dancing and ballet and acrobating – I'd got medals for acrobating. So I finished up dancing with them round the clubs.

We married in 1942 when we were 19, so we were married 54 years. They used to call him Young Garth at work, because if they'd got anything heavy they'd get him to lift it. He was a very strong bloke. He'd not been ill that long. It all started with him fainting. Frightened me to death when it first happened, frightened me to death. Because he looked like death, you know. It happened about five times, love, and the ambulance would come and take him away, bring him back in two or three days. I went to the doctor and said, 'Why can't they keep him in longer?' And the doctor put his hand out and said, 'Your husband is dying. There's nothing they can do.' They said it was the muscles round his heart were diseased. That was about a month before he died.

He couldn't get upstairs – he used to crawl upstairs – so I said, 'I'll get you a commode. Social Services will.' He said, 'Who's going to empty it?' So I said, 'Me.' He said, 'I'd die first.' That was my Bill. He was like that.

What happened – this night, I was sat on the settee where you're sat now, and he was sitting on this chair by the door, and he said, 'You've got a lovely little face, you.' That's the first time I've said this to anyone, love. Anyway, he said, 'Why don't you go to bed? You look knackered, love.' So I gave him a cup of tea, a glass of water, and his tablets were there, like, where he could reach. And I went to bed.

It must have been about seven when I got up, because I'd had hardly any sleep. I knocked on that front room door, lightly, and there was no answer, so I thought, 'Well, I'll not wake him up yet.' So I came in here, even had a cup of tea and a slice of toast. Then I knocked on that door again, and no answer. Well, I panicked then. So I opened that door, and he's laid on the floor in front of the fire, which he'd turned off. He hadn't even got his blanket round him. I saw the note and tablet bottle on the table, and that was it. He'd left it there where I couldn't miss it.

He was still alive, though, so I got on the phone, and I said, 'Come here, quick, my husband's tried to kill himself.' I was going off alarmingly. And they came and they carried him out.

Next thing I know, there's police at door. One was quite nasty. I showed him the suicide note and he said, 'Margaret, can you just give me a copy of your writing.' I said, 'What for? You don't think I've done this?' I said, 'Do you mind, I want to go to the hospital.' But I had to write this thing. Then I phoned Larry, Bill's nephew, and I said, 'Bill's tried to kill himself and the police are here, I think they think I've done it.' Well, he was down here in 20 minutes and swearing at them. He said, 'If she'd done that, she'd be laid at side of him.' I was trying to tell him not to swear. But he was fond of Bill as well.

Apparently, they have to do this with suicides. A few days later, one of the policemen brought the suicide note back and apologised for upsetting me.

My brother came up from Birmingham and we went up to the hospital. I said to Bill, 'They only thought I'd tried to get rid of you!' So he winked at my brother and said, 'I shall have to think of something better next time.'

He was determined. He didn't want me having to carry him about. He was worried over me, because I was looking rough. He'd say, 'Get to bed, Mag, you look terrible, love.' I mean, we'd been joined at the hip since we were about 12.

A couple of days after, we were up at the hospital – me and my brother and one of his lads – and Bill was chatting to us lovely. When we were coming away, I said, 'We're going home, love, me and our Ted, to make sure the animals are all right, and we're coming straight back.'

So we came home, made some sandwiches, and the phone went – he'd passed away. He'd passed away in that time from us going up there to coming down here. He was only in hospital a few days. I do not remember driving back to hospital and driving home. I do not remember.

I felt terrible, love. Terrible. I didn't feel angry with him, because I think it takes a few guts to try and kill yourself. I've got a lot of admiration for people who do it. He was trying to save me from all the problems we were having, because he just sat there, he couldn't do nothing, love. He had his tea and watched television. He didn't want me to watch him getting terribly ill. They must have told him there was no cure, see. I don't think he wanted me to see it, didn't want me carrying him about. Because I couldn't even go to bed. I'd sleep on the settee, or sometimes I'd sleep on the floor in there. I think it was worrying him.

I've been sat on that seat – I sometimes fall asleep on it with a dog on my knee – and Bill didn't like you to sleep like that. He'd say, 'Get to bed if you're tired.' And I've opened my eyes and heard this door go, and I looked up – whether I was dreaming or not, I don't know, but I was wide awake, I think – and he was just walking out of here. I thought he'd got narky about me falling asleep, so I went out and I'm halfway upstairs and I thought, 'Where's he gone?' And I shouted at the bottom of the stairs: 'Bill!' Then I remembered he's not here. Things like that have happened once or twice since. So I just know he's doing what he said he'd do, watching over me. I love you, Bill.

The dog's brought me a lot of comfort, because Bill loved him. I get a lot of comfort out of animals, and they're good company to me. We didn't have children. If anyone asked us, we'd say, 'No, it's best to let our breed die out!'

We were two of a kind, love. We understood each other perfectly. I used to swear a lot, and he'd say, 'Mag! A nice little woman like you, it's terrible.' And he was funny – we had lots of laughs. I once fell out with him and I landed out at him, and he put his hand on my head here and I couldn't reach him! We both finished up laughing.

I don't know about life after death. I was brought up strict Catholic, but I'm nothing now. It's made me think, that experience I had. He'd always tell me, 'I'll always be looking after you.' I talk to him. He's anywhere and everywhere. I talk to him in bed, before I go to sleep – it's as good as praying.

K atie Boyle was a regular on television panel shows during the 1950s, 1960s and 1970s. She also introduced the Eurovision Song Contest and was a magazine agony aunt. An Italian marchesa by birth, her first marriage ended in divorce, and her second husband died suddenly of a heart attack in his mid-fifties. In 1979, she married the theatrical impresario Sir Peter Saunders – the man responsible for many West End shows, including *The Mousetrap*. He died in 2003, aged 92.

It was old age, really. Peter was deteriorating, but I remembered him only as he was, and I just ignored the fact that he was getting older.

You don't prepare. You can't prepare. I realised that his memory wasn't as good as it was, but he was always interested in everything, and one of the things I miss most of all is coming back home and thinking, 'I must tell him that' – and he's not going to be here. That is one of the things I feel terrible about and I could never prepare for that, never. Even when he was really ill, he was always interested. His face would light up when I walked into the room, and he'd say, 'Any malicious gossip?' I'd say, 'Yes, darling, lots! Let me tell you all about it.' So it wasn't the kind of deterioration that was a complete black, far from it. He could always talk, and was always willing to talk.

We talked about his dying, of course, lots of times. Because I'm a Catholic, I have no doubt at all that we will meet again, no doubt at all that there will be a contact.

Ours was an extraordinary marriage. I don't think we ever had a row. If one of us disagreed, we roared with laughter. I used to ring him up when he was at work and say, 'Are you playing tycoons or may I talk to you?' We had a tremendous influence on each other. I was much calmer and he was much more outgoing – which I think is great, to have a marriage of that kind at that age, at that stage in our lives.

He was the easiest and sweetest person. Yes, he was a businessman, but he had kindness towards so many people, so many people. He gave pleasure in lots of ways. I know there was one woman who couldn't have afforded to have any tickets to go to the theatre, but he always made sure she had tickets to go to his first nights and things like that. Kindness, thoughtfulness, these were things that people I don't think realised. Because he never talked about himself, whereas I'm outgoing by nature, being a Latin.

Peter and his first wife, Anne [who died after a long illness], built this house. And there is an atmosphere of peace and happiness here, isn't there? I've felt his presence tremendously. I still put out my hand to say good morning to him or to say goodnight to him. So many things hurt. I miss him. We were so close. And the void is agonising.

I was with him as he died. I knew he wanted to die, yet he didn't want to leave me. He used to say to me, 'I don't want to leave you.' And I used to say, 'But it won't be forever.'

When he died, I did go to pieces. I couldn't walk, really. I couldn't write, I couldn't really talk. I still have some difficulty with numbers, rather as though I'm dyslexic.

He always said he wanted me to go on living. I find that very difficult. It's over a year now that he's been dead and I find it just as difficult, in fact more difficult sometimes, than I did at the beginning. The emotion and the pain is still as bad.

I sank into a terrible depression. I've got a letter here from a doctor who was recommended by my doctor. [She fetches the letter.] Here it is: 'I feel she has probably had a very severe depression, but this began well before her husband died…at least two years previous to his death.'

And it did. I was frightened of him dying. Terrified. I knew how much I was going to miss him and I wasn't disappointed. I just knew that I'd be lost without him.

According to this doctor, when he did die, I 'suffered the normal bereavement reactions superimposed on the pre-existing depression… She has made an excellent recovery in her own time, helped by all the support around her. It is normal for depression to get better over time.' A lot of people have said that – but it doesn't.

My faith helped. I was brought up a Catholic and my faith is a very important part of my life. Peter didn't have a faith, but he said so often that he felt we would meet again because I had such faith. I have no doubt at all that one goes on. It doesn't make sense if we don't.

He's cremated, and I have his ashes, and I want them to be mingled with mine. His life was very much the theatre. Maybe I'll suddenly want mine to be scattered among the West End, I don't know! I'm not thinking quite along those lines yet, but I have no doubt that we'll be together, no doubt at all.

There are no rules or regulations for grief. We all have to get through it as best we can. I get through it by being alone a lot. I appreciate people coming but I'm very happy with my animals. I feel they're such a link. There are times when I know I don't want to go out in a crowd. Somebody I know very well decided when she was widowed that she wanted to go abroad, to a different country, to shop until she dropped. To me, that would have been absolute hell. I couldn't have stood it, all those people. Not that I'm anti-people, but not at that moment. I wanted to be alone.

And I found that I wasn't frightened of being alone. I wasn't frightened of the dark. I felt he was so close to me all the time, so close. I had no feelings of fear. I knew I couldn't touch him, yet often I'd reach out and think, 'Yes, that was your hand.' The most extraordinary feelings of closeness I had with him, and still have.

I still talk to him, a lot. I talk to him when I'm going round the garden. Oh, yes, very much so, no question about that. I never feel cut off from him.

I find it terribly difficult, though, to laugh as much as I did. But – how do we get through it? I don't know. Ask me in a year's time and maybe I'll feel better. How can anybody put a time limit on grief?

People sometimes said to me, 'Are you feeling better?' That drove me mad: 'You must be feeling better now.' I'd say, 'But I haven't been ill. I've lost Peter.' I resented making the comparison between illness and bereavement. It's nothing to do with that at all. So to say 'Are you feeling better?' didn't help.

I can't think of starting again in any way. I've got so many memories, so many happy ones, that I'd rather concentrate on those. I was always thinking how lucky I was: 'My goodness, haven't I been blessed?' I don't know what I'd put first – the kindness or the humour. So many things that people list that they want from a marriage, and I had them all, so how lucky I've been.

I seem to be terribly busy. At times, when I'm so tired, I go to bed at seven o'clock in the evening, and I find that a great relief. I'm a great believer in staying in bed. It's therapeutic, no question about it.

I'd be very wary of giving advice about grief, because it's something one has to do at one's own pace. The only thing I'd say is, 'Don't feel guilty.' We've all got to find our own way and not feel guilty. There are some people who want to talk about it, and others don't. That's why I would never, never say to somebody, 'Get it out, talk about it.' You've got to be awfully sensitive. Don't force anything on people because *you* felt it. You must not. Get them to talk about how they feel. And there are some people who will rally to the call and want to talk about it. Others won't.

My first husband [Lord Boyle, now the Earl of Shannon] and I divorced, very amicably. My second husband, Greville Baylis, died very suddenly. We'd been married about 20 years. We'd talked on the phone a long time that night about what a wonderful holiday we'd just had in Kenya [she was in Cardiff, he was in London], and I said, 'Isn't it lovely? So many years to look forward to.' The telephone went at four o'clock in the morning. It was a doctor: 'Is that Katie Boyle? I've got some bad news. Your husband's dead.' And he put the telephone down. He didn't give me any sympathy or under-standing or anything.

I remember I let out a scream that I'm sure was heard all over the hotel. We were in Cardiff doing *The Hostess with the Mostest*. I couldn't make head nor tail of it. I remember getting into the train, and my producer came with me. I couldn't work out why he had pyjamas on under his overcoat. I just sat on the train, tears pouring down.

I remember we got to the station – Paddington I think it was – and I remember seeing headlines saying 'Katie Widowed', 'Katie Boyle Widowed'. And I remember thinking, 'That's me. He's dead.' Complete lack of under-standing of the facts. I wanted to know why, how.

A sweet woman called Julie Clements, the flower arranger, came and brought me a lovely bouquet. And I remember flinging it at the door and crying, 'I'm a widow, I'm not a bride!' It didn't make any sense to me. There was resentment and fear and shock.

And there are two memories, very similar but both of different husbands. With Greville, they locked me into the drawing-room of our flat. It was because they were taking the body out of the flat, I suppose in a bag.

When Peter died, I saw two men coming with a black bag and taking him out of the bedroom. That was one of the worst moments. I should have moved from this room, but I couldn't. I couldn't move. So I saw them carry him down on a stretcher – oh! the memory of that! – just a black bag. That has stayed with me so long. It still stays with me. That's when I really went to pieces. There was nothing I could do, nothing.

But I don't remember that all the time, because I look round here and I think, 'He always sat in that chair' – he loved the terrace, and he always had a dog with him. And I remember that wonderful feeling of loveliness when the magnolia came out and the Chinese cherries came out – those are the things I must remember. Those are two of the many things that have helped me. Not the memory of that terrible day when they took him out. We all have moments when we can cry, so easily, even now. Don't you?

Cheryl Craggs's husband, Glenn, died in 1999 when Cheryl was 17 weeks pregnant with their first child. She was 35 and he was 41. They both worked in sales and they were away at different conferences when Glenn collapsed. Cheryl is a committee member for the WAY Foundation, a national support group for young widows and widowers.

We were very excited about the baby. When we found out I was pregnant we were crying and laughing and hugging each other. One of the first things we did was drive over to his parents to tell them they were going to be grandparents. We couldn't have been happier.

Glenn and I had been together for 13 years and we were married for nine. We'd got to a stage in our lives when we decided we wanted to have children, but it wasn't happening, so we'd gone through IVF. We were happy together, so if it didn't work it didn't really matter. The IVF brought us very close together and it worked first time.

I think I'd just started to feel a little tiny flutter. I wasn't sure, but Glenn would shout through my tummy, 'It's your dad! I'm your dad!' He was the kind of person who would spoil me. Anything I wanted, I could have. When I went away for this meeting he even packed me all sorts of goodies, packets of cereal and milk to drink, because I got hungry in the night. He was a very giving, kind person.

I was at this sales conference in Cheltenham and he was at one in Northampton. At 10.30 in the morning I was called out of a meeting. I hadn't heard from Glenn the night before, which was unusual, so I'd been leaving him messages saying, 'I'm worried. Why haven't you phoned me?', but I didn't really think anything was seriously wrong.

The general manager ushered me into a boardroom and asked me to sit down in a chair next to a big boardroom table. At the time I didn't notice the box of tissues and the glass of water. I just thought, 'Oh, this looks a bit serious', wondering whether I was going to be fired or given a warning of some sort.

Then my manager just put his hands on my shoulders and said, 'I've got something terrible to tell you. It's Glenn. Something's happened. He's had a heart attack.' He actually couldn't come out with the words and say, 'He's dead.' I think I might have said, 'Is he dead?' There was a woman from HR [Human Resources] in the room and she just nodded and I think I screamed. It was just disbelief, shock, like something you'd see in a film going, 'No! No!' but screaming it out loud. Just complete disbelief.

All I was told was they thought it was a heart attack and he was in Northampton General Hospital. People said, 'What do you want to do?' and I remember saying, 'I don't know. Somebody tell me what to do.' I thought, 'Do I go home? Do I go and see his parents, my in-laws? Do I go to the hospital where he is?' It was just shock.

He died in his hotel room at midnight the night before and people from Glenn's work had tried to get hold of me, but our head office doesn't have anyone manning the phones at night so I didn't find out until he'd been dead for 11 hours and we didn't find out till another 24 hours later exactly what he'd died from. It wasn't a heart attack in the end. It was a brain haemorrhage.

I didn't cry much. I just remember thinking, 'I need to keep myself together, because otherwise I'm going to end up in hospital hooked up to monitors and things, because of the baby.' And I didn't want that. I just had this permanent shiver, this cold kind of shiver. I felt total disbelief. We'd been in the gym together on the Sunday. Fit as a fiddle, he was, no problems at all.

It was decided that I'd be driven to Northampton, but what I didn't realise was that I was going to be identifying him. Nobody told me that. I was left on my own with him for a few minutes, but it wasn't Glenn. It was his body that was lying there and it sort of looked like him, but he'd gone. His expression was wrong – fixed. It was horrible. I didn't want to touch him. I didn't want to kiss him or anything like that. None of those things. But I had to see him, otherwise I wouldn't have believed it.

I don't know how I got through the next five months. When I got back from Northampton, my sister stayed with me most of the week. I remember she comforted me for hours while I just wept in utter despair, but in the end I just wanted everyone to go.

I went into practical mode, organising the funeral like it was some kind of wedding, and there was none of the excitement or anticipation of the baby. I'm choosing a coffin when I should be looking at prams. I'm staring at the Yellow Pages trying to find a funeral director, when I should have been buying a cot. I couldn't stop saying to people, 'I'm pregnant' and when I was registering the death the registrar stifled her shock. She was embarrassed, but she was a human being at the end of the day. A pregnant woman registering the death of her husband would be a shock to anybody.

I didn't even have any clothes that fitted me for the funeral, so I had to go shopping for some. I wandered around this shopping centre for hours, thinking over and over again, 'My husband's died.' Eventually, I walked into a shop and said, 'I need something to wear for my husband's funeral and I'm pregnant.' They were really kind.

The funeral was held a week later in the chapel where we'd been married. It was so packed people had to stand. In his coffin, I placed scan pictures of our unborn child.

People would say, 'At least you'll have the baby' and 'Everything will be better when the baby comes.' They're looking for something to say. The window cleaner said, 'Still, life goes on, love, doesn't it?' You can't believe someone would say that to you three days after the funeral, but they do.

I felt like a freak. Whereas I'd been really proud of the pregnancy and really excited, I didn't want to talk about it at all, because it wasn't a happy event. I would have given anything not to be pregnant if I could have had Glenn back, because I had never had a baby before. I didn't know what the impact would be of having a child.

From wanting to buy every single pregnancy magazine, I didn't want to buy any at all. I hated all the references to comfortable love-making positions and asking your partner to rub your feet. And I remember trying to put the cot up and I realised I couldn't do it on my own, so my friend's husband came round and I just sat in the corner of this room looking at the cot, just crying because it seemed so bloody unfair.

Grief is exhausting. It doesn't leave you alone. You can't escape it. You're driving along and the tears are just misting up your eyes. You're wandering around Tesco and you want somebody to say, 'Cheer up, love. It might never happen' so you can turn round and say, 'Well, actually it has.' You want to scream at somebody.

When Alexandra was born I was scared to look at her at first, but when they put her in my arms, I loved her straightaway. Even so it all felt so wrong, because Glenn should've been there with us.

The next morning there was almost a bit of euphoria, I think. I remember going up the ward and saying to one of the nurses, 'I've learnt how to put mascara on with one hand.' Holding the baby with one hand and putting mascara on with the other. She must have thought, 'What's she bothered about her mascara for with a new baby and no husband?'

I cried a lot throughout the day, but I never just sat and wallowed in it, except for when it became so bad I was just sobbing, shouting out his name. And everywhere I looked there seemed to be couples holding hands or a proud dad holding his newborn baby in a carrier. I hated them.

I think some of the grieving was put on hold once Alexandra was born, because I was so wrapped up in dealing with her. Then there'd be times when I would just be feeding her, looking at her little face and suddenly find myself crying, thinking, 'This is just awful. This isn't how it should be.' It's having no one to share those momentous occasions like her first tooth or learning to crawl. There was no one who loved her as much as me to say, 'Come and look', when she was sleeping.

I remember being in the park one Sunday morning and there was a couple there and I just found an excuse to bring it into the conversation and talk about it. I felt the need to tell people about what had happened to me, because I didn't want them to think that I was a normal single parent. I might be alone, but it was not out of choice.

As well as losing your husband and lover, you've lost your best friend because you share everything. Nobody knows you more inside out than your husband or your wife. You know exactly what they're going to say before they're going to say it. You can finish each other's sentences. It's that intimacy. The little touches as you walk past each other, stroking each other's heads when you're lying on the sofa. It was everything: the emotional, the physical, the everyday normal boring stuff, the stuff that you argue about. You even miss the grumpy side of them.

Glenn was an only child and his parents idolised him. I sometimes felt that they thought they were suffering more than I was. What was really happening was that we were grieving for two different people – they were grieving for 'their baby' and son – I was grieving for my best friend and lover. They were also grieving for their loss together, and could go home together, and their day-to-day lives could 'appear' to remain the same. I was living and breathing the loss every minute of every day. I'd never gone longer than a few days without him, where they'd go three or four months and not see him.

Just after he'd been gone a year, I asked his parents if they would come and stay for a couple of days, because I was feeling tired and Alexandra had been out of sorts. I felt – this is my interpretation of it, not theirs – that I was putting them out by asking them to come. I asked them at nine o'clock in the morning and they didn't come till nine o'clock that night.

So I'd been getting more and more tired all day and when they arrived my emotions were frayed and there was an argument. Well, an outburst, where a lot of emotional things were said which maybe shouldn't have been said, and I found myself screaming and crying. His mum will say now she thinks I had a breakdown, but I was fully aware of everything that was being said. At one point Glenn's dad said, 'We had him for 41 years, you know. If something happens to Alexandra, you'll know how we feel.'

I felt they were more into comparing grief than I was. They thought their grief was the worst. I thought mine was. This is a common thing amongst people who are young widows. The in-laws think they're the chief mourners at the funeral, but in fact you all are. We're all grieving.

I had a lot of anger towards my mother-in-law, because even before we buried Glenn, she made a comment about me being young and probably meeting someone else and I was absolutely outraged.

I didn't intend to ever be in a new relationship. Having said that, I think what his mum had been trying to say was, 'We realise it might happen and we support it.' But she didn't have quite the right words to say it. I think they felt – certainly his mum felt – she could never say the right thing to me.

Over two-and-a-half years after losing Glenn, I did meet someone else. We've been seeing each other for about two years now and we're going to get married.

There is the worry that if you give yourself to someone else again, you might lose them, too, but I have a distinct memory of walking to a park with my new partner and our children and actually holding hands, thinking, 'This is how it should be. This is how it's meant to be. This is what I had been cheated out of, but now I've got it and it's so lovely.'

Karen Harrison's husband, Bob, was a GP. In 1998 he died suddenly of a heart attack at the age of 39. Their son, Oliver, was six at the time and their daughter, Abigail, was just a baby. Oliver tells his story in Chapter 4: Sons and Abigail in Chapter 3: Daughters.

I got in from work about seven o'clock and I went to get a meal ready and he was upstairs with the children. They were getting ready for bed. Everything was normal, then I just heard him shout, 'Karen! Karen!' and I went, 'What?' He shouted it again and I dropped the plate and went straight upstairs. He was collapsed down the side of the bed and then the children – they were in another room – they ran in. Abigail was crawling, so she was starting to crawl over him. Oliver's screaming, 'What's going on?'

So I get on the phone – 999 – 'I think he's collapsed.' He was six foot three and 13 or 14 stone. I couldn't physically move him. I remember having to kick the baby gate down to try and get him into the ambulance quickly. You just remember flashes of it. You know, Oliver screaming, 'You're not going to let him die, Mum, are you?'

I remember blue lights and going through red lights at the traffic lights. And then it was casualty and they just whizzed him off. I phoned my mum and dad and said, 'You've got to come. He's dying.' I knew in my mind that he was dying. I could hear in the background people saying, 'Oh, it's a local GP.' They all knew him at the hospital. It was a bit like going into labour. You're in a dream. It's all going on around you and it's unreal.

Your life's changed completely and I can only describe it as I can imagine the feeling of if you've been shot – or if you've ever had a really near miss in a car – and you've had that horrible shock of adrenalin, almost to feel sick with it. I just felt like that. Instantly they told me the news that he'd died, I had awful stomach pains like indigestion. The worst thing was Oliver looked at me pleadingly. That was the hardest thing. I spent the whole night with him in my arms. That's all I wanted to do.

People didn't avoid us. We probably had the opposite. I had strange people coming up to me in the supermarket and say, 'I know all about you' and 'I can't believe this has happened' and 'How are you coping?' They were shocked for us. It was often my husband's patients. They would recount funny stories and loads of people wrote cards and letters. I found that really helpful – that people told you what they liked about him.

I knew he was popular. I knew he did wonderful things that he didn't always tell me about and when people came and told me some of the things, that gave me comfort and I've got a sack full of letters. I've not been able to face going over them, but they're there if I ever can do that.

You felt quite special at first. The newspapers wanted to speak to us and we had visitors constantly. We were being phoned up at all hours of the day and night. But after that people very quickly – and I don't mean maliciously – drop you. But all they've done is gone back to their normal lives. People used to ask, 'How do you feel?' There's only one thing you ever did feel. 'Do you *really* want to know how I feel? Have you got three days?'

It's so enormous – the impact – that people have no idea unless they've been through it. They put a timescale on going back to normal, but it never does. It was like I was walking along one path and I can describe the shock, feeling as though I'd walked into a glass door. Suddenly you now have to turn and go in a different direction. During that night I knew that I'd got two choices: I could either give in to the whole thing or I had to get up the next day and face it.

I really had a strong protective maternal instinct for my children. That was my driver. I thought, 'My children are going to lose the qualities of somebody who's so important to us. They're going to be without a father. So you're going to have to get up tomorrow and this is the start of the biggest battle of your life.' And that's how I treated it.

I didn't really grieve as a wife, I don't think. I didn't collapse. I just focused on my children and kept thinking, every day and every hurdle I came across, 'You're doing this to try and help your children have the best life they can possibly have.'

I tried in the early days to be two people. So I did all that I was doing and then I was trying to do everything he would've done as well. But you get to a point where life isn't sustainable. I remember once, with Abigail in my arms, falling down the stairs because I was rushing that much to try and do everything and I thought, 'You'll have to stop this.'

I don't always like admitting to people that I'm a widow because you look at the shock on people's faces. I'm now 43, but I was 36 at the time with a baby in my arms and people are completely shocked by it, so now I often introduce myself as 'I'm on my own with the children.' People always assume it's a divorce or that you've chosen to be single.

I craved desperately to find somebody who was in the same position. I didn't want to meet another widow who was 75. I needed to meet another 36-year-old ideally. Or someone that had a baby and that had a young child. Just to not feel alone and alien, unique.

What's helped me is allowing myself a bad day every now and again, and I think it's important to show the children that I need that as well. I needed to show them that I was grieving, that I could cry and that I was upset. I had almost drowning feelings at times. I sometimes thought, 'I'm going down and down and down. I can't get my head above water here.' I'd have my half an hour when I'd get on my own and I had a good cry and then I'd be all right to pick the kids up and make tea. I had to do things like that to keep myself going.

You get the horrible physical symptoms that nobody, unless they've been through it, can understand. Complete insomnia. I could go days and days with maybe one or two hours sleep, and not really feel that bad for it. On a complete adrenalin high. I'd have a tremble. I couldn't hold a hot cup of coffee for a long time. Waking with night sweats, a bit like a panic attack in the middle of the night, waking up not knowing what's going on. Your skin's affected. Your hair's affected. Everything.

It's with you 24 hours of every day and it's a slow 24 hours. It's everything you touch. There's no need to open twice as much food. You don't buy the same things in the supermarket. There's no ironing of shirts. On Christmas Day there's an empty seat.

It's when you're taken unawares that it's hard. Oliver was at a soccer school and they announced that he'd won some soccer tickets for the best behaved child. I was there clapping. Then the guy who was presenting them said, 'So, will your dad be able to take you to the match on Saturday?' And the room fell silent and some bright spark chirped up, 'Oh, his dad's dead. He can't take him.' And because I wasn't prepared for it, I just went, 'Ohhh!' But it was a child – he was only being factual.

It's not the big things that are hard. It's watching other couples going to the pub on a nice summer's night. It's the companionship and sharing decisions. It's that comfort that somebody else is there. I miss the best friend thing, the having a laugh, and it's all the goals and the plans we built together. We'd been together 20 years and we knew roughly where we were going, what we would like to do. Gone.

CHAPTER 8

Husbands

Ed Farrelly's wife, Nadia, died just after the birth of their second child, Teddy, who is now three. Their elder son, Jacob, is five.

About ten days after Teddy was born, Nadia became ill, went into hospital and was in intensive care for about ten days. It was actually necrotising fasciitis, which is the flesh-eating bug, so it wasn't particularly pleasant.

The birth was fantastic and the next week was fine – as fine as you can be with a newborn baby and a 22-month-old. It was a bit chaotic. But she had a sore leg and we called a doctor in the night before who said, 'Take two paracetamols and see how it is in the morning.' In the morning she had quite considerable pain in the leg, so we called the hospital, because she was still under the midwives and they said, 'Come on in.'

She was actually breastfeeding Teddy in the hospital while saying, 'This is getting very painful.' They increased the painkillers over four or five hours, then eventually she was on morphine and she lost consciousness through the painkillers. The last words I ever heard from her were something along the lines of 'I could really do without this at a time like this!' She was very practical. Shortly after that she arrested and she never regained consciousness.

They gave her a hysterectomy that night, because the source of the infection was there. A couple of days later they amputated the leg and it was always going to be downhill really. It was another five or six days after that before she died. It was like walking into a brick wall, just suddenly sheer horror.

Walking up the aisle behind the coffin with a small baby in my arms was pretty incongruous. The funeral is just a haze. The church was packed – absolutely packed. There must've been 300 people there. I did cry at the time, but I remember thinking afterwards, 'I don't think I cried enough. I'm not reacting the way people do in films. There's something wrong with me. Am I retarded emotionally?'

But I don't think that's the case, because I never used to cry. I used to watch a weepie film with Nadia and I used to just absolutely mercilessly laugh at her when she started to cry, because it was like waterworks switching on with her. And now what I find is, I'm more like that.

I think I went through all the classic stages of grief, but not in classic ways. I was very, very angry early on – literally from the day after. Bizarrely, I remember driving around, arranging the funeral and that kind of stuff, and thinking, 'I just hope somebody gets into an argument with me. Just give me the opportunity!' I'm five foot five and not remotely violent. I'd probably have been beaten to a pulp!

Sometimes I felt there was a big neon sign over me saying, 'This disaster has happened to me' and you think everybody is looking at you, which, of course they're not. You go to Sainsbury's with the two boys and you're the only man there with children – or one of very few men – and you're thinking everybody must realise that I'm a recently bereaved parent.

It didn't enter my head that people would think I was a divorced dad. There was a time when I'd go to the checkout and the woman would say, 'Is it your turn with the kids today?' or 'Nice to see you doing your turn.' And a couple of times I said, 'Well, no, actually. My wife just recently died.' That is worse than hitting someone in the face as far as I'm concerned. It's just not fair to do that.

Having the children was an enormous crutch. Your mind is so numbed by what's happened that to have that enormous task is a pretty damned good thing to have, in a way. You know what it's like with a newborn baby – you don't have time. There were sleepless nights, but not necessarily through the grief.

If I hadn't had the children, I think I would've packed up, sold stuff off and gone off round the world and lost myself in that way. But you just bury yourself in the enormity of the task – the odd glass of wine might have assisted from time to time!

Nadia was not in a great shape when she died. She'd been ten days in intensive care and the disease had really taken its toll and the undertakers tactfully said, 'Would you like the coffin open or closed in the chapel of rest?' I said, 'I think closed is probably a good idea.' But when I went in I remember thinking, 'I'd like just one last look' and I tried to undo the screws and I couldn't. I undid one and then I couldn't get it back in and it was just farcical. I went out and said to the lady at reception, 'Thank you very much. That's really kind. By the way, there's a screw loose on the coffin lid. Can you sort that out, please?' and I fled!

Genuine friends who stuck through thick and thin did help. You just think, 'What sterling people.' People who came – not to help, not to Hoover – just to have a drink and watch the footie. I'm a bloke and if someone says, 'We'll come round with a curry and a couple of beers and watch the footie', you feel, 'Right. I'm having a normal life.'

I was worried that the kids would be traumatised. What's painfully apparent to me is that kids are hardier than that and they were too young, and there is a danger of putting your guilt and sorrow onto them and saying, 'You should be sadder. You must feel the same way as me.' I try desperately to avoid that.

The danger is to look at other people and say, 'That's how I should be feeling' and you can't. 'Time is a healer' is the classic and there's an element of truth in it, in the sense that you have other experiences intervening between you and the death. But it doesn't heal. Nothing heals.

I miss everything about Nadia. I miss having a soulmate. I've got two soulmates to love – the children – and so in some respects I'm luckier than most, but I was with Nadia for ten years – a third of my life. We had the same sense of humour. It's a bad sense of humour. It's a terrible sense of humour! Terribly corny.

I hope – I very much hope – that I will still in 20 or 50 years, however long I live, I will still get sudden uncontrollable bursts of grief, because that is a genuine reflection of my love for Nadia.

J eremy Howe's wife, Elizabeth, an academic, was murdered 12 years ago while teaching at an Open University summer school at the University of York. She was 34, the mother of two small daughters, Jessica and Lucy, and the author of a newly published and much-acclaimed book, *The First English Actresses*. Jeremy is a producer at BBC Bristol.

At the end of July 1992, when Lizzie was killed, it was like being at the centre of an atomic explosion. What happened to her and its effects on us were so gargantuan, I'm still experiencing the aftershocks. It's like dropping some massive stone in a pond and seeing the ripples go out – and actually that pond is the size of your life. As you get further from the epicentre, time-wise, the ripples get less, but it doesn't mean that they've gone. They're always there.

Grief is no longer the dominant feature of my life. I've remarried – to Jennie – and that's fantastic and it's turned my life round. I haven't replaced Lizzie, but I do have another wife. Our two girls were four and six when Lizzie was killed, and now Jessica's about to go to university, so – in terms of their lives – it's three times Jessica's life and even more for Lucy, the younger one. So we've all moved on.

But, you know, I had a conversation with Jessica the other day – there's a leaving ball at her school, and you need to be sponsored by someone who then has to go to the ball. She asked me if I wanted to go, and I said, 'No way' – it's just not something I want to do. It's not a big issue, she'll get someone else – but she came home the next day and she said, 'Some of the mothers, the mummies, are going to be the sponsor.' And we had a perfectly reasonable conversation about that. About an hour later she came up to me in tears and she said, 'I don't have a mummy. I felt so left out.' And she doesn't have a mummy. Her mummy's dead. Jennie is her stepmother. And I realised that it was something that Jessica could only really articulate to me. So in that sense the grief is still a secret, because to all intents and purposes we look like a perfectly ordinary family, but there's a secret there that Jessica does not tell anyone, which is that Jennie is not her mother, that her mummy died.

The thing is, when it happened, it was so incredibly public. There we were on the front page of *The Daily Mail*. So it was very difficult to be secretive about it at all. There was no hiding place. But, although it was so public, it's not something you can share with people very easily. You know, it's a real party-pooper, telling people your wife's been murdered, so you find all sorts of ways of not saying it. You don't want to burden people with it. Also, when you rehearse the details, it affects and infects you as well.

You try and achieve a balance between being truthful to yourself and not upsetting other people. But if you begin to tell lies, you begin to live a lie, and it screws you up, actually. I mean, it's a long time ago now and it's not part of my everyday strategies any more, but in the aftermath of her death I absolutely had this kind of mantra, particularly for the children, that you've got to tell the truth. Because if you tell the truth, you have a clean wound and a clean wound can heal. If you don't tell the truth, there's crap in the wound, and that's when you get infections and it won't heal, or it heals wrongly.

One of the things that's really strong is the need to articulate it and tell people about it, and I don't know why. I've spent forever working with writers, developing scripts – since I joined the BBC 20 years ago that's been, by and large, what I've done. And the writer you're really on the lookout for is the person who's got something to say and needs to say it – and I never thought I had that at all, but that changed in July 1992, when there was something I really needed to talk about. It's very private, but it's almost unstoppable.

About 18 months after Lizzie's death, I got the job here [at BBC Bristol], and I upped sticks and moved house from Oxford to Bath. I basically reinvented myself. In London, I felt slightly stigmatised. You know, you go down the corridor and you can see people looking at you – and that's my perception, not their perception. People were incredibly supportive of me, and even more so in Oxford where we used to live. They were absolutely bloody brilliant, fantastic. But actually it was stifling me. But the bizarre thing was, I moved here and after two years here, I then made a film about what I'd been through [*A Moving Image*, transmitted on BBC2 in 1996]. So I might as well have had 'Jeremy Howe – Victim' all over me. And yes, it's weird, because I don't want to be labelled as 'victim', and for 98 per cent of the time, I don't think I have that at all.

It was such an incredibly lonely experience for me, I really needed someone to share the burden with, and there isn't that much literature about it. It's a subject where a good book or a good programme or whatever can help people. When I made that film, I had severe doubts about what I was doing. And you know, I usually only ever receive about four letters for a programme. With *A Moving Image*, I would say I got about 200, two of which were saying, 'This is disgraceful', the other 198 saying, 'Thank God you made that programme, it was so helpful.'

I do think it's an individual experience. There's no checklist you can go through. It's just not that simple, I don't think. I certainly never had any phases of grief. Retrospectively, you can see it was either bloody awful, awful, painful, less painful, like that, but I was never able to recognise the classic phases of grief in my behaviour.

Some people have very slow metabolisms, some people have very fast metabolisms, and I think it's to do with age. My mother was widowed in her sixties and I think it's been very hard for her to adjust – though she's done fantastically well. Lucy was four when she lost her mother and 12 years in her lifetime is massive, so she's adapted much more quickly. But people have different temperaments, different circumstances – everyone is different.

One thing you can say about grief is it is shattering. I had no idea just how shattering it is. It was traumatic, it was devastating, it was life-changing. My father died shortly before Lizzie was killed and I was very sad, but nothing prepared me for when Lizzie was killed.

You just have to trust your instincts. By nature I'm an intelligent, articulate, thinking person. When Lizzie died, I stopped that. Instinct took over. The instinct I had was: 'I've got to shore up our lives.' And that's what I did. I went out and tried to shore up our lives, tried to make them as regular as they could be, given the circumstances.

I can't begin to tell you just how devastating it was. I had to go and identify Lizzie's body in York and that was traumatic (a) because it was Lizzie's body and I then knew it was her. You know, you always have some hope that it's not the person they've told you it is. And (b) then the police interviewed me immediately, to see if I was a suspect, which was pretty… well, I don't thank the police for that. They were pretty shitty.

Anyway, I was driven home that evening by my brother-in-law from York down to Norfolk, where I'd left Jessica and Lucy with my sister. And I said to him, 'I don't think I'm going to be able to sleep tonight.' Miraculously, he managed to get an appointment that night with his GP – and I can tell you, at seven o'clock on a Sunday evening, he was not best pleased to be called to his surgery to give someone sleeping tablets. He said, 'What's the problem?' and I told him, and you could see his jaw dropping, and that's when I realised the enormity of it. He was probably the first person outside the family group to know – it hadn't been on the news then – and then I realised this just doesn't happen in normal life. It was just extraordinary.

I realised then what it was like to be in a Shakespearian tragedy – and I don't mean that flippantly. Because Lizzie was an academic, one of the first people I told was her PhD supervisor who's a Professor of Shakespeare Studies, and her reaction was that it reminded her of Cordelia's senseless death at the end of *King Lear*. And I thought, 'That's exactly what it's like.' You see those things on the stage and suddenly you're part of it – it was monstrous.

But you get through it. You do get through it. And the advice I'd give to people – and it's terribly pat – is, it will get better. It doesn't mean you love that person any the less. It's just that time passes and you adjust to it.

The other advice I'd say is, just take each moment as it comes. I was incredibly blessed by all the support I got from friends, neighbours, from the NHS. I saw this brilliant clinical psychologist, and he said, 'What you've lost is your map. You've got no future, it's mapless, it's gone. My job is to find the tracks for you and by the time we've finished I will find you a map. And the way you find that map is, you just put one foot in front of the other. And you live in the moment.' The weird thing is, it was awful, but it was exhilarating. I basically had to go and reinvent my life at whatever age I was – in my mid-thirties. The adrenalin was just extraordinary.

So that's my advice: trust your instincts. And just put one foot forward at a time. Don't be too ambitious about it.

I still grieve, of course I do. I still miss Lizzie. I think the thing I miss most about her was that she had her life cut off at the point where she was about to really reap the benefits of all the hard work she'd put in. She wanted to be an academic – she was a very gifted teacher and she was a very good researcher. Her doctoral thesis – the research was just extraordinary. It was published as a book about four weeks before she was killed, and I'm sure that she would have had a very good academic career and that book was a really good foundation. It won prizes and it's been turned into a play and a film for television – and she didn't see any of that. She didn't reap any of the benefits of that. As Lucy said, 'It's unfair.' And it is. Life is very unfair. It was for Lizzie.

The other immortality that Lizzie has achieved is through Jessica and Lucy. And, though they're absolutely their own persons, there's Lizzie in them, obviously genetically, but also in every way. So her presence is there, and it's not a ghostly or weird or fetishistic presence, it is irrefutable and undeniable that Lizzie is present in Jessica and Lucy – and will continue to be. And, if they have children, she'll continue to be present there.

One afternoon, a few weeks after her death, I was driving back home through Oxford and I'd swear Lizzie cycled past me. That image stayed with me for days. And I've had dreams about her. So she's there, but she isn't there, at the same time. She's there in my head.

When my father died, I knew someone who had a baby about four hours later and that was quite a comfort, really. You did feel the universe had some kind of purpose. I'm afraid when Lizzie died, all sense of purpose just was smashed to bits. Her death, in my head, is terribly like the death that starts off Camus's *The Outsider*. Just randomly, someone is murdered. And it just destroys – for me, it destroyed the world order. How do you explain it? I suppose the closest you can get to it in religious terms is it was an evil act. But

I don't even think it was that. I think she was the wrong person in the wrong place at the wrong time, and this person [the man who murdered her] was completely out of their head. You can't explain that. It just happened.

I don't think you can make sense of something that has no sense. You get on with life and you remember, but that's it – there's no sense in it. She was a good person who had a good life, but it was terminated brutally. And if you can be snuffed out that easily, then all life is dangling by a thread.

Going back to the comparison with Shakespeare, you hit that Shakespearean tragic moment for one brief insightful moment, but ordinary life – particularly when you're trying to bring up two children – runs over it very fast, and you just get on and lead life. I've normalised life, really. Our lives are no longer Shakespearian, thank God.

The really positive thing about it was, because I became the prime carer, I've got an extraordinarily close relationship with Jessica and Lucy, which I'm not sure I would have had. It made me prioritise. Before, when Lizzie was alive, I would hang around at work afterwards, have a drink with colleagues and then come home. After her death, I would literally stop a conversation at twenty to six, get my coat on and go straight to the station to come home. I didn't care who I was talking to – the Director General of the BBC or a mate – that was the end of the conversation. I just knew I wanted to get home to say goodnight to the children. So yes, I think I am a very different person to the one you would have met in 1992.

I think the most depressing thing – and that's all changed now, thank God – was that the heart went out of our house. That was the other reason I wanted to move from Oxford. Because at best our home was a kind of place where people went through, and at worst it was just a soulless place because I didn't have the time or the energy to recreate it as a home. It was beyond me.

It's quite hard camping in a house, but it's really hard camping in a house that had been a home. So then we moved to Bath. I did my best, but the house was just shabby chaos, frankly, but at least it was our home, we created it ourselves.

Jennie and I have been together seven years, married for five. She came into our lives and she, with my absolute blessing, reorganised our house in Bath in order to turn it into a home, so minor details – like carpets and curtains – appeared. It was another major, major step on the road to normalisation. You look at our family now and I don't think you'd think, 'God, that's a tragic family.' We're just an ordinary middle-class family. We're fine.

Lizzie bequeathed us a very, very secure family. Another person we saw at the time was this fantastic woman called Dr Gillian Forrest who was head of the child psychiatry unit in Oxford. I remember she said, 'In psychiatry we always say, "Each year that a child has of stable growth is money in the bank", and your two have got gold in the bank.' That's what Lizzie left us, and that's what I needed to pick up and keep the investment working.

One of the interesting things that happens is you lose all perspective of anything, and trying to get that perspective back is really hard. The thing that helped me do it is I had to bring up two kids – and they don't half interrupt your lonely vigil with 'Can we have some breakfast now, Daddy?' I can't imagine otherwise what would have got me up in the morning.

But you totally lose perspective. People must have thought, 'This guy's a nutcase.' I must have behaved very oddly. A lot of the strange things I've done were to try and find out where Lizzie had gone to. I'm sure that's why I made that film. I kind of needed to go and see where she'd got killed, and the only way I could think of doing that was by taking a television crew with me! That's such a strange thing to do. Complete tunnel vision. God knows what my crew must have thought – what kind of madness was I in the grip of? I was unstoppable. *It* was unstoppable. And that was a good four years afterwards.

I went to the room where she was killed and it wasn't at all like I'd imagined it. It was just a room. We then got into a taxi and went back to York Station. That journey was probably the most desolate 45 minutes of my life. It didn't make it more real, but it does make you confront something. You put yourself through the worst experience you can, and you either break under it or, like steel, you're tempered and get stronger. And I think I did get stronger.

One of the hardest things I've ever done in my life was edit that film. We cut it for four weeks, and week on week it got tougher and tougher, because I was having to make choices. Then we put the film to bed and I spent the summer doing other things. The film went out while I was abroad – in August – and by Christmas I was living with Jennie. I think the process of editing the film had enabled me to put everything into an order. And once you've put something in order, you can begin to understand it and then you can begin to move on. 'Moving on' is a bit of a pat term, but I did make an enormous leap with that film, with coming to terms with what had happened. There was less chaos in my life.

We still talk about Lizzie, but not as much as we used to. It doesn't mean we've all forgotten her or that we don't love her. We got a royalty cheque from her book the other day and Jessica and Lucy were very keen to know what I was going to spend the royalty cheque on. They wanted something to remember her. And we make a point of buying something for the house to mark her birthday – one year it was a punchbag! But she's still part of our lives. She has to be because, as I said before, she's genetically encoded deep in Jessica and Lucy.

It was only when Lizzie died, I realised what an extraordinary person she was. I've never met anyone who was capable of working quite so hard and in such a focused way. She had amazing energy. She was half-Serb, so she had that Eastern European temperament, and that Eastern European determination. She was just great – a great person to share my life with. We were intellectually and emotionally very evenly matched, so we paced each other. And she was a great mother.

It's weird though, because bits of it fade. She does seem a long, long way away now. It's strange that you spend all that time with someone and there are so many things you can't remember. For the first time in 12 years – because I certainly didn't read them while she was alive – I started looking through her diaries the other day, and I don't remember the half of what was going on. It's like the chatter that GCHQ picks up that doesn't tell you what's going on. But one of the interesting things is – I was remembering one of the first times we were together. And – it's not a picture, it's a feeling, of her smile. There's a whole kind of hinterland to that smile which is not visual, it's not tactile, I don't know what it is. It's the memory of a smile, which is pretty intangible, really, but it's locked in my system.

And there are some fantastic memorials to Lizzie. Not least is her book. Receiving a royalty cheque from the Cambridge University Press 12 years later – it's not bad, is it? And St Anne's College, Oxford, put up a memorial stained-glass window in her memory, which all our mates from Oxford put up money for. But the best memorial, the best memory, we've got is Jessica and Lucy.

Paul Whiteside's wife, Maria, died suddenly at a St Valentine's Day dance eight years ago at the age of 53. They had been married for 25 years and their two teenage sons, Matt and Jamie, were 18 and 14 at the time. Paul has since remarried.

It was towards the end of the evening and we were just coming off the dance floor and she said, 'I've gone all hot.' And I just said, 'You've got one of your hot flushes, you daft bugger.' Anyway, she went down and she never moved again. They said she was dead before she hit the ground. She never had a day's illness in her life. Never. It was unbelieveable. Absolutely unbelievable.

There was a surgeon, a nursing sister and a nurse actually at the 'do'. The surgeon came up to me and said, 'Paul, there were three of us and if we could've saved her we would've done.' All I can remember is people getting hold of me and dragging me away. One of the lads at the golf club said I was running round, punching the walls in temper. That was only what I was told. I still don't know what happened – how I got home or anything that night.

We'd left the boys at home. They'd said, 'Go on and enjoy yourselves' as they normally did. Of course, the sad thing is they never got the chance to say goodbye. Nobody did. The whole family was just in total shock. The world was over as far as I was concerned.

We just all fell to bits. Jamie, the 14-year-old, walked out of school and never went back. I couldn't even bear to stay in the house. I'd just wake up and go out. I could smell her. I couldn't even open a wardrobe.

We were lost souls. We just sat round the house. Didn't do nothing. For ages. The boys got themselves into wacky baccy and I hit the bottle. It was just crazy. It was madness. I didn't care if I ended up dead in the gutter. What I wanted was a mugger. I wanted to unleash this feeling that was in me and I thought, 'Where are these bloody people when you want one?' There were times when I didn't care if I didn't wake up. The house was in a bloody mess. Three blokes living and grieving. That was the last thing I wanted to do – put the bloody Hoover round. But who cared?

If Maria had walked in she'd have slapped us senseless. She'd have beat us up. Oh, my God, she'd have gone mental. Fiery woman. She had a lot of Italian blood in her and she ruled the family. She hit me with a milk bottle once. Been stabbed with tweezers, scissors. I used to have to grab her wrists when we were arguing before she could pick anything up!

The funny thing was me and Matt were sat at the kitchen table one day and there was this bloody waft – it's true – waft of perfume. And I looked at Matty. I didn't want to say anything and he looked at me. He said, 'Did you smell that?' I said, 'Yes.' It was her perfume without a doubt. It came right between us and it wasn't just me. Matty was there as well. Now why it happened or how it happened, I don't know, but nobody can tell me any different. That's fact. Whether it was a comfort or not, I don't know, but it was a nice feeling at the time.

Then two-and-a-half years after Maria died, I met Gloria. She was my saviour. She had a pub and she put on a beer festival. One of the lads I knew told me about it and I went in and I saw Glo. From there it all picked up. It got better. The worst thing about it was that my two boys couldn't accept it when I met Gloria. They do now, but at the time they didn't, which I can understand. But I needed somebody and Glo pulled me straight out of it. If it wasn't for Gloria, I'd have been gone and that's a fact.

I used to get good days and bad days and anything would trigger it off. You'd end up bawling like a bloody kid, storming off somewhere. I still get the odd day. It's just something – anything. One particular song on the radio and that's it – you're off.

The pain is like nothing I've felt before in my life – ever – ever. It's like somebody's taken your left arm away or the left half of your body, because when you've lived together and had children and you've lived as one, it's as though something's been literally hacked off and you don't know how to cope with this missing bit. It's all right for people to say, 'let go', but you can't let go. If you've spent half your life with a person every day and you know them inside out, how can you just let go? It's impossible.

My outlook on life has changed to the extent that – if it could happen to Maria, just like that – what's in store for anybody? I've never been frightened of death. I've always accepted that one day you're going to die and whether that's sooner or later, God only knows. If I die tomorrow, I can say, 'thanks'. All I wanted to do at the end of the day was see my children grow up, which I have done. So, there must be someone up there looking after me.

CHAPTER 9

Partners

Vera Percy's husband died in 1976, leaving her to bring up their three teenage sons. In 1999, aged 77, she began a relationship with James, a widower of the same age who also had three children: a son and two daughters. The relationship continued until James's death in 2001.

When I was almost 78, James, a man I'd been writing to for over three years, decided he wanted to come and see me. And that was it. We had three-and-a-half years together – weekends and going out – not being together all the time. Then we went on holiday and he died. He had got heart trouble, but we didn't expect him to go so suddenly.

We were in Northern Italy with his daughter who's in her thirties and has learning difficulties. On the Monday, at the hotel, we went out and about. Then that night – he'd had these attacks before and he'd take a tablet and it would go off – but it seemed to be worse than usual. So early the following morning, we sent for a doctor, and he tested his heart, his blood pressure, his pulse – everything seemed quite normal – and he said it might be better if he stayed in bed all day, which he did.

The following day, we spent the day together, and it was a lovely day and the scenery was beautiful, and he was all right. Then during the night he had another attack, and we got over that, and he was talking about when he was little and so on. Then he started in the morning about six-ish, and it seemed to get worse and worse, and the hotel arranged for an ambulance to take him to the nearest hospital.

The ambulance men couldn't speak English and I couldn't speak much Italian, and they brought a chair, not a stretcher, to put him on. I realised afterwards that they probably thought he was too ill to be moved. And he suddenly shouted, 'I'm dying!' and slumped in my arms. I'm telling him not to, he can't be dying, that he had to hang on. Then they came back with a stretcher and laid him down flat, and I knew then he must be dead.

I'd got his other daughter's work phone number, so I got hold of her and asked would she tell her brother, which she did. The rest of the people on the coach were very kind, and they all signed a sympathy card for us, and the lady who owned the business was with us, and they were all very kind, all the way back.

We went back to James's house at the end of the holiday – his daughter and I – and I stayed there a couple of days, to do all the washing and ironing and put everything straight. Then I went, but I said I was there if she wanted me. I came round the following day, and the brother arrived and didn't want to speak to me at all. Then he shouted and said his father shouldn't have gone on holiday. I said, well, that was up to him, surely? And I handed over everything belonging to their father.

I wasn't invited to the funeral, but I went. I was rung and told when it was on, and the older sister said it would be from the house and I could go with them. But when I mentioned that, the son said, 'Oh no, certainly not, we've got far too many going as it is.' And nobody looked at me. At the crematorium the minister turned to James's daughter and said, 'You were with your father when he died, weren't you?' And I wanted to shout, 'No, she wasn't. I was with him.' But I didn't.

But I was. And he died in my arms. In a way that's a lovely feeling. It would have been a lot worse if he'd died at home and I hadn't been there. That's the feeling that keeps me going, really.

We were writing to each other for over three years and after we met we still wrote quite a lot. Not as often, but they were more love letters than the originals. And we rang every day. Quite often when it wasn't his turn he'd ring up and say, 'It's me', or sing to me. He'd leave a message on the answerphone, and sometimes I wish I hadn't wiped them all off. Then I think, maybe it would have made it worse, if I could have heard his voice. But I can still feel him in bed, touching me – still. It's as strong as before he died. We neither of us believed in the afterlife, so it's not that. But it's something.

I've cried a bit. I don't listen to love songs and whatnot because they upset me a bit. At first – because we used to ring each other unless I was going out – I had to change the times of my meal and that sort of thing, so I wouldn't be waiting for his call. And weekends are rotten because we were always together weekends. But I can feel him with me – even though he's not with me.

He's been dead now over two years, so it's nearly as long as we were together, isn't it? I did keep his diary – I wasn't going to leave it for anyone else to see. And in there, on 16 June, he wrote that we celebrated three years of knowing one another, and he put, 'I wonder what will happen over the next three years. We are both getting rather decrepit!' I thought that was lovely. And he'd put in the dates and times when I'd been there. 'Vera came at four o'clock', and then he'd put when I went. That's nice as well, to read that.

He didn't believe in anything after death and I agreed. I think people live on in the memory of other people. I shall live on because of contacts I've made and he lives on through people he's known. Apart from your own immediate family, that's how you do live on.

It has hurt that I couldn't talk about him to his family, yes it has hurt, that. It hurt a lot at first, then it gradually dims. But I've always got this thing that he died with me and not with them. I think that's partly at the bottom of his son's attitude. Perhaps he blamed me for him dying.

It helps – instead of saying, 'Why did he die and leave me behind?', this sort of thing – I say to myself, 'Well, we shouldn't really have had this wonderful love experience at our age, out of the blue, when he was 78 and I was almost.' It sounds a bit silly. At first, people laughed about it, and then they thought it was nice and lovely and different – well, maybe it isn't different, but you don't hear about it, do you?

I felt it was wonderful to think that maybe elderly people do make love, but they don't talk about it so it's always understood that they don't, that they're past it, that it's too much like hard work. Which it is. I've put on weight since, because I don't get the exercise!

My husband died of a heart attack when I was 56. He was 12 years older. This grief is different from that grief. Because with my husband it was having three children as well, and being married and living together and the lot. Whereas with James it was a straight one-to-one thing more. Before we went on holiday, he said, 'In all my life, I've never known such tenderness as you've shown to me.' It was a lovely thing to say, because he'd had a happy marriage and he'd had children, so it wasn't that he'd had a rough time before. I suppose it was because there were just the two of us, more or less, apart from his daughter. But we hadn't any responsibility.

After my husband died, that's when I started writing, doing a column every week in the local paper. James wrote to me because of a letter I'd sent to the paper, about what we used as toothpaste when we were kids. That's what we had in common. We both came from ordinary working-class families, a similar age and so on. I answered it and we just kept writing about our families, what we did. And he always said, 'Don't stop any of the things you do, never give up anything for me' – and it's paid off, really. Otherwise it would have been a bit deadly. There are a lot of couples, especially if they've been married for years and they always do everything together, and when one of them dies, it's absolutely dreadful.

I miss him more than anybody I've ever known in my life. Before my husband I had a man friend and I used to say he was the love of my life. But James eclipsed it. I used to look at his profile, you know, if he was watching telly, and it just stirred me, physically, like nobody else I've ever seen. It just got my hormones racing. I can still see his profile at the side of me sometimes. I found him very attractive physically. It wasn't one of these things where we just sat reading a book together. It was physical. He had an aura about him.

If you're older, you haven't got the time to get over it and you can't replace them with someone else, either. Whereas if you are younger, there's all your life in front of you and there's more chance of finding someone else and make a similar relationship.

I still can't get over the surprise of the relationship. What's given me comfort is the fact that I am absolutely wonderfully lucky for it to have happened. I'm sure it must have happened to other people, but I don't know of anybody else. That photograph of him that I've got, I took two days before he died, and he's laughing, on the verandah in Italy. I used to talk to him at first, to his photograph. I don't now. But I feel it – on Fridays at half-past-three, when I used to go to his house, I try to be doing other things, like shopping. That bit hurts.

It hasn't got any better so far, no. It still hurts. Like Sundays I do any cleaning that needs to be done, I occupy myself, because I know I would have been with him otherwise. Sunday's not a good day. And there are certain songs I can't listen to. I don't cry normally, but something like that can spark me off. Daft silly love songs.

At first, after he died, I thought if I'd never met him, I would have been spared all this heartache. But that was just the odd thought. It's better to have loved and lost than never to have loved at all.

Richard Scarborough is 42. His partner, Paul, died of an AIDS-related illness eight years ago at the age of 28. He now lives in a platonic relationship with Barbara Law, who was their befriender. She was a volunteer with George House, a charity working with people affected by HIV and AIDS.

Paul and I met when I was just finishing university. I'd done a degree in Sheffield as a mature student and he lived over towards Manchester. He told me he was HIV positive when I met him and I suppose with typical optimism I thought, 'Well, he's only been positive a year or so. He's got another ten years before it even becomes a problem.' But unfortunately he was one of the unlucky ones and he actually started getting ill quite quickly.

After I finished my course, I moved over to Manchester and not long after that I became his carer. He had a stomach bug which meant he had sickness and diarrhoea all the time, so he basically starved to death. But it went on for two years before he died. He had continual sickness and diarrhoea, going into hospital with dehydration, unable to eat, then getting back on his feet again. He had different drug therapies and halfway through them he sometimes came very close to dying, but then he'd bounce back. Then he just went down and down and down.

My relationship with Paul's family was very good. I was one of the lucky ones from that point of view. Whilst Paul was ill and in and out of hospital, I made friends with lots of other people in the same situation. There was another couple who were going through the same as us. Andrew's partner hadn't spoken to his family for something like five years, because they disapproved of his lifestyle, as they put it. But after he died, they actually turned up and took the body. That was the last Andrew saw of his partner, even though they'd lived together and he'd cared for him. He didn't go to the funeral; he didn't even know where it was.

My experience was totally different. I think Paul's family were grateful that I was the one that cared for him. I was existing on just a couple of hours' sleep, because I was up in the night taking him to the toilet with severe diarrhoea. I was as exhausted as it was possible to be.

Friends used to say, 'I don't know how you cope', and I used to want to scream at them, 'Well, we're not coping. Perhaps we would if you turned up and did something.' But most of the friends couldn't cope with seeing one of their peers dying – he was only 28 – and there were quite a few people who we didn't see for the last few months of his life.

Paul talked about death very openly. We used to laugh and joke about it. I used to go to a support group and I remember conversations like, 'I wish he'd hurry up and die. It's about time.' Things that you couldn't say to anybody else.

When I look back, I can't believe that I coped with the dying, let alone the death. While it was happening, I would've said that death couldn't be worse than coping with the caring. I thought I'd done the grieving before he'd died, but it wasn't true at all.

He died at home in our bed with me there by his side. All I remember at that time was feeling exceptionally tired, almost like I'd done a massive walk or something. Unbelievably tired and not just physically, but emotionally and mentally. But it was only tiredness that I felt. Nothing much else.

After a few weeks I went back to work, but I actually didn't do any work. I just got up in the morning, got dressed, went in, sat at my desk, did nothing, they said nothing and I came home again. I really did not do anything at all, because I was just incapable of doing it.

My parents didn't come to the funeral. There's always been this tacit agreement that my sexuality isn't mentioned. They knew I lived with Paul, but we spoke about 'my friend Paul'. They'd met him, but they would never refer to him as my partner. I rang my mum to tell her that he'd died and she was in tears and distraught, but I think that was because I was upset. She'd just had a cataract operation and couldn't travel so that was the reason for not coming to the funeral, but they didn't even send flowers and I still feel really angry about that. I've never forgiven them for not at least sending some flowers. If Paul had been my wife, it would definitely have been different.

My sister, who lives in Greece, didn't come to the funeral, either. She actually asked me to buy some flowers from her, which I did, but she's never paid for them. I know it's stupid, but it's something that's always going to be there. I'm never going to mention it to her, but it's always going to be there.

I live with Barbara now. She used to be our befriender and she probably saved my life. We live together as friends, but to anybody outside they would think we're a married couple. We do everything together – we own the house together, we pool all our resources and since we've lived together, I haven't seen my parents without Barbara being there. If I visit, she goes as well. We do everything as a couple. I'm sure if Barbara died, they'd be over here like a shot, because they see her as my partner.

I don't know what they think, but they know we have separate bedrooms. They, like everybody else, can make their own minds up. I don't really care. One of the results of Paul's death is that I don't give a toss about most things now.

I think when somebody dies, you realise we're all going to die sometime, so you can actually do what you want. I can be bloody rude to people, but before I would probably have been mortified at the thought of upsetting somebody. I remember once being out with Barbara and this guy who I had once worked with came and talked to me. I just simply didn't have the patience to talk to him. He kept saying, 'I must be going. I must be going.' Eventually I just turned to him and said, 'I really do think you ought to go, because you're boring me now.' Barbara was mortified.

I think it's made me realise in some respects how fragile a person I can be. I went from being a gregarious person to someone who couldn't bear to be with other people, except for strangers. I could sit with any complete stranger and chat to them. But I couldn't bear the thought of being anywhere near people that knew me. If I was in a bar and somebody I knew walked in, I walked out. I couldn't bear the look on people's faces when they saw me. I couldn't bear the fact that I looked absolutely shit and I only knew that by looking at their faces.

I got out of bed some time in the afternoon, dressed, left the house and then I stopped out till the last pub or club closed. I didn't eat much, so I wasn't really looking after myself. I lost a hell of a lot of weight. Now given that my partner had basically starved to death and the symptom of people being HIV is being skinny, I don't think it was very kind on my friends.

When Paul died, from that point on all I wanted was to die. I didn't realise how bad I was until I got a letter from the benefits people asking me to come in for an interview. I sauntered off to the local Job Centre thinking we'd just have a chat. I was totally unconcerned until they called my number and I started walking towards this woman at the desk and it suddenly occurred to me that I was about to crack up. All I said to her was, 'Is there a private room?' I just felt myself collapsing on the spot – absolutely imploding.

I'd had nights of crying my eyes out – all those sorts of things – but this was a collapse. I suddenly realised I dreaded the phone ringing. I couldn't cope if it rang, because I'd have to speak to the person at the other end and they may ask me to do something like, 'Do you want to go out for a drink?' And I wouldn't be able to give a reasonable explanation for why I really couldn't. I could cope with absolutely nothing.

I was exceptionally lucky because the woman [at the Job Centre] had just started work there and her previous job was as a counsellor, so I hit the jackpot. She knew exactly what was going off and she was absolutely brilliant.

In any relationship you're defined by other people, so you are the son of, the daughter of, the husband of, the partner of, and you lose some of your identity. In a gay partnership, for you, it's like losing your limb, but for other people the relationship never existed in the first place. But also, there were a lot of people dying of AIDS then, so from other gay people you got, 'Well, you were lucky. At least you had somebody and you had a relationship.' There was also, 'But loads of people die. Get on with it. I know somebody who's lost three partners.' Or, 'We don't want to talk about AIDS and acknowledge it, because, if I do talk about it, I have to admit that this could be me.' I think that's why I virtually never saw any of Paul's friends again after that. They didn't want to acknowledge that what happened to Paul could very easily happen to them.

Even people who seem to be quite 'PC' about it still don't see it as a proper relationship. Maybe it's similar to people who feel that with a girl- and a boyfriend, if there's a death, somehow they'd be treated differently if they were married. But in our few years together, particularly with the intensity of the caring – and we spent every minute of the day together – that consumes my whole life and I can't see that loss being any less than if we'd been together 70 years.

I've had one relationship since Paul with another man. That lasted just a matter of weeks, because I knew I could not forgive him for not being Paul and I had to end it because I knew it wasn't fair on him. I haven't had another relationship since and I think it's unlikely I ever will. I just can't bear being without Paul.

If either my mother or my father dies – and they're both now in their late seventies or early eighties – I can't imagine that it could possibly be worse for either of them losing the other than it was for me to lose Paul. They would never, ever understand that.

Jane Shepherd met Sam at a personal development workshop in February 1998. He was 42, she was 44. They were together for just over a year, until June 1999, when Sam took his own life with an overdose of drink and prescription drugs.

I'd had bits of flings and holiday romances, but for whatever reason, at 44 I'd never really had a proper boyfriend. I'd kind of given up really.

I met Sam on one of these personal development weekends and it was love at first sight. I did think, 'Oh, he looks dangerous.' He was covered in tattoos, six foot two, very well built and muscular and this No.1 haircut. I ended up sitting next to him and he was just amazing.

Within ten or 15 minutes, we'd swapped our life stories. He told me he was widowed – in actual fact, they weren't married. His former partner, Debbie, had died in tragic circumstances, he was one of four children and his other siblings had all died in tragic circumstances – a sister had died at two, a brother had died of complications following flu, another brother had had a brain haemorrhage on a building site and had fallen off the scaffolding and died – just unbelievable. Also Sam had been in the Army, done two tours of duty in Northern Ireland and seen some of his friends blown up in front of him. So he'd had this really tough life.

There was just this immediate connection. I felt he was looking right into my soul. And I remember thinking, 'This is what it must be like when people say love at first sight.'

We had to do these different exercises on the course, in pairs, like a sort of Reiki, putting hands on someone else's shoulders. You had to look for a partner and we did it together. But he said, 'I can't bear to be touched', so I said, 'I'll just put my hands above your shoulders and I'll hover.' Afterwards, I said, 'Was that all right?' And he said, 'Yeah, it's less bovver with a hover.' That was the thing – he was just so funny.

The very first thing, when we had to get up and move about the floor, and my sticks were on the floor [Jane contracted polio when she was five months old and now walks with calipers and sticks] – he leaned down and picked them up for me. And I thought, 'Bloody hell! He's kind, he's funny, he's bright, he's sensitive and caring – blimey!' So that was it really. Oh, and he kissed my hand – I gave him a lift to the bus station and he kissed my hand.

I met him on 7 February 1998 and he died on 22 June 1999, so I didn't know him long really at all. It was very brief but very intense, and some people go through their whole lives and don't have that. But sometimes it's difficult to keep that in your mind.

That first day I met him, he told me he had been drink dependent and seven months before he had attempted an overdose. He thought he'd taken enough to kill an elephant, but he woke up the next day.

I think he'd made a decision, long before he even met me, that that would be what he would do. Because Debbie, his previous partner, had died in tragic circumstances in the hospital, and he was fighting on behalf of her family to get some kind of redress for that.

The conference with the barrister was coming up and it was a very big deal for him. I did my best to support him in it, but he'd told me that if he couldn't get justice for Debbie, he didn't know what he'd do. I think he knew exactly what he'd do, but he wasn't telling me. Then, when the barrister said they hadn't got a case, I think he decided that was it.

We'd spent a wonderful weekend with Debbie's family in Liverpool and then I had this phone call from Debbie's sister's partner. He rang up and said, 'Sam's been found dead. It looks like suicide to me. He's taken tablets and drunk vodka.'

His mum said, 'No, he had his bag packed to come over to you.' She kept saying it wasn't intentional. I'd have been better thinking from the start that he did intend to take his own life, because that was in the June and the inquest wasn't until the November, and you know how you believe what you want to believe? Well, I was believing it wasn't intentional and then it all comes out at the inquest – and that was horrific, actually, because he'd crushed up tablets between two spoons, and put them into this glass and drunk them like that.

So then you've got to try and make sense of it and come to terms with the fact that he has left you. And that is difficult, when someone has taken their own life. He didn't leave a note or anything. It's very easy to go down the route of, – 'Well, it doesn't say much about me, does it? If I was so marvellous, why did he leave me like that?' Because he always used to say, 'I'd never do anything to hurt you.' But I can see that he was in such turmoil, he probably thought I would be better off without him. And there was also a sense that he probably had decided before he even met me that that would be his course of action. He was a very resolute person.

Then you get the guilt – 'I should have gone over' – but I try not to beat myself up too much about it. It's not healthy or helpful. He'd set his stall out ages before he met me. And that weekend, we'd had such a brilliant time, it was the best weekend ever. When I left on the Monday to come back here, he got really upset – he was emotional anyway – but he was really upset and crying. And – you know how you get these feelings? Well, as I left his flat, and he was standing there, I thought I might never see him again. I actually had a premonition.

I was angry in a way. You think, 'You've left me to deal with all this.' It wasn't just about Sam and the fact he died in the way he died, it's the overall sense of being cheated. That I waited until I was 44 to meet him and then 15 months later he's dead. So I think, 'What have I done to deserve this?' Then I try and turn it round and think, 'Well, there must be a lesson in this.' And some people go through their whole life and don't have a relationship like that.

When it's the right person, you put up with a lot, don't you? I mean, if you'd told me that I'd fall in love with an alcoholic who was covered in tattoos and who wasn't working, an unemployed scouser with a drink problem – I was telling that to a friend, and she said, 'You really know how to sell someone, don't you, Jane!' On the face of it, it's not that appealing, but...

My mum wasn't so bothered about the drinking or the fact that he wasn't working, but she wasn't keen on the tattoos. She said, 'Can't he get rid of them?' But he was very proud of them. I said, 'Look Mum, I've looked beyond the tattoos and he's looked beyond the calipers.' And she went, 'Yes, you're right.'

It did me good, in that he made me feel beautiful. He showed me that I am lovable and desirable, which I'd had doubts about before because, frankly, you think, 'Well, if I'm so bloody marvellous, why am I still on my own?'

One thing that helped was writing our story. I started writing it when he unplugged the phone [a few days before he died], in the form of a letter to him – which was never sent. I was bloody angry – I was saying, 'Nobody could have been more supportive to you than I was.' But I don't think anyone could have stopped him.

But my friends have been great. My friend Stephanie was really support-ive. She wrote a poem:

> 45 and never been kissed
> Least not
> By a real man
>
> One who understands...
> Despair

A Man
Who wants to hold her hand
And walk as lovers do
Reaches out
to touch Jane's pain
And buoyed by her angel from the North
The one walking-stick
Will do

Because he'd said, could I manage with one stick, because then we could hold hands and then he'd feel he was really going out with me. And I thought, 'I'm 45 and no one's ever wanted to hold my hand.' You know, I was going through at 45 what I should probably have been going through at 15. And when you do get to 44 and it's not happened, you think it's not going to. But it has.

As I get older, I find I have more empathy with people who've suffered, and that's what Sam said. When I met him that first day, we had to write down the negative messages people had given us over the years. Most of the things I wrote down were things like, 'You're so fat.' When I read them out to Sam, he said, 'I am appalled. You are not fat.' I said, 'Yes I am, I'm a size 20.' He said, 'When you walked in this morning, I didn't think, "Oh, she's fat". I looked at you and saw your smiling face, and I just thought, "That lady has suffered".'

He taught me a lot, about all sorts of things. Chiefly about how to be a human being. I think about him every day.

He had so many talents: he was a wonderful cook, he was musical, had a wonderful voice, taught himself to play instruments, he could draw, paint, pretty much do anything – all that talent gone to waste. And kindness, in this cruel world we live in. Trying to make sense out of that is quite a challenge.

CHAPTER 10

Grandparents

Connie Ainsworth's granddaughter, Amy, was diagnosed with the genetic condition Batten's disease when she was two. Her parents, Connie's daughter, Debbie, and son-in-law, Stephen, were told she might survive until she was five, but she died in 2002, aged nine. Batten's disease is a genetic condition which causes loss of muscle control, and eventually blindness and deafness.

We were devastated when the hospital told us Amy had this genetic disorder. We just hugged each other – the four of us: me, my husband, Debbie and Stephen. The thing with grandparents is you've got to be strong for the parents. When Debbie cried, I cried; when she was up, I was up.

My husband and I were never away from the house. Every night we'd go down to see Amy. It was hard because sometimes Debbie used to get upset if I spoke about it, but I think it depended on the mood she was in. While I was with Amy, I was all right because I was nursing her and loving her. The problem is when you leave them. I used to come home and do nothing but cry – sit on the bed and cry.

I've got daughters-in-law and it isn't that they didn't care, but they were afraid of going to see Amy. They used to go at Christmas and her birthday and take her a present, but I don't think they went much in between times. I think it was because they got upset. I know they cared. One of them cried buckets when Amy died, but as a grandma I felt they should go all the time.

I used to look at Amy and think, 'I can't believe I'm only going to have you until you're five or six.' So many times we thought we were going to lose her. We've sat hours and hours in the hospital. She developed pneumonia and she was very poorly. I remember the paediatrician asking us did we want to hold her, because he didn't expect her to last the night out. But she lived another three or four years after that.

When it did happen, we didn't expect it. She'd had a really good day the day before. My husband and I were up at our caravan when we heard the news. Amy was in the hospice and Debbie was going to pick her up that morning, but they phoned her and told her she'd just gone to sleep. I was up at the caravan and Debbie rang us up and she said, 'Mum, she's gone.' I just screamed and the lady in the next caravan heard me and she knew.

I lost a little boy myself. He was five. So I know what it's like to lose a child. Debbie could never say to me, 'Mum you don't understand.' I *did* understand, because I'd been through it all myself. I was only 25 when I lost Stephen. That was an accident. He fell in the canal and drowned. I couldn't do anything for Stephen. I didn't even have the chance to say goodbye to him. But with Amy I had time to spend with her. I just wanted to be with her all the time. I felt I did for Amy what I wanted to do for my own child.

Sometimes I'd go to talk to Debbie, but after she lost Amy she didn't want to talk about it to me. Maybe she couldn't say to me what she wanted to say in case she hurt me. I just couldn't get near and I resented the fact that it was friends she spoke to and not family. She had a friend who only lived up the road from her and she did her crying there. But I wanted to be the one to console my daughter. I wanted to put my arms round her and cry on her shoulder and say, 'I know exactly how you feel.' I felt as if I'd lost her for a while and that I was grieving on my own.

Debbie was really poorly after losing Amy. She was so depressed, she just wanted to sleep and she didn't want to live. She said, 'We won't see Amy getting married. We won't see her having children.' Those are all things I'll miss out on. I'd have liked her to have said 'Nana' like the other grandchildren, but she never did.

I feel as if I've lost something that I'll never get back. When I go down to Debbie's I look for her. I still think when I walk through that door I'm going to see her. She's going to be lying down on that settee like she always was.

Her quality of life wasn't good, but she was loved – she was loved so much. I couldn't have done any more. You never expect to lose your grandchild. I don't think I've ever got over it. I've never been the same since Amy died. It's like your world's come to an end when you lose your grandchild.

Rose Dixon's younger daughter, Penny, and her husband, Paul, have two children, Joshua and Zoe. Their third child, also called Paul, died a few weeks after birth in 1997. Rose's elder daughter, Avril, died aged 22 in 1991 and Rose talks about that loss in Chapter 1: Mothers.

When Zoe was about 15 months old, Penny and her husband were here with the children and I remember her saying, 'Mum, I think I'm pregnant.' I knew she'd had the coil fitted so I said, 'Don't be so stupid, you can't be.' But she was. They tried to remove the coil, but they couldn't get it out, so the doctor said, 'Don't worry about it. When the baby's born, it'll probably have it in its hand. They often do.'

She wasn't terribly well through the pregnancy and obviously I was like a raving lunatic, because I'm seeing Avril going to happen all over again. Then when she was about 20 weeks pregnant, she contacted me and said she was very shivery so I said, 'Get the doctor immediately'. The doctor said she was OK, but shortly after that she was admitted to a small hospital in Birmingham.

They thought she had an infection in her womb caused by the coil, so they put her on intravenous antibiotics and they were hoping against hope that it would make everything settle down. Shortly after, I had a phone call to say she was in labour.

The hospital had no intensive care cots, so they decided to transfer her to a hospital in Staffordshire. She was put in an ambulance with an obstetrician to look after her and a paediatrician to look after the baby if it was born *en route*, and two midwives. There were so many people in the ambulance that her husband couldn't get in, so he was driving behind.

It was the day the IRA said they'd planted a bomb on the M6, so the motorway was closed and all the traffic was on the ordinary roads. I believe she had eight motorcycle policemen trying to clear the route, but one of them radioed to say, 'We can't get through the traffic. Open the motorway.' That evening on the national news they showed the M6 motorway completely empty except for this ambulance with a police escort. That was Penny.

I sat there in the evening, looking at the clock. I think it was about half past seven and I became aware that my knees were shaking. I tried to stand up, but I couldn't and I remember thinking, 'She's going to die.' I was saying,

'Please, God, don't let her die. I can't lose another one.' I knew in that moment she was very close to death.

About an hour later her husband rang and he said, 'Penny's had the baby. He weighs one pound 12 ounces and he's in an incubator.' I said, 'How's Penny?' And Paul said, 'She's OK now. She collapsed. I've never been so frightened. She went blue and the doctor actually said to me, "Your wife or your baby? You can't have both. Quick! Make a decision." And I said, "My wife. I've got two other children. They need their mother."'

As soon as the baby was born, he was taken to intensive care. He was on a ventilator and his little eyelids hadn't opened – they were fused together. I remember sitting next day with Penny and she was stroking the baby. You could only stroke him with your finger, he was so tiny.

They were absolutely wonderful in the hospital. I've never met such lovely people. I was included in everything. Penny had obviously told them about Avril. They were very, very concerned for me. But a few weeks later they transferred the baby back to hospital in Birmingham and I was treated appallingly there. Penny and Paul were considered, but I was ignored. It was as if I was a nuisance. Nobody acknowledged that, as the grandmother of this child, I had any needs at all. They'd barely speak to me.

The baby was doing so well that he was moved from intensive care to high dependency and he was off the ventilator. But then we got a phone call to say that he'd been moved back to intensive care. We were never really told what had happened. He had a problem with his bowel and gradually he seemed to deteriorate.

Penny, Paul and I were called into the office with the consultant and he said the baby had had a haemorrhage in his brain. They'd done a scan and said that, if he lived, he'd be severely handicapped. They wanted to turn the ventilator off. I was in a terribly difficult position, because I wasn't the next-of-kin, but I wanted to say, 'No, you can't do this! I'm not allowing you to do it!' But, of course, I couldn't. It was like trying to walk a tightrope.

Paul and Penny said they didn't want the ventilator turned off, either, but the consultant said they would turn it off the following day. Paul said, 'Over my dead body.' But the consultant said, 'We have to turn the ventilator off and let this baby die. There's nothing we can do and we need the intensive care cot for another baby.' But Paul said, 'It's my wife's birthday tomorrow and if you think you're killing her baby on her birthday, forget it.'

The next day was Thursday and the agreement was they would leave it till the day after her birthday, so on the Friday I went down and went in to see the baby and say goodbye to him. I left and Penny and Paul were there. The consultant was coming at 12 noon to turn the ventilator off.

I believe they turned it off at 12.30 lunchtime and we were told that the baby would be dead within two minutes to two hours at the most. About seven o'clock I rang the hospital and said, 'What time did Penny and Paul leave?' and the nurse said, 'They haven't left. The baby's still alive.' So I waited and waited and about 11 o'clock I rang again and they said, 'The baby's still alive.'

They put Penny and Paul in a side room that had a double bed in it and they'd sat there all day with the baby. About ten past 12, Penny rang me and said, 'Mum, he won't die. We're going to stay the night with him.' So they slept in the double bed in the clothes they stood up in with the baby in a Moses basket between them.

The next morning Penny rang me and said, 'We feel dirty and smelly. Will you come and mind him while we come home and have a shower and change our clothes. Then we'll come back. I don't want to leave him on his own in case he dies. I don't want him to die on his own.' I got there about 20 past ten and I just sat with the baby, cuddling him. Then just gone half eleven, he just died in my arms.

It was just like nightmare number two, just like after Avril had died, undertakers and everything. It was so hard watching my daughter grieving for this baby. You almost put your grief on hold as a grandparent, because you have to support your child. I think the hardest thing for me was that my husband never saw that baby. He wouldn't go and see him. He said, 'It will kill me if I see this child. As long as I don't see him, he's not real. If I see him and he dies, I can't do it.'

When he did eventually die, it was so hard. I am grieving – I'm torn apart – because my grandchild is dead, but I'm also grieving and torn apart because my child is hurting and going through what I went through. If I had just been a bereaved grandmother, I'd have been grieving terribly for this little baby and for my daughter's grief at losing her child, but it was this knowledge that I had in my heart for how it feels to lose a child. Knowing she was going through that was like being doubly crucified.

I felt that the death of my parents was very much the death of my past and my childhood. I think that the death of my husband – if it happens when I'm still alive – I see that as the death of the present. My present way of life would have to change, because we'd no longer be a couple and I'd be on my own. But I see the death of my child and my grandchild as the death of my future.

J oe and Iris Lawley's daughter, Lisa, gave birth to her first child who was stillborn. Thirty years before, their 12-year-old son, Kenneth, was killed riding his bicycle to school. They talked about the experience together at their home in Nuneaton. Joe and Iris are founding members of The Compassionate Friends which supports bereaved parents. They have two surviving children: Angela was 14 when Kenneth died and Lisa was born almost two years after his death. Joe talks about the experience of losing Kenneth in Chapter 2: Fathers.

Iris: Lisa had an accident when she was three months pregnant. Her car was struck by another car. We took her to hospital and they just said, 'No problem.' There was a slight tear in the placenta, but they said that was nothing and if she didn't lose the baby within the week she would carry on as normal. The consultant never even examined her.

Through the whole pregnancy she was swollen up like a whale and her feet were huge. She was a very slim girl and I kept on and on about it, saying, 'What is the midwife thinking?' I was thinking of pre-eclampsia.

In the end she was 15 days overdue, and she came home and said to her dad, 'I've not felt the baby move. Will you come with me to the hospital?' So off they went. They put her on the monitor and left the room. Joe saw this instrument thwacking back and forward, but they had no idea what it meant.

That night she went into labour. I'd taken her to the hospital that morning and I said to the doctor, 'What about this swelling?' and he said, 'Oh, we don't worry about that' and they sent her home. But later she said, 'Oh, the baby's really going mad.' Well, that was the baby dying, fighting for her breath.

That night Lisa was having pains every four minutes. She had a bath and when she got out, she was vomiting, then she collapsed on the floor. Her husband rang the hospital and they said that was normal. In the end her husband took her in and a young girl came to examine her. She said, 'The baby's dead.'

It was just horrendous. It was like going back to Kenneth again, yet it was my child going through this and I didn't know what to do. They shunted us into a room and our other daughter, Angela, came, Lisa's in-laws came and we were in this room the whole day. We kept pleading for them to operate. I really thought we were going to lose her as well as the baby.

So about five o'clock at night they eventually took her to theatre, started to operate without any anaesthetic. They thought the earlier epidural from seven o'clock in the morning would still be effective and she went into shock and I really thought she would die. But she didn't.

Joe: We were able to hold this beautiful child and look at her. And she was perfect, yet she was dead. She couldn't open her eyes, she didn't breathe. And yet you would hold her against you and she was still warm.

Iris: Her little hands went round yours.

Joe: And you think, 'Oh, my God! How is this? What is the life thing that's not there in her?'

Iris: When it's your child you want to take the pain away. Like when they fall over and get hurt, you kiss them better and you never want them to be hurt. And after losing Kenneth, I never wanted anything to happen to them. You're actually overprotective. I was with Lisa. And here she is, going through this and there's nothing I can do. Just be there for her and love her.

But, you see, she needed someone in the same position as her. Another mother.

Joe: I felt very much this inability to do anything other than put our arms round her and try not to be saying to her the things that people had said to us, like, 'You'll be all right. You're still young. You'll have other babies.' Nothing like that. To try and be with her in the grief.

Iris: [While Lisa was pregnant they'd called the baby 'Buttercup'.] I think of her as much as I think of Kenneth and I miss her. Lisa has two other beautiful little girls now and when they come – Buttercup's two little sisters – I think she should be here, too, and we're always saying she would be at school now, she'd be doing this, she'd be doing that. You miss them terribly.

Joe: It's a two-staged grief when you're a grandparent. You're grieving for your own child, because you know she's going through what you went through, and you're also grieving for this beautiful child – your grandchild.

CHAPTER 11

Grandchildren

Amy Ahmad is seven. Her Pakistani grandfather died when she was five. He was her father's father and he lived in London. Amy lives in Lancashire with her parents and her younger sister, Emily, and brother, Leo.

We used to call him Grandad Munir and I remember he was really kind to us. When he went to visit the family in Pakistan he always brought us something back, like a teddy bear or pictures. Once he brought back this toy house with lots of little dolls in it. He used to play with us quite a lot. He used to have dominoes and he bought us this paint set. I think of him when I play with it. And he made me laugh, because he sat on the bed and told us jokes.

I think he got cancer. I went to the funeral. I saw them putting him in the coffin. Then we went to a house where we all said goodbye to Grandad Munir and they put him in the car. Then we went to put him in the grave. At the end we got a drink and biscuit.

I remember I wore a white dress with lots of pink flowers on. I've still got it now and I still wear it. That day was really, really special to me and I thought it was a really special dress to wear. I think children should go to the funeral, because they've at least said goodbye and been there for the person.

Once I came home and Mummy and Emily were crying thinking about Grandad Munir. Emily was really sad because Grandad Munir never got to see Leo. That's my new brother. Emily and I talk about it. We just think about lots of different things and we remember the happy times.

I knew that he was really close by to us because whenever we were at home – this was after he died – I knew he was really close by. His feelings were landing on me and Emily in our house. It's like an invisible person by

your side. It makes me feel much happier because I know I've got someone
there with me when I feel scared and alone. It's like he's watching over me
when I want him to be there and need him.

M atthew Douglas is 17 and his grandmother, Bernie, died when
he was 15. Matthew's grandparents emigrated from Lancashire to
Canada when his mother was five and, when his parents divorced,
Matthew and his mother moved in with her parents. The whole
family came back to England when Matthew was four.

I saw my grandma as kind of an anchor of normality. No matter how crazy
things were, Grandma would always be the same. She'd have a smile on her
face and a cigarette in her hand. It was a bizarre bond, really, because I'm
close to Mum, but I would say I was closer to my grandma. When I was five
or six maybe, I was calling my mum 'Grandma' and my grandma 'Mum'.
Mum used to get pretty ticked off about it.

When we came back from Canada, we used to live on a caravan site and
Mum had to work long hours just to keep us going and I used to stop with
my grandma in the caravan next door. And every Sunday I used to have my
breakfast with my grandma and grandad.

My gran was a very cuddly person. I always knew if I needed to talk to
somebody, Grandma was there. Mum isn't the first person I'd go to. I was the
only grandchild – I *am* the only grandchild – and I was special. Because they
only had one daughter and one grandchild, both me and my mother were
smothered by Grandma. I used to get everything I wanted. She used to make
the best coffee as well. She knew exactly how I like it: with whole milk and
four sugars, so it's really sweet and creamy with a bit of coffee at the bottom.
It was fabulous.

In the four months up to her going into hospital she was always in bed
and I found that rather confusing really, because I didn't understand why she
was in bed. I used to go home and say to my mum, 'Grandma's ill again.'
Nobody seemed to know what was wrong with her.

I think she knew that whatever was wrong wasn't a small thing.
Thinking back now – it might sound a bit odd – but I think she knew she
was going to die. I think she thought it was cancer and she wanted to die at
home. That's why she was so damn adamant that she wasn't going to go to
the doctor or the hospital.

She did go to the doctor's in the end and she had a blood test. Then a few hours after that we got a phone call saying, 'Please can you come to the hospital.' They'd obviously found something that was wrong, but it wasn't cancer. It was her kidneys and they also found that she had pancreatitis [an inflammatory disorder of the pancreas].

I just dismissed it really. It was just Grandma. She's tough as nails. Everybody in my family is tough as nails. We're all supposed to be 'hard'. That's what I always thought, anyway. I remember having an argument with my mum. We'd both had a drink and Mum got rather emotional, because I hadn't started crying. That's because I wasn't willing to accept that my grandma was going to die – ever.

In the last week she was looking dreadful and I realised she might die. She didn't make much sense really and it was kind of upsetting. Then they made the decision to turn off the life support machine. It was either fend for herself or she was going to die, but we knew there was no way she was going to fend for herself.

The day she died, everybody was there: me, Grandma's sister Irene, Irene's husband, Grandad, Mum and Mum's boyfriend. Everybody who should've been there was there, but when you're seeing your grandma struggling to breathe it was just horrible and I didn't want to remember her like that. It's a good job I have so many photographs otherwise I'd probably burst out crying now.

I found going for walks helpful. I used to say I was going out with my mates, but I wasn't. I was going by myself and I was walking over the tops above the town, just sitting in the pine trees and thinking.

I hang around in a close-knit family of friends. There are four of us and we're like brothers. We would never judge each other and if I want to burst out crying I know that they're not going to judge me in any way. I have cried with them. Only one of them has lost anybody close and he kind of knew what I was going through.

I wanted things to go back to normal, but when people are trying to be nice round you it kind of bugs you, because it's just reminding you that there's something wrong in your life and you're missing something.

I'm a very open person, but I would rather curl up in a ball with myself and say, 'That's that. I'll try to find something to anchor myself to, to make things feel normal again.' So I did. I've become a lot closer to my grandad, because he was very upset and he used to cry all the time about it. He still does, sometimes. So me and him now are like best friends in a way. I still go and have lunch every so often on a Sunday and we go to the pub together. I walk in with my spiked hair and my trainers and he walks in with his blazer and everyone stares at us. Yeah, me and Grandad are good friends – better friends than before. It's the only positive thing that has come out of losing Grandma.

A grandparent is different from your parent, because your parents shout at you all the time. It's their job. It's quite amusing, because you know if it was the opposite way round and she was your mother, she'd be shouting at you. There is a bond there. It's the only loss I've experienced really, apart from a friend that got knocked over, but I was only about nine and it wasn't the same. I'd probably think differently if I lost one of my friends now.

I think people do underestimate the grief of grandchildren. It's often the first death and you can be very, very close and you always think they're going to be there, but they're not and you have to try and cling onto something else then.

I used to believe in something after death, but now I don't. Her death changed my view. I thought, 'If there's a God, why would they let somebody die in such a horrible way?' I believe that the only thing that we have left of her are pictures and your own personal view of what the person was like. I know that I've got everything to remember Grandma in here: in my heart and in my mind – and in photographs of her when she was well and happy. Providing I don't lose those, I don't lose the feelings, and she's with me.

Michael Jackson was 14 when his grandmother died. He is now 21. His father, Gerald, tells his story in Chapter 4: Sons.

My grandmother had a wacky dress sense. She was the kind of person who, if you saw her walking down the street, would always have that extra thing on that people wouldn't think about wearing. She had thousands of hats and always had a lot of make-up on.

The night she died, she was cooking a meal for me and my dad, and all of a sudden she said she felt a bit dizzy and I told her to sit down. My dad was trying to get an ambulance and she was saying, 'No, no, no, I'm fine.' But things just went worse. The ambulance took her to hospital and I jumped in the car with my dad and followed it.

I felt really bad inside, but what really worried me was my dad's reaction, because he was really close to her. He's a bit of a soft person anyway. He cries at the world's worst movie. But even when we were just waiting to find out what was wrong, I could tell he was upset and worried. Then when she died, it got really bad. I didn't think he'd ever get over it and it wasn't easy for me because it's the first close death I've experienced.

I remember the funeral and it was just horrible – the whole day. Seeing my dad so upset and it was pouring down with rain and it was on the top of a hill, really windy. I remember we all had to shovel some mud – all the grand-children had to do it. It was really bad.

You usually lean on your parents and they're usually your support when you're hurt, but to see them hurt is difficult. It really upsets you. I try and comfort Dad if he gets upset, but it's a funny situation. You can't shout at him to get on with it. I was bad as well, because when he got upset, I got upset, then he was trying to comfort me. It was just a vicious circle. It seemed to be years of crying all the time. I felt it just couldn't get any worse.

At first he couldn't bear to go down to the house to sort out her posses-sions, taking all the ornaments down and packing them up. From what I remember it was a year or maybe two years before he'd go down and empty the house out. But when he finally did sort all my gran's stuff out, I think that was a big stepping stone for him.

Allan Struthers is ten. His paternal grandfather died before he was born. His maternal grandfather died 18 months ago.

My father's father died two years before I was born, but my dad has told me loads about him. We call him 'Uppa' because that's German for 'Grandad'. He wasn't German – he was Scottish – but my Grandma was, so I call her 'Omi' and Grandad 'Uppa.'

My dad told me he supported Glasgow Rangers and he was very funny. When he was at school he always made a joke out of everything. He used to tell the oldest joke in the book, 'My dog's got no nose. How does he smell? Terrible.' When anyone tells that joke, I think of him. Sometimes I feel like I am him, because I'm funny and that's what he was like.

It seems weird that he died before me and I haven't seen him, but it's like I have, because I know so much about him and I've still got one of his pipes that he used to smoke in the study. Also I've seen him in photographs, so I've seen him in loads of different places. I know he had a Ford Anglia and drove around all Europe. He went to the Swiss Alps and Lakes quite a lot. I'll look at the picture and that shows me exactly what he was like. He had black hair and his name was the same as mine. That's why I was called 'Allan.'

My other grandfather – my mum's dad – died about a year ago. He was a really good artist and I've got his old cartoon book, because he cut out all the cartoons he did for newspapers and stuck them in a book. I've got that now and I was reading it last night. There was one that made me laugh a lot. It was a picture of a man and – you know how they walk along the edge of a building and jump off because they don't like their life? Well, he's doing that. He's in mid-air and there's a woman in his office with a phone in her hand, looking down at him and saying, 'It's your wife. You've just won the pools!' That's just one of them. There's loads and loads of them in there.

I remember his smile because he always used to smile a lot and laugh. He was really kind. We used to visit my grandma and him a lot. He liked playing with me. When I was little – about six – I was always asking him to come and play football with me in the garden. He came out in his slippers. He knocked the ball around with me. I always seemed to beat him.

We played a lot of board games like Monopoly and Rat Race, and I played card games with him and my grandma. There's one card game that went on for ever and ever and ever called War. If you draw the same card, you say, 'War!', put another card face down above it and then draw your card face up and whoever wins that gets all the cards that are there on the table.

He had a couple of heart attacks. He stayed alive and then he just died. I think it was a stroke. I went to visit him in hospital. My mum always went down to the cafeteria – I don't know why – and bought some chips. And I was sat there offering him some chips – 'Do you want a chip, Grandad?' It took him ages to eat it, though. He changed a lot when he was ill. I was very sad, because I thought he was going to die and he did. I think he was 72.

I had sleepless nights knowing I'd never see him again. You can tell young children like my little sister a story that's not as upsetting, like Grandad's gone away forever. Not like – he's just dead. I felt extremely sad, because I was crying in the night. I used to think about his smile. There wasn't anything bad about him.

I went to the funeral at the cemetery. At one point they were going to leave my sister, Rachel, behind, but I said that she should come because she has a right to. I just knew how she felt. If your grandad dies, it's a big thing, isn't it? It's a really big thing. The kids want to see their grandad for the last time. It's like showing him you really love him. Sometimes adults don't understand that.

Grandparents are more playful than parents. You say, 'Do you want to play a game, Dad?' 'No, I've got work. I've got to do this – and that.' With old folks, it's, 'Oh, yes, of course, I'd love to play a game with you.' My dad offers to play games with me sometimes, but not as much as my grandma and grandad did.

They always took me to the cinema and I watched lots of films with them. They enjoy it too, because they enjoy their grandchildren being happy and the grandchildren enjoy them being happy. I don't remember anything bad about them. I don't think they ever have done anything bad.

I miss my grandad a lot. I won't be able to tell him I graduated or I get a new job or something really important. I'd tell him that the local football club won a match on Sunday and I nearly scored a goal. I would have told him all the really important things.

CHAPTER 12

Friends

Debbie Barton met her friend, Ian Matthews, when they were students at Liverpool University. They were part of a large group of friends who met in their first year. Ian married Kate, another member of the group, and they had two children. In 2002 he committed suicide. He was 38.

[The names in this interview have been changed.]

Ian and I met in our very first week at university. He was a medical student. There must've been about 20 of us who were really good friends and in my last year we all lived in a couple of houses near each other. I used to share a house with a girl called Kate, who was also a medic. We were all so close, because we used to see each other every day, right through university.

Over the years quite a few of the group became couples. Kate married Ian and I married one of the other medical students, Peter. People moved all over the country, so we didn't keep in touch that much, but we did see each other at weddings and christenings.

We hadn't seen Ian and Kate for probably about 12 months and then we just got a phone call one evening from another friend, to say that Ian had died. It was a big shock, because he was only 38. I immediately thought he'd had a car accident. But, no. He'd killed himself.

He was a consultant anaesthetist, so he was able to get hold of these drugs, lock himself in an 'on call' room in the hospital and shoot up with whatever it was he took. They broke the door down eventually and he was found dead. He knew what to do to make certain he'd succeed.

When we spoke to Kate, she knew that he'd been depressed and apparently – none of us knew this, but she knew – before he went to university with us, he'd been to another university, but he left there after a term because of depression. He told her that just before they were married.

He'd had the odd episode of depression over the years, but that summer he'd been quite bad and she'd said to him, 'Look, I'm going to book you an appointment with the GP.' But before she could get him down there, this is what happened.

Ian was very conscientious, very bright and everything in his life seemed perfect. He'd sailed through all his exams first time, he was a consultant probably younger than any of the guys in his year, he was married and had kids. At the time his two little girls were six and three, and he absolutely doted on them. But with hindsight I think he believed that nothing he ever did was good enough. He was a real perfectionist.

We all went to the funeral. It was devastating. Total shock, really. You don't expect it to happen at that age, do you? And I think for all of us it was the first time anyone in our generation had died. Some had lost parents or grandparents, but for it to be one of your own generation, you think, 'That could have been me.' Also the way he died was so upsetting. It was the saddest day I can remember.

What was really sad was thinking back to their wedding. Kate and Ian had been married 12 years before and they'd left the wedding by train to go to wherever they were staying. They had to go down the hill to the station in the village and some of the lads who were mucking about picked Ian up and carried him on their shoulders. Then at the funeral two of the guys who did that were now carrying his coffin.

Some of our group are godparents of the children and I felt that both Ian and Kate's parents were conscious that we were a very supportive group and for Kate's sake they were glad of that. I'm sure they realised it was hard for everybody.

Other people don't expect you to be that upset by the death of a friend. Even the people you work with. If I walk into work and say, 'I'm going to be off work tomorrow. I'm going to a funeral.' They'll say, 'I'm so sorry. Who is it?' and I'll say, 'A friend.' People go, 'Oh, well, that's kind of OK then.' If I'd said it was my father or my husband or something, it would be different. Then you burst into tears and they go, 'Oh, right.'

Ian's death did make us appreciate each other a lot more. After the funeral we said, 'We've had all the weddings and the christenings now and if we don't make the effort to get together, we'll be meeting at another funeral.'

So now once a year – for no particular reason – we all get together with all the kids and have a good time. Kate and the children come as well. It's not mournful at all. We have a good laugh really. And yes, we talk about Ian. In fact we realise that we wouldn't have got round to organising this if he hadn't died.

S ally Goldsmith is a singer-songwriter in Sheffield. Her great friend Fi Frances died in November 2001 of ovarian cancer. She was 61.

Fi had been ill for a while. Her mother had died of ovarian cancer, the same thing she died of, at about the same age. About three years before Fi died, she suspected something was wrong with her and she went and had lots of tests, and they said no, it wasn't ovarian cancer, so she was given the all clear. She was feeling pretty poorly from October 2000, but at first it was mis-diagnosed. In the end, she saw a different GP and was whisked into hospital and it was diagnosed as ovarian cancer in February 2001.

She said it was a great relief to know. The consultant came in and said, 'I'm afraid it's bad news', and – she was such a bolshy old fart really – her reaction was, 'How dare you assume it's bad news!' I think (a) she felt it was a relief to have a diagnosis and (b) it meant she was bloody going to get on with what she wanted to get on with! For years, she'd considered herself an artist, but it was hard to do what she wanted to do because she had to earn money, you know? So she never really got stuck in properly to her own artwork. Then, she decided she was going to go all out for it.

I'd known her for years, ever since I moved to Sheffield, when my son, Ewan, was little, so I suppose almost 20 years. And she was a difficult woman. She was bolshy and eccentric and very feminist, very socialist, and she'd fall out with people, but we never fell out. Somehow, we comple-mented each other. We used to co-mentor each other about our work, as well as talk about our love lives and lack of love lives, whatever. She was a very good listener and she could really help you.

She'd done lots of things through her life, lots of arty things. She'd been a teacher, she'd gone to LSE, she was very, very bright. She'd trained to become a graphic designer, she'd set up a women's card company, she'd become a photographer, she'd become an artist, she wrote, she did commu-nity opera with kids. She was a potter, she lived in the wilds of Wales, she lived in the middle of Liverpool, she was a busker – she'd done everything really. And she was the sort of person that people found very fascinating. Some people found her difficult, and judgmental, but she was never judgmental with me. I think she used to find me quite soothing – that's what she often said.

She was 61 when she died, under a year after the diagnosis. She thought she had longer. She had chemotherapy, and there was a period during the summer when she felt a lot better, was able to get out and about, but then it all came back and hit her again.

All during that time, she made artwork about what was happening to her. Like the chemotherapy, she took a whole series of photographs of all of that, which were incredible. You look at one series and they're all very blue – it's hard to describe – you're not quite sure what they are. Like there's a drip bag and there might be a tiny drop of blood, but it's also very beautiful. So they're both disturbing *and* very beautiful.

She was doing all that all during the time she was ill, and she was going to go on this course with Fay Godwin, the famous photographer, but in the end, she was just too poorly. They did discuss her work. I sent stuff down for her – I was acting as her curator – and they discussed it, and they videoed the discussion and sent it back up. At that point she was in the hospice and we – her friend Maggie and an artist friend Angela Martin and I – were able to look at the video and discuss it too.

We were actually working towards an exhibition and she knew when she was dying that it was going to happen somehow. She knew she was working towards that and it was extraordinary. In the end, it was this posthumous exhibition, called Cancer Series 2001 at Cartwright Hall in Bradford as part of the Yorkshire Photography and New Media Awards. It was wonderful.

The theme of the exhibition commission was new ways of looking at landscape and her work was really about looking at the landscape of the body. And it was bizarre – you started to see things through her eyes as well.

By the time she went into the hospice, she rallied. She was so poorly, but it was so wonderful in there, they looked after her so well. It was such a relief. And she liked it and found the other people interesting, and as well, all during her illness she used to take Polaroid pictures of the consultant, the nurses, the visitors – it was about taking power for herself really. Because, when you're so ill, your control shrinks.

The consultant having his photograph taken means she ceases to be the person in the bed, she's the observer as well. She was doing that when she went to the hospice, taking pictures of the other patients. And she had these beautiful little Polaroid diaries that she'd made, that her visitors could come and leaf through.

I ran her funeral. She wanted this alternative funeral, one of these green ones, where you get buried in this woodland burial site out near Rotherham. She wanted me as MC and wanted an emerald green shroud, and she drew a picture of it – a beautiful little drawing. She'd give me tapes of what she wanted at the funeral – you know, it had to be the Pablo Casals' version of the Bach cello suites. She was very particular about what she wanted.

At the funeral, I had to go into performer mode and there she was in her cardboard coffin at the front. People who wanted to speak had lined up. The service was in an old thatched barn somewhere out near Rotherham. We had her old friend Maggie talking from her early life, Maya [a fellow artist] talking about her artwork, a song, her brother Al read out a letter from her brother Rob in America, so we just did it ourselves. And one of the things she wanted – she drew this for me as well – on top of her coffin she wanted a huge bunch of bananas! So on the morning of the funeral we had to stop at Banana Bob's fruitshop and I said, 'I want a big bunch of bananas, Bob!' I told him what it was for and he couldn't believe it. A friend who's an artist put them on the top of the coffin, and hung them off the handles. Then they got thrown in the grave – though Fi's daughter Rosie ate one, I think.

It was like her last laugh. It was both ridiculous and really sad, and I had to lead this bloody thing. So I had to hang onto myself and go into performer mode, and I did. It wasn't until we went to the burial ground that I felt I could let myself go.

Then I got up really early the next morning and I went to her grave and I talked to her for well over an hour. I just sat there and cried and talked to her, because I hadn't been able to do that at her funeral. All the ridiculous things – like I looked round and told her about all the other oddballs who were buried there in this eccentric graveyard with wind chimes in the trees and God knows what.

There have been points in my life where things have been difficult, where I've thought, 'This is the sort of thing I'd talk to her about.' It was a few months afterwards that I suddenly felt that really strongly. And I wrote her this letter: 'Dear Fi, where the fuck are you?' I felt angry with her for going and leaving me, I think, because I needed her.

I also had a close friend, Jeanette, who died in her thirties, and when that happened I thought, 'We're all mortal and you've got to make the most of it'

– like these bloody fridge magnets people have: 'Tomorrow is the first day of the rest of your life'. You do realise you've got to get on with stuff and that actually life is really wonderful.

I still hear in my head the sort of things Fi would say. If I see a film, I think, 'Oo, I know what Fi would think about that!' And I want her to be there saying it. She is still in my head. One of the things I was worried about when she died was I wouldn't remember her how she was. You know, I thought, 'Will I forever remember her as this gaunt aged person, when she wasn't?' She was a bit overweight and full of vigour. I did get that back, but you have that overlaid as well, really.

I was working part-time in Doncaster during her illness and death – an arts and health job employed by the health authority. My manager was quite good about it and said, 'If you say it's stress, you can have time off, but compassionate leave is for close relatives. You might get time off for a funeral but you can't have time off as a friend.' I felt quite angry about it. I thought, 'How dare they prescribe who I love?' Because even when she was in the hospice, it was quite a job – overseeing everything, about her house, her dog, her work, bringing food in – though she couldn't eat, really.

It's a cliché, but sometimes I can't quite believe it, even now. It seems mad that she isn't here and I do still get angry with her for not being here. I think, 'How can she just have gone?' How can someone go? You can't believe that that consciousness, that way of being in the world, has gone. And it's two years ago. Like, we used to talk together on the phone and she'd always say, 'Oh, hello Big Sal.' She was the only person who ever called me that. And I feel deprived of it. Why can't I just pick up the phone? And for a while I couldn't go past her house – I didn't want to see that someone else was there. So it still seems very odd to me that she's not there.

S tephen Kelly is a journalist and writer. He has had two friends die suddenly. The first, Tony [not his real name], took his own life in 1990; the second, David, died in 2002 of non-Hodgkin's disease.

Tony was somebody I'd known all my life. He and I were very close friends, particularly when we were teenagers. We did all those things teenage boys did – chatting up girls, going to pop concerts, pot-holing and climbing, and going away camping for weekends.

He and I were very, very close. I probably have not been as close to anyone as I was to him. He was somebody I could always talk to – he probably was quite unusual as a guy because we could talk quite openly about our feelings, though, I have to say, it was usually me talking about my feelings rather than vice versa. Tony was a great shoulder to cry on. This was back in Birkenhead, when we worked together. Then we went our separate ways in our twenties.

Later, when he'd moved to Scotland to run a youth and community centre, I would go up and see him a couple of times a year and we'd end up going out in the car and sitting chatting and smoking cigarettes.

From the age of 25 to 35, I had numerous girlfriend and emotional problems. I was not a particularly happy person during that period, and I would constantly ring him up when I was in London just to talk things through. He was very good at that.

Tony, I should also say, had married – a lovely girl who's a couple of years older than him. But they didn't have any children. Going into my forties, I also got married, and because I was a lot happier and very busy working as a journalist in Manchester, and he was up in Scotland, so the contact between us wasn't as much as it had been in the past. I hadn't seen or heard from him for – it must have been six months. Then suddenly, out of the blue, I got a phone call from my mother, on a Sunday evening about six o'clock, to say that she'd had a phone call from Tony's cousin to say he had committed suicide. This must be ten years ago now.

It came as an enormous shock. I immediately rang his cousin and rang his wife and – to cut a long story short – Tony had taken his Mercedes into the wood – he loved cars – he'd plastered up all the windows, put the hosepipe into the exhaust and had committed suicide. He'd disappeared on the Saturday night – he'd gone out allegedly to see a friend and had never come back. His wife had alerted the police on the Sunday when she hadn't been able to track him down, and he was found by somebody walking in the woods early on the Sunday morning.

I was totally shocked, because it just wasn't like Tony. He was an amazing character in many ways. He was very charismatic. He was a big guy, very athletic – he did a lot of gym, pot-holing – and everybody liked him. He was always the centre of focus. He was great fun.

He was also the most positive person I've ever met in my life. We'd go pot-holing and I'd say, 'I can't go down there', and he'd say, 'No problems, Steve, it's dead easy. Come on, just stick your foot on that ladder...' I did things with him I probably wouldn't have done otherwise. He was incredibly positive, and a very good teacher, and that was the way he operated in the youth club.

So I was totally and utterly shocked, because it was the last way anyone would have expected him to die. Had my mum rung and said he'd been killed in a car crash, I could fully have understood that, because he did drive his car far too fast. But not suicide.

The minute I rang his wife, the first thing she said was, 'He committed suicide because he didn't want to get old.' That was the only explanation, which seemed bizarre to me. He didn't leave a note at all.

I simply do not accept that he would have committed suicide because he was getting old. So even to this day I don't have an explanation for his death, which kind of bugs me, because I feel there should have been an explanation. But there wasn't.

My feelings at the time were almost anger, rather than sadness. I guess I felt, 'Why the hell did you do that? Why did you not pick up the phone and talk to me if you had a problem? And what a stupid thing to do. You've left all these people who were close to you, particularly your wife, without any kind of explanation.' I felt a bitterness and an anger towards him for doing that.

I still feel an anger. I feel angry because (a) he never telephoned me to confide in me – and, given our long, long friendship, which was based on us talking to each other, I felt he could have done that. And (b) I felt that he had done something which was appallingly selfish, because probably the most selfish thing you can do is to commit suicide and leave a lovely wife without a husband and income and so on.

I remember shedding tears in the church and feeling very angry. And I remember another old friend, when they brought the coffin in, saying, 'For fuck's sake, Tony, why did you do that?' We both felt that, that exact emotion. But I didn't feel the sense of upset and sadness and the tears as I did with David's death.

David was a lovely guy. He was very, very bright, he'd got a First from Cambridge and he'd actually gone to Cambridge when he was a year or two younger than everybody else. Then he'd become a civil servant and he subsequently shocked everybody by chucking that in and becoming a production manager at a theatre. He made a great success of that, and made lots of friends in the arts world. I met him probably in about 1980.

Every Sunday morning we'd play football together – a dozen dads and their kids. Then we'd go back to his house and have a cup of tea, so we became really close and I liked him a lot. He was a very open person and a very cultured person – you could talk about novels with him, you could talk about theatre, and films and so on.

He was also a very gentle person, well liked and respected. Everybody liked David because they saw him as a decent, civilised human. He was a genuinely decent guy.

At the beginning of 2002, we went round for dinner one Saturday evening and he'd got bad pains in his stomach and he said he couldn't sleep the previous night.

We played football on the Sunday morning and he scored this wonderful goal, chested the ball down, ran down the field and slammed it into the net. I said to him, 'If you were to die today, David, that would be your epitaph, that you'd scored that wonderful goal.' It was probably the last goal he did ever score.

This was now June 2002, and the World Cup was on and he rang me one Friday to say had I watched the game. And he said, 'I'm going to hospital this evening to try and sort out these pains in my blessed stomach.' That was the last I heard of him. He went into hospital with pains in his stomach and within 48 hours he was dying.

I was chair of governors at my children's school and where his wife was a teacher, and I was talking to the headmistress and she suddenly said, 'I've got a problem with another member of staff whose husband may have cancer.' She didn't know I knew David. So I asked who it was and she told me. I said, 'Christ! I know David really well.' She said, 'It doesn't sound good to me.' I always remember she said, 'It sounds exactly the same thing that happened to my father, and he was dead in eight weeks.'

I ran straight from her round to the classroom to see his wife. She wasn't saying very much, just that he was going to have an operation the next day. It must be very difficult for someone like that, a wife, to say, 'Yes, he's got cancer. He's going to die.' There was a lot that was being thought about but not said.

I immediately said, 'Can I come and see him?' But in fact the only people who got to see him were immediate close family.

One day I rang up and his wife's brother answered and he said, 'It's non-Hodgkin's disease and it's as bad as it can be.' He was in tears and I was in floods of tears. I sensed from the beginning that this was life-threatening and once I spoke to his brother-in-law I just knew he was going to die.

It dragged on for about ten weeks. I'd gone to France for the summer and I was ringing up every couple of days and he was gradually going downhill. We were out one night and got back late and there was a message on the answerphone from a mutual friend to say could I ring him as soon as possible. I did and he had died. He was 48.

I think men take it in different ways. There are some guys who don't talk about their emotions very easily and certainly don't talk about their emotions about death so easily. Women will expose themselves much more. I think, in a macho world, men feel they shouldn't expose themselves. They shouldn't cry in public. I was certainly very upset about David's death and I found myself frequently in tears over it.

We'd tried to continue playing football when David was taken to hospital and even after his death we continued. We had a minute's silence, stood in a big circle with our arms all around each other, and that felt right and suitable. He'd have liked that.

I would have liked to have had the chance to say goodbye to him. But I don't blame anybody for that. The family obviously didn't want everybody descending on the hospital and I can understand that. At least I had that last phone call with him, that Friday.

I'm not a religious person. I'm a militant atheist. I don't believe in religion at all, I have no belief in an afterlife. At least if you believe in the afterlife, you have an escape clause. But I do not believe in any kind of afterlife at all. So death therefore for me is very dramatic and very final. It's more difficult having that point of view. And when David died, it did make me think about my own mortality. You realise life is short.

I remember when he died, my wife saying, 'You must enjoy yourself more, and keep cheerful.' And for a while we did have an attitude of – 'Yes, let's enjoy ourselves, maybe we can't afford this five-day trip to Rome or whatever but sod it, we might not be here next year.' Of course, these things don't last. But it hammers home the vulnerability and that tightrope we all walk in life.

Useful Contacts

The Alder Centre
For those affected by the death of a child.

Royal Liverpool Children's Hospital
Alder Hey
Eaton Road
Old Swan
Liverpool L12 2AP
0151 252 5391

The Compassionate Friends
For bereaved parents.

53 North Street
Bristol BS3 1EN
0117 966 5202
info@tcf.org.uk
www.tcf.org.uk

Cruse Bereavement Care
Cruse House
126 Sheen Road
Richmond
Surrey TW9 1UR
020 8939 9530
0870 167 1677 (helpline)
info@crusebereavementcare.org.uk
helpline@crusebereavementcare.org.uk
www.crusebereavementcare.org.uk

Help the Hospices
Information about hospices.

Hospice House
34–44 Britannia Street
London WC1X 9JG
020 7520 8200

The Lone Twin Network (LTN)
For surviving twins over the age of 18 to make contact with other twins for mutual support.

PO Box 5653
Birmingham B29 7JY
Contact by post only

Mothers Against Violence (MAV)
Manchester-based support and lobbying group for relatives of young people affected by gangland crime.

Room 113
23 Newmount Street
Manchester M4 4DE
0798 5490333

The National Association of Widows
National Office
48 Queens Road
Coventry CV1 3EH
0247 663 4848

PAPYRUS
A voluntary organisation committed to the prevention of young suicide and the promotion of mental health and emotional well-being.

Rossendale General Hospital
Union Road
Rawtenstall
Lancashire BB4 6NE
01706 214449
admin@papyrus-uk.org
www.papyrus-uk.org

Samaritans
Confidential emotional support 24 hours a day.

The Upper Mill
Kingston Road
Ewell
Surrey KT17 2AF
020 8394 8300
08457 90 90 90 (helpline)
www.samaritans.org.uk

SANDS (Stillbirth and Neonatal Death Society)
Provides support for bereaved parents and their families when their baby dies at or soon after birth.

28 Portland Place
London W1B 1LY
020 7436 7940 (10am–5pm, Monday–Friday)
www.uk-sands.org

SOBS (Survivors of Bereavement by Suicide)
Centre 88
Saner Street
Hull HU3 2TR
01482 610728
0870 241 3337 (helpline)
sobs.admin@care4free.net
sobs.support@care4free.net
www.uk-sobs.org.uk

The Way Foundation
A self-help social and support network for men and women widowed under the age of 50 and their children.

PO Box 6767
Brackley NN13 6YW
0870 011 3450
info@wayfoundation.org.uk
www.wayfoundation.org.uk

Winston's Wish
Helps bereaved children and young people rebuild their lives after a family death and offers practical support and guidance to anyone concerned about a grieving child.

The Clara Burgess Centre
Bayshill Road
Cheltenham GL50 3AW
01242 515157
0845 20 30 40 5 (family line)
info@winstonswish.org.uk
www.winstonswish.org.uk

Useful Books

The following books were recommended by interviewees:

Abrams, R. (1999) *When Parents Die: Learning to Live with the Loss of a Parent.* London: Routledge.

Collick, E. (1988) *Through Grief: The Bereavement Journey.* London: Darton, Longman and Todd Ltd.

Ironside, V. (1997) *You'll Get Over It: The Rage of Bereavement.* London: Penguin Books Ltd.

Kohner, N. and Henley, A. (2001) *When a Baby Dies: The Experience of Late Miscarriage, Stillbirth and Neonatal Death.* London: Routledge.

Parkes, C.M. (2004) *Bereavement: Studies of Grief in Adult Life.* London: Penguin Books Ltd.

Pincus, L. (1989) *Death and the Family: The Importance of Mourning.* New York: Schocken Books.

Stokes, J.A. (2004) *Then, Now and Always.* Cheltenham: Winston's Wish and the Calouste Gulbenkian Foundation.

Tatelbaum, J. (1990) *The Courage to Grieve: Creative Living, Recovery and Growth through Grief.* London: William Heinemann.

Wertheimer, A. (2001) *A Special Scar – The Experiences of People Bereaved by Suicide.* London: Routledge.

Whittaker, A. (ed.) *All in the End Is Harvest.* London: Darton, Longman and Todd Ltd.